Memory and the Built Environment in 20th-Century American Literature

Memory and the Built Environment in 20th-Century American Literature

A Reading and Analysis of Spatial Forms

Alice Levick

BLOOMSBURY ACADEMIC
LONDON • NEW YORK • OXFORD • NEW DELHI • SYDNEY

BLOOMSBURY ACADEMIC
Bloomsbury Publishing Plc
50 Bedford Square, London, WC1B 3DP, UK
1385 Broadway, New York, NY 10018, USA
29 Earlsfort Terrace, Dublin 2, Ireland

BLOOMSBURY, BLOOMSBURY ACADEMIC and the Diana logo are trademarks
of Bloomsbury Publishing Plc

First published in Great Britain 2021
Paperback edition published 2023

Copyright © Alice Levick, 2021

Alice Levick has asserted her right under the Copyright, Designs and
Patents Act, 1988, to be identified as Author of this work.

For legal purposes the Acknowledgments on p. vi constitute an extension
of this copyright page.

Cover design: Namkwan Cho

All rights reserved. No part of this publication may be reproduced or transmitted
in any form or by any means, electronic or mechanical, including photocopying,
recording, or any information storage or retrieval system, without prior
permission in writing from the publishers.

Bloomsbury Publishing Plc does not have any control over, or responsibility for, any
third-party websites referred to or in this book. All internet addresses given in this
book were correct at the time of going to press. The author and publisher regret
any inconvenience caused if addresses have changed or sites have ceased to
exist, but can accept no responsibility for any such changes.

A catalogue record for this book is available from the British Library.

A catalog record for this book is available from the Library of Congress.

ISBN: HB: 978-1-3501-8457-2
PB: 978-1-3501-8465-7
ePDF: 978-1-3501-8458-9
eBook: 978-1-3501-8459-6

Typeset by Deanta Global Publishing Services, Chennai, India

To find out more about our authors and books visit www.bloomsbury.com and
sign up for our newsletters.

Contents

Acknowledgments	vi
Introduction	1
1 The Garden and the Grid: D. J. Waldie and Raymond Chandler in Lakewood and Los Angeles	17
2 The Imago City: Joan Didion, Hisaye Yamamoto, and Alison Lurie in Los Angeles and Sacramento	65
3 The Suture: Marshall Berman and Robert Moses in the Bronx	107
4 The Palimpsest: Paula Fox and L. J. Davis in Brooklyn	137
Conclusion	173
Notes	191
Bibliography	197
Index	221

Acknowledgments

I am indebted to Bloomsbury for accepting my book for publication, and would also like to thank the anonymous reviewers of my proposal for providing key criticisms that greatly improved the text. I would like to express my gratitude to Lucy Brown at Bloomsbury Academic for her early interest in my book proposal, for her encouragement throughout, and for her patience with my many questions as we proceeded through the writing and editorial process. This book is based in large part on my postgraduate thesis and I am hugely grateful to my PhD supervisors, Professor Jo Gill and Professor Joe Kember, both of whom provided a huge amount of insight, constructive criticism, and stimulating conversation over the course of more than seven years. Jo Gill, my primary supervisor, was endlessly patient with my re-writing and ever-increasing word counts and guided me through the process with immense steadfastness.

I conducted a significant amount of archival reading in the New York Public Library, where I read through the myriad papers in the Robert Moses collection, which proved invaluable, in addition to several other collections. At Columbia University I made use of the Rare Book and Manuscript Library in particular, and I am indebted to Thai Jones for dexterously guiding me through the Marshall Berman papers, to Ben Serby for his early, painstaking work on their itemization and collation, and to Shellie Sclan for giving me her blessing to look through the collection at a very early stage and for her generosity in the time she spent with me. I also spent a lot of time gathering material in both the Brooklyn Collection at the Brooklyn Public Library and at the Brooklyn Historical Society, and I am grateful to both institutions for their help. On this side of the pond I have to acknowledge the British Library, which provided a second academic home for me for seven years, and would have provided more had it not been for the lockdown in early 2020. Without this reflective space in which to study, think, research and write, this book would not exist.

Amazing librarians, curators, and archivists in New York helped me in innumerable ways, guiding me to truly valuable and at times surprising resources. Special thanks to Erin Butler at the Municipal Arts Society Reference Library; Sady Sullivan and John Tofanelli at Columbia Butler Library; Laura Tosi at the Bronx County Historical Society; June Koffi at the Brooklyn Public Library; Joanna Lamaida at the Brooklyn Historical Society; Thomas G. Lannon at the New York Public Library; the Schomburg Center for Research in Black Culture; and Geri Solomon at Hofstra University Library Special Collections. I also received particularly generous help from Christopher Niedt, Ina Katz, and Laurence Levy at Hofstra and special thanks must go to Susan Opotow and particularly to her son Nate for driving me around Long Island! I am grateful also to Dustin Tamsen and his family. The writing I was able to do because of the archival material, people, and places I had access to, has made an indelible mark on my work.

Portions of this book have been published elsewhere in different iterations. A version of Chapter 1 (parts of the Raymond Chandler section only) was published in *HARTS & Minds*, Spring 2015: 2.2 Crime and Concealment, under the title "The Big Sleep, Uncanny Spaces, and Memory." Parts of Chapter 3 can be found in "Looking for Moses in NYC," a short personal essay published in *US Studies Online* (March 28, 2016). Parts of Chapter 2 appear in the *European Journal of American Culture*, volume 40, number 1 (Spring 2021), edited by Dr. John Wills, under the title "Damnatio Memoriae in California: Joan Didion's *Play It As It Lays* and *Where I Was From*." An essay which draws from Chapters 1 (the Waldie section) and 3 has been published by Palgrave Macmillan as a chapter, titled "Marshall Berman and D. J. Waldie: Memory and Grief in Urban and Suburban Spaces," in the collected work, *Time, the City, and the Literary Imagination*, edited by Dr. Anne-Marie Evans and Dr. Kaley Kramer.

I owe a huge debt to the people who shared their experiences with me through interviews and conversations. Their personal histories breathed real human life into this book, and I am so grateful for their patience, honesty, and generosity with their time. They are David Allen, Andrew Berman, the "Brooklyn Transitions" book discussion group at the Brooklyn Public Library in Park Slope, Richard Fine, Sam Goodman, Vivian Gornick, Amy Hass, Howard Kaminsky, Lee Koppelman, Lawrence Levy, Francis Morrone, Margo Moss, Jack Putnam, Naima Rauam, Rebecca Reitz, Joe Rosen, Shellie Sclan, Lynne Sharon Schwartz, Geri Solomon, Joseph Svehlak, Gilbert Tauber, and Lee Zimmerman. In particular I must thank Shellie, Howard, Richard, and Amy—I am so lucky to have met them and so grateful for their kindness and inestimable insight. I am grateful also to Howard's family for giving me permission to use his words in this book after his passing.

Finally, I would like to thank my friends for making me laugh and bringing me back to the real world every now and then. Most of all, I am thankful to my family, who provided support and a room of my own in which to work, both equally precious things.

Introduction

Since 2011, when I first began this book (in its previous incarnation as my postgraduate thesis), I have moved out of one house and into another, moved my grandmother out of her flat and into my family's house, packed up and sold the house my grandparents lived in after they had passed away within a few months of one another, lived in New York during which I moved from student halls in Midtown to a friend's studio apartment in Chelsea to my then-boyfriend's flat in Elmhurst, Queens, moved back home, then a year later moved in with said boyfriend elsewhere in Elmhurst, Queens, on a temporary (ninety-day) basis before moving back home again, considered which personal items to bring my grandmother when she was moved to hospital, put my grandmother's belongings into boxes when she passed away, and finally barely moved from said home for several months during the lockdown necessitated by the coronavirus pandemic. Every move, whether I was moving myself or other people, or relegated to one domestic space from which I could not move, deepened my sense of anxiety about home. What did it mean to me, that word? After my family and I had moved out of the house we had lived in for more than twenty years, I wrote in my diary that I had a feeling of discombobulation: "as though you have come home and someone has rearranged all the furniture in your absence. Someone, some interloper, has been in your house. Which is funny because right now we are in someone else's house, and someone else is in our house. We are the interlopers." I don't think I ever really stopped seeing that house as "our house," fancying myself a Marianne Dashwood in *Sense and Sensibility*, saying goodbye to her dear Norland: "when shall I cease to regret you, when learn to feel at home elsewhere?" (I did in fact scrawl her farewell on the inside door of the boiler cupboard before we left the house) ([1811] 2004: 21). I felt an echo of this anxiety each time I had to separate myself from familiar places with which I had long-term, mostly familial, ties, and attempt to feel at home in a new a-historical location. Home became, for me, a place that was no longer tethered. Part of the reason I never went back to my old neighborhood, let alone my old house, circumnavigating entire sections of my borough just to avoid doing so, was that

I feared I would return and find nothing to return to, as though the locus for my formative years had been erased from both the actual physical landscape and that of my memory.

Throughout my life I have grown increasingly frustrated with the failure of my total recall, keeping a diary for many years as an attempted corrective. Home has always been important to me for this reason: it became a place where I could store as many tangible remnants of my history as possible for the posterity my unconscious mind was incapable of preserving. Before leaving my old house for the last time, I itemized every part of it that had given me continued access to my past. The colored lines drawn on the wall in my sister's bedroom to measure her increasing height and mine; the stained-glass panel made by my mum in our front door, the door that I was always nervous about opening after the time we had been burgled and I discovered that the chain had been left on from the inside; the loose banister in the staircase that had been broken at one of my sister's house parties; the passion fruit that grew along the fence in the back garden that I would pick every summer; the small wooden cross that marks the place in the garden where our beloved 16-year-old dog was buried.

In the midst of this outpouring of sentimentality for bricks and mortar, I read Marshall Berman's *All That is Solid Melts into Air* (1982) and felt an immediate connection to him. It was only much later that I understood this strange magnetic pull I felt toward a book that was about (in part) growing up in the South Bronx. When Berman wrote about memories of his childhood in terms of a kind of locational mourning ("As I saw one of the loveliest of these buildings being wrecked for the road, I felt a grief that, I can see now, is endemic to modern life" ([1982] 2010: 295)), it struck me that I had felt much the same way, and that this feeling was not just a result of the move, but an accumulation of everything that had been lost during the months before and after it.

I started to collect other authors who seemed to me to be trying to articulate the same experience—of a lost home, misplacement of memory, vulnerable spaces which did and did not remember or memorialize according to one's expectations. I read Walter Benjamin's "A Berlin Chronicle," ([1932] 1986) in which I discovered the importance of specific houses to his plan to construct a sense of his past through the use of a series of signs on a map. Each of these signs would represent the various "houses of my friends and girl friends, the assembly halls of various collectives [. . .] the hotel and brothel rooms that I knew for one night [. . .] the sites of prestigious cafes whose long-forgotten names daily crossed our lips" (5). Susan Sontag (1979) writes that Benjamin is not attempting to "recover his past, but to understand it: to condense it into its spatial forms, its premonitory structures" (13). Benjamin's spatially contextualized images of specific locations form an autobiographical montage of these condensed "spatial forms." Inspired by this approach, which touched on my fixation with familiar houses, throughout this book I look at the meaningful spaces—houses, apartments, rooms—in each of my chosen primary texts, examining their summative effect in terms of what they tell me about the representation of memory and history in the urban spaces in which they appear. In these meaningful spaces, the past is concentrated and imagined materially. As Benjamin puts it in his *Arcades* (1927–1939) project, in such places the past is able to "*become* space" (393 emphasis added).

Benjamin prompted me to consider what role *my* city might have played in the construction of my own self-narrative. I reduced this complex mass of urban connections down to my more immediate neighborhood, and, in the midst of my domestic uprooting, this question gave me pause. How could I perceive the reality of my own home, what it had meant to me, the way it enabled me to memorialize, amid the fog of the quickly deepening nostalgia that now surrounded it? I was reminded of something the author Bernard Malamud wrote about his old home in Brooklyn, a flat above a grocery store where he had grown up. When he married he moved away from the borough, and he writes: "Years went by. But that was another country" (Note in Letter from HA to RG: n.p.). I considered the way that my house, my street, my neighborhood, became a place so far away it was as though it had retreated, been entirely uprooted and moved to a different land I could no longer access, and thought about how this experience might feed into my academic pursuits.

Urban Thirdspaces

Integral to this book is the discussion around how the city is "read" and interpreted; the particular way in which narrative form and voice have shaped the representation of city narratives. Raymond Chandler's heartsick letters and Joan Didion's elegiac, mournful *Where I Was From* (2003) necessitated the expansion of both time-frame and map to Los Angeles and Sacramento, California. In the case of Chandler's letters, his simultaneous attraction to, and repulsion from, Los Angeles, the place he made his home for almost five decades, instills an intriguing ambivalence. This is also in evidence in the way he describes his domestic arrangements after his wife's death in 1955: "Perhaps when I get away from this house and all its memories I can settle down to do some writing. And then again I may just be homesick and to be homesick without a home is rather poignant" (Chandler 1955: 206). The need to be home even if it is not really a home anymore, or perhaps never was, is also a characteristic of Philip Marlowe, his most famous character. Marlowe's apartment, detailed most memorably in *The Big Sleep* (1939) when it is invaded by the toxic presence of Carmen Sternwood, is the one place where the detective can store his sense of self in the little items which he packs away. Marlowe's constant sense of alienation from a landscape with which he is also intensely intimate says as much about him, and about the man who created him, as it does about the city.

In *The Culture of Cities*, Lewis Mumford ([1938] 1940) writes: "In the city, time becomes visible" (4). I apply Mumford's maxim regarding the visibility of time in the city to Los Angeles, Sacramento, Lakewood, the Bronx, and Brooklyn, from 1939 up to the early 1970s, examining the ways in which they each speak to the complexities involved in visualizing and retaining a tangible connection to the past. Studying these five American locales, memory and forgetting are often evident in the compartmentalization, subdivision, and fragmentation of internal and external urban space. Related to this wider argument is the idea that personal and individual histories are layered on to wider urban histories and, like memory and history, the city is often "soft," malleable and palimpsestic. How do authors project their ideas about history and modernity out into their textual representation of urban space itself (for example, D. J. Waldie and the rigid organization of the grid system, Berman and the suture wound of the Cross-Bronx Expressway)? The time-frame of this book takes in the years leading up to the Second World War, going further into the mid to late twentieth century rather than its opening act. Chandler's work demonstrates that what happened postwar went further back than the economic boom, with seeds planted earlier in the 1900s and even before this. Waldie and Didion then articulate the progression of urbanization and modernization through the mid-twentieth century, its material impact on the landscape (from the idea of the garden to the imposition of the grid to the expansion of the suburb to the construction of the freeway), and the resultant textual representation in a selection of Californian texts that sought to internalize or extrapolate these transformations in various ways. The New York texts in subsequent chapters project us forward into the 1970s, enabling us to understand how modernizers like urban planner Robert Moses would ultimately be framed.

Through reading Berman's descriptions of the postwar Bronx, it becomes evident that there was a movement toward the renewal and reconfiguration of urban spaces, at least in New York, providing a very tangible example of change in the built environment of the city. In her obituary of the Pulitzer-prize-winning architecture critic Ada Louise Huxtable, Suzanne Stephens, deputy editor of *Architectural Record*, notes that when Huxtable was first writing for the *New York Times* as their architecture critic during the "boom years after World War II," it was in the context of "the banality of commercial Modernism, the demolition of historic buildings, and the destruction of the urban fabric [which] dominated the formation of the man-made environment" (Stephens 2013: 26). Both the construction of the modern city and anxieties regarding its preservation and renewal pre-date this period of urban renewal, but in the years afterward the debate regarding the cycle of construction and destruction grew louder. This continued into the 1970s, by which time urban renewal was indelibly ingrained in the built environment and architectural attitudes of both Los Angeles and New York, but had also proved increasingly controversial, with the thinking of Robert Moses for example largely discredited.

Among the writers who most absorb the attention of the book, Raymond Chandler, Marshall Berman, D. J. Waldie, Joan Didion, Alison Lurie, L. J. Davis and Paula Fox provide evidence that in the prewar and postwar urban spaces of New York and Los Angeles (and beyond, in the case of the latter) it is possible for history to be both displayed and displaced. Each of these authors, alongside Gil Cuadros, Hisaye Yamamoto, Paule Marshall, and Alfred Kazin, reflect and represent the rich ambiguity involved in writing about something so seemingly intangible, frequently layering their own personal histories with these cities into their work. The book examines these authors from a novel perspective; in the past they have been read for particular reasons related to the area or genre for which they are renowned, for example, Chandler as a crime writer, Berman as a commentator on Marxism and modernity, Didion in relation to the New Journalism, and Lurie for her "witty and astute comedies of manners" (Wroe 2003: n.p.). Waldie, Davis, and Fox are not quite so well-known, so they do not carry with them the same weight of expectation. I did not wish to simply reiterate the expected approach, but rather to consider them in the context of what they have to say about the experiences I mentioned earlier. Namely, history, memory, and how both are and are not expressed in the urban and peri-urban spaces about which they write with so much personal authority. Most importantly these are spaces in which each of them have, or have had, a personal stake.

This book offers an interconnected series of close readings of these works of fiction and nonfiction, coupled with interpretations of archival, autobiographical, and theoretical texts that will cast new light on representations of the past in particular urban spaces. In an attempt to process and articulate the ways in which memory itself is characterized by a simultaneous degree of fluidity and discontinuity, I also chose to draw on a host of city planners, developers, architects (and their critics), urban historians and theorists, psychoanalysts and philosophers, all of whom helped me to map the relationship between urban space, policy, and people's daily lives and experiences. I use the interviews that I conducted in New York as a way to humanize very abstract ideas, seeking another method of interrogating the literature concerning a highly emotive subject, that is, the construction of felt experience (unfortunately, it was not possible to do the same on the West Coast, purely for practical reasons). Throughout the writing of this book I have sought ways to make each chapter accessible and personal, including using my own experiences with memory and history in the built environment.

The book traces the trajectory from the control and effacement found in modern city planning and organization as established in New York and Los Angeles (and by extension much of California too), all the way to the resultant spatial and temporal rupture and attendant anxiety regarding coherence in personal history. First the modern city imposes its rigor on the landscape, interrupting its pre-urban origins, starting with the paving over of rivers and gardens (Chandler, Didion's *Where I Was From*) and the grafting of a gridded system (Waldie), continuing with further plans such as the imposition of an integrated system for automobiles (evident in Chandler's novels, Didion's *Play It As It Lays* (1970), Yamamoto's "Wilshire Bus" (1950) and Lurie's *The Nowhere City* (1965), and in *All That is Solid*), the clearance of unwanted housing stock in favor of newer, at times quite thoughtlessly incongruous, models (in the poems of authors like Gil Cuadros and Manazar Gamboa; in *All That is Solid* and *The Nowhere City*), the substitution of historically significant structures for a more modern convenience (the Grand Concourse turns into the Cross-Bronx Expressway), and finally in both the preservation which necessitates the dismantling of aspects of history and the restoration which is more like a total reimagining (Davis' *A Meaningful Life* (1971)). Built-up spaces cannibalize their own histories (for example, the Embarcadero in Didion's "Notes from a Native Daughter" (1965), with its firehouses turned into bars), until only signs of the past remain that no longer have any meaning in the de-contextualized present.

Throughout this book, the use of the word "urban space" relates to cities (as distinct from rural areas and also, with one exception, from the suburban), but also to types or typographies of space. The types of space that characterize each city are not always defined by boundaries that delineate, for example, the borough from the city proper, and even the fictional from the autobiographical.

There is a gravitational pull exerted by cities upon adjacent physical spaces both within and without their jurisdictional and geographical/legally defined outlines. As Ben Highmore (2005) argues, "our real experiences of cities are 'caught' in networks of dense metaphorical meanings [. . .] It is the tangle of physicality and symbolism, the sedimentation of various histories [. . .] that constitute the urban" (5). The city is also in theory a tangible representation of our individual immaterial or sensory memories which are specific to place, but in practice the urban landscape does not always reflect back, to our minds, an accurate representation of these memories. The arrangement and navigation of space in the modern city affects what and how we remember. Urbanization can and will find ways, intentionally or unwittingly, of erasing traces of the past in the city. As the shape, scale, and specifications of the city change, so does our perspective and indeed our material familiarity with it; as our familiarity is eroded, so is our connection to the past as physically locatable. The discovery of absences in lieu of an expected presence creates a feeling of discontinuity and loss; of rupture. The fissures and gaps in the narratives of both the city and one's own sense of the past reflect the processes of urban renewal, slum clearance, displacement and gentrification instituted in the city during the postwar years.

Despite this, the past persists within (and without) its spaces. The repressed can return, and it presents itself spatially. This notion that what has been repressed can re-emerge in various disturbing forms is described by Sigmund Freud ([1919] 2003) as the experience of "the uncanny" (121). The experience of the uncanny has much in common with the trope of spectrality and both Jacques Derrida's theory of hauntology and his concept of the trace, all of which are concerned with the conjunction of the absent and the present and the return of the repressed. This book refers primarily to the uncanny, but I also found it fruitful to reflect on the ways in which Jacques Derrida's theories relate in similar ways to memory and haunted spaces. Gayatri Chakravorty Spivak ([1967] 1997), in the explanatory notes for her translation of Derrida's *Of Grammatology*, in which he outlines his poststructuralist concept of the trace, recounts that "his word is 'trace' (the French word carries strong implications of track, footprint, imprint), a word that [. . .] presents itself as the mark of an anterior presence, origin, master" (xv). Derrida's "trace," she continues, is "the mark of the absence of a presence, an always already absent present" (xvii). The idea of the trace is rooted in the Saussurean concept of language being structured around difference: words are defined through their difference from other words. Each word has meaning, but that meaning holds the implication, the *trace*, of its opposite—what it does *not* mean. This trace of alternative meaning haunts a word like a ghostly presence; it is both there and not there, the parallel track of something absent. For Derrida there are no fixed meanings in language, no single point of origin, only "an interplay of absence and presence" (Derrida [1967] 1978: 294). In *Specters of Marx*, Derrida ([1993] 1994), in a thesis which centers around the spectre of Marxism haunting Western society, builds on the idea of the trace in his exploration of hauntology, a homophonic play on ontology (if one adds the magic of a French accent): the study of being. In the same way that words are haunted by the intimation of other words, hauntology marks an overlapping of being (or presence) with not-being (or absence).

Colin Davis (2005) explains that hauntology replaces "the priority of being and presence with the figure of the ghost as that which is neither present nor absent, neither dead nor alive" (373). The idea of the spectral presence in all representation, Fredric Jameson ([1995] 1999) elaborates, does not revolve around a literal belief in ghosts, but rather that "the living present is scarcely as self-sufficient as it claims to be; that we would do well not to count on its density and solidity, which might under exceptional circumstances betray us" (39). This notion of all that is solid potentially melting into air is central to Marshall Berman's thesis of things falling apart in the newly modernist New York, where he finds himself haunted by the past that he can no longer see, but only feel its traces. Likewise, the realization of Esther in Hisaye Yamamoto's ([1950] 1998) "Wilshire Bus," when she narrates that, in the insubstantial air of Los Angeles, through which she passes like a ghost, there is "nothing solid she could put her finger on, nothing solid she could come to grips with" (37). The past may not be past, to coin a phrase, but it certainly is not complete in its presence. What Berman is pursuing matches the silences of the noplace in which Waldie makes a home; like Berman, he seeks "another kind of history, a history of the submerged, a history of the layers below the nondescript" (Waldie and Campbell 2011: 237). As Andreas Huyssen (2003) notes in *Present Pasts*, it had been the job of the built environment to represent "the material traces of the historical past in the present" (1). However, thanks to industrialization, urbanization and modernity, these "formerly stable links" to the past as representable in and anchored to space, have lost their groundings, and now the past takes place within "the register of imaginaries" (4). Such spaces, which "shape collective imaginaries," are "lived space" (7) argues Huyssen, arguably a nod to Edward Soja's concept of *thirdspace*, that is, space which acquires meaning not through cartographic quantification but through being lived.[1] An urban imaginary, such as envisaged by, for example Berman and Waldie, in their "temporal reach may well put different things in one place: memories of what there was before, imagined alternatives to what there is. The strong marks of present space merge in the imaginary with traces of the past, erasures, losses" (6). Remembered space is a place of absent presence, haunted by other versions of itself, just as texts like D. J. Waldie's *Holy Land: A Suburban Memoir* (1996) contain spectral traces of Waldie's own memories, as though continually in the process of overwriting itself like a palimpsest. Indeed, there are some literary texts, claims Huyssen, which are able to "mix language and image" in such a way that they speak to "the palimpsestic nature of all writing" (9, 10). These texts, into which category I would place *Holy Land*, *All That is Solid*, "Wilshire Bus" and much of Joan Didion's work, are "fundamentally concerned with haunted space and spatial imaginaries" and "acknowledge that [...] representations of the visible will always show residues and traces of the invisible" (10). They "haunt us because they themselves are haunted." Notions of haunted-ness and the trace persist throughout this book through my excavation of the urban, spatial, and architectural uncanny embedded in each text.

In the two quintessentially modern American cities on which this book places its focus, the new replaces the old, the familiar is eroded, and traces of time passing seem to have been erased. Each urban space and its accompanying text(s) tells a story about the evolution of the built environment during the (mostly) postwar period, and each illuminates key perceptions about how history is and is not displayed in these spaces as a consequence of the material modifications imposed upon them. Los Angeles, despite the fact that it is one of the most cultivated, contrived places on earth, can exhibit pockets of a more ancient natural history in its physical make up, while New York, though it is a most vaunted synecdoche for a historical East Coast, is nevertheless capable of expressing a more manufactured, regurgitated history in its material, architectural form than one might imagine. On the surface it seems invested in its own sense of heritage and lineage, though at the same time it is the American metropolis that most typifies ideas surrounding modernity, progress, density, and shared space. An additional reason for its central focus is the fact that, as Samuel Stein (2019) notes in *Capital City*, the city has long served "as an example for many other places. Planners from around the country look to New York for new patterns and practices" (6). Two other urban spaces are examined: Lakewood, California, a classic postwar American suburb (technically now a general law city) where the aforementioned Waldie lives, and the city of Sacramento, Didion's place of birth and center of gravity. In Greater Los Angeles and Sacramento, which provide a counterpoint to New York, an apparently oppositional space can be found, against which to juxtapose its East Coast counterpart—its spatial composition, form and landscape is antithetical to that of New York, and ostensibly looks to the future rather than its place in history.

Despite the proliferation of sites which speak to the past, New York can be just as affected a city as Los Angeles when it comes to its narrative of the past, and Los Angeles can be just as demonstrative as New York of a secreted sense of history. Both cities reflect an attempt to extract, control, and suppress the past. My work on each of these spaces focuses on the processes by which memory unfolds within a spatial framework and asks what happens when that framework is dismantled. How do these spaces attempt to impose order on the chaos of memory? How do they provide access, in textual and architectural forms, to the past? How does memory and forgetting *work* in my chosen texts? Both memory and forgetting are particularly visible in the compartmentalization, subdivision and fragmentation of city spaces both internal and external; in the ambivalent binary of oppositions juxtaposed against one another; in the empty or derelict open spaces which speak silently of the past; and in the subtle seeping of one space into another.

From Chandler's vision of a fraudulent Los Angeles riddled with façades and fronts which attempt to sequester a willfully repressed history, to the dilapidated tenement buildings, empty houses and entirely hollowed out neighborhoods of Berman's ghostly Bronx communities, and the inauthentic, co-opted history of Davis' brownstone Brooklyn dreams, I examine the texts which contend with the material landscape of the city and its relationship with the protagonists' own sense of the past. I do so in order to come to an understanding of the distinction between history and memory, how they are alternately preserved and ignored, and how this manifests itself spatially.

A Note on Chapters

The book begins with a discussion of D. J. Waldie's *Holy Land*. Waldie has remarked that his task when writing *Holy Land* was "not to write a history but something essentially different" (Waldie and Campbell 2011: 230). The work was constructed through a process of "accumulation by association," and this *something different*, placed by Waldie in contradistinction to history, was an articulation of "everyday existence, considered within the physical structure of a place, and how that conjunction shapes an imagination," a rather perfect description of memory. In Chapter 1, it is in *Holy Land*, and its setting of Lakewood, that the importance of the suburb and the grid system to discussions about the Californian landscape first makes its mark. This chapter presents as its central focus the only dedicated suburban text, which may render it somewhat incongruous. It has been suggested that suburbs like Lakewood can tell us nothing about history, being too blandly uniform to speak to the past with any depth. In fact, Waldie demonstrates the remarkable similarities between the suburb and the city as spaces characterized by a sense of absence that can in fact make the past visible. It would be remiss not to include an appraisal of the connection between suburbanization and urbanization in the postwar United States, given its mutually defining relationship; the fundamental place of the suburb in the story of the city as a palimpsestic space.

In this chapter I examine the ways in which the grid system came to be so embedded as an expression of modernity and control over the land, with consequences for communities of color such as the Mexican neighborhoods of Boyle Heights, Chavez Ravine, and City Terrace, as authors like Gil Cuadros, Helena Maria Viramontes, and Manazar Gamboa articulate. The city's propensity for change, expansion, development, displacement, effacement, is visible in its landscape in the form of its irrigation system, the grid, the suburbs, the freeway system, the powerful invisibility of long-departed urban structures, visible only to those who once called them home, and above all the levelling, subdivision, and selling of the land as real estate. Despite his attempts to cultivate his personal history in textual form, a sense of loss is what is long remembered and hard to control in Waldie's Lakewood reminiscences; he tries to manage his memories but grief creeps over the borders of his home like the vines that quickly cover the houses on the deserted Mar Vista street in Lurie's *The Nowhere City*. Nothing seems to be permanent in this place. What was future is past almost instantaneously, what was past is quickly ancient history, and ancient history is hard to come by unless you are adept at spotting the signs.

Next, the scope widens to take in the Los Angeles of the late 1930s to early 1940s, examining the city through the prism of *The Big Sleep* (1939), by Raymond Chandler, with references also to *Farewell, My Lovely* (1940) and *The High Window* (1942). The standard view of Chandler seems to alternate between two perspectives. The first is the belief that he was tough yet sentimental and an Angelino by nurture if not by nature, whose intimacy with his adoptive city was as entrenched in his character as it was in that of his authorial avatar, Philip Marlowe. The second is that Chandler never took to Los Angeles, and that his novels express a yearning for the green grass of the England in which he spent his formative years. The latter is a contention upheld by Paul Skenazy (1984), who details the sense of ostracism and alienation in Chandler's work. Chandler's outsider perspective, Skenazy contends, stems from the fact that he was not a native of Los Angeles, but an import, first from Chicago, and then from England. His novels deal therefore with "exile, cultural duality and dislocation" (93). Chandler saw California as "both a new and an old territory," one rich with a history of exile. David Wyatt (1986) argues that Chandler's England may in fact have only existed in his mind, creating the sense of home being somewhere else, somewhere displaced, that permeates his novels. For Wyatt, Chandler's longing for home manifests itself in his depiction of the perversion of nature in Southern California. For him this longing was a form of nostalgia for what W. H. Auden calls the "Great Good Place" that "Eden-like" nature should provide, which Chandler had known in England and lost in Los Angeles (409). I agree that nature has been subverted, but that is not to say it has entirely disappeared in the rush to urbanization; its ubiquity and ability both to hide and reveal the past proves that nature is still a place of authenticity where the history of Los Angeles lives. The past is never entirely gone; it is always somehow both absent and present.

Chandler articulates a potent sense of both location and dislocation; of the significance of artifacts found within city spaces; and of the multiplicity and fragmentation of his interiors and the uncanny sense of absence which characterizes his exteriors. Fundamental to my analysis here is the aforementioned experience of "the uncanny" and Anthony Vidler's (1992) exploration of the ways in which this is experienced architecturally.

Los Angeles is a city built on a repressed natural landscape, where there has evidently been a failure to connect the past to the present. In continually pushing back the frontier and re-shaping itself, the city unwittingly leaves traces of its path, written in the land itself. History is not preserved in Los Angeles so much as it is endlessly renewed and reimagined in various alternative forms. Nature, though repressed and built over, finds a way to make itself noticed, cannot be ignored, and pushes back against the encroachments of modernity by sporadically revealing criminal acts and dead bodies. External spaces are vast, obscure, uncertain, devouring. The man-made environment is fragile, short-lived, precarious, and at the mercy of the nature it has trammeled.

Chapter 2 looks at two novels set in mid to late 1960s Los Angeles. Alison Lurie's 1965 novel *The Nowhere City*, one of the archetypal pieces of fiction about Los Angeles, is either "hate mail or ironic love letter" to the city in which she, a native Chicagoan, spent time as an interloper, furtively gathering material (Fine 2004: 241). In the pockets of what remains of Los Angeles' pre-urban spaces, occasionally illuminated by accident like a torch light in a dark basement, a different, discarded version of the city can be found. The land, its troublesome history with water and its ability to produce a sudden resurgence of green, is proof that there is history at work in this city, however subterraneous, that will outlast the fragile constructions of humans which, throughout the novel, we find stuck pathetically, and temporarily, into the earth. In Joan Didion's 1970 novel *Play It As It Lays*, Maria Wyeth rejects her own personal history and the people associated with it, trying to repress, curtail and edit her memories. For Maria, the city's incoherence and a-temporality is a blessing—she can forget herself and erase her own memories if she tries hard enough. Instead of the intimacy and familiarity of domestic interior space, she chooses the freeway, where she can remain in the present and blank out painful memories by looking ahead. "Never look back at all" is the California mantra that Maria personifies (Didion [2003] 2004: 199). But by submitting herself to the perceived freedom of the freeway, she is not entirely leaving behind history, but re-living it in terms of her continued journey West, onwards to meet the forever-deferred horizon like the so-called pioneers before her. The crossing story, scrutinized by Didion with increasing alarm, is one example of the mythologization of history in California. Other historical traces, like the internment of Japanese citizens after Pearl Harbour in concentration camps throughout the state (and across the country), are not so easily distinguishable in the spaces through which Esther Kuroiwa travels in Hisaye Yamamoto's ([1950] 1998) "Wilshire Bus," published in her collection *Seventeen Syllables and Other Stories*. Yamamoto, who herself had been placed in one such camp in Arizona, moved to Los Angeles in the late-1940s, and this collection reflects on her experiences, funneled through the conduit of fiction. Published in 1988, it spans forty years and begins after the Second World War. Los Angeles is presented as a flimsy landscape, structurally unsound, prone to a deep sense of unfamiliarity, which does not seem capable of retaining a sense of its own history. Is it possible to feel at home in such a city? Is it possible to leave traces?

Several works of nonfiction from Didion are also included in this chapter: *Where I Was From*, a genealogical work which looks back at California through the prism of the author's family history, in addition to several texts from her collection of personal essays on things falling apart in California, *Slouching Towards Bethlehem* (1968). In the latter, Didion writes of generational settlement and exodus in California, and of impermanence and exhaustion in New York. For her, the memory of the "Old California," (1984a: 29) like that of Berman's Bronx, is no longer something tangible, yet though she cannot find it, still she sees it. Through an examination of *Where I Was From*, in addition to "Slouching Towards Bethlehem" (1967d), "Notes from a Native Daughter" (1965), and "On Going Home" (1967c), we find that Didion's idea of California is based on two myths: that of the crossing story as romantic pilgrimage, and the notion of the state as America's Holy Land, a latter-day Eden that is therefore sacrosanct. This way of seeing the land in California gives Didion continuity with herself. But as she dismantles these myths, she begins to see that she cannot rely on this particular image of California to keep her sense of the past safe. The land, the garden, is commodified, franchised, sold. The crossing story leaves blood on the hands of her antecedents.

In Chapter 3, Marshall Berman examines the material form taken by the past in New York, with a specific focus on the Bronx during the late 1950s and early 1960s and the impact of master builder Robert Moses on the borough. Primarily I focus on evaluating *All That Is Solid Melts into Air*, while making use on a secondary basis of some his other publications, such as *On the Town: One Hundred Years of Spectacle in Times Square* (2006a) and *New York Calling: From Blackout to Bloomberg* (2007a), in addition to archived material housed at Columbia University and the New York Public Library, and the personal interviews conducted with Bronx residents. What we remember of the *places* linked to our past, in the form of localized, geographical, at times compartmentalized memory, is the subject at hand here. The theme of the uncanny wends its way from Chandler to Berman, manifesting itself both spatially and in terms of the split between memory and history. Waldie, Chandler, and Berman all make use of the familial home as a locus of the past. For Chandler the family pile is a place of repressed history and buried crime, whereas for Berman and for Waldie, the old neighborhood and the childhood home, respectively, are places haunted by memory crises.

Integral to this chapter is the theory of modernity as put into practice by Robert Moses, representing a desire to escape and erase history. It was Moses' wish to impose a sense of control and regulation on the urban landscape. Moses' plans for the Bronx specifically led to huge displacement and the tearing of the fabric of neighborhoods in the borough that would otherwise have maintained a continuous thread from past to present. This rupture led to the increased appearance of "the uncanny" and the separation of memory from history. Berman perfectly crystallized in his writing the way that the postwar economic boom, and its concurrent galvanizing of the trifecta of urban renewal, slum clearance, and highway construction, had very visibly altered conceptions of history as made manifest in the built environment. He demonstrates the ways in which Moses and his modernity remade urban space, unpicked its cohesive tapestry, and imbued the landscape with unfamiliarity and disorientation. Berman's thoughts on this are applied to conceptions of memory and the creation of the symbolic city, and the book considers how his conceptualization of modernity works for the other writers under discussion. In the California chapters for example, evidence of the postwar boom feeding into and enabling ideas behind modernity (such as a sense that the rationalization of the land was a necessity, and its movement away from the agrarian toward the urban) can be found in the construction of the freeway (see Chandler's novels and Joan Didion's *Play It As It Lays*) and the new suburbs (per D. J. Waldie's *Holy Land*), and the accelerated development and selling-off of farmland and the erosion of the agrarian way of life (as in Didion's *Where I Was From*). In Brooklyn, meanwhile, the brownstoners, depicted by Paula Fox and L. J. Davis, in seeking the original, authentic city, instead recreate Moses' modernist impulses to eradicate history, paving the way for the most damaging expression of urban modernity—gentrification.

The final chapter moves to Brooklyn in the early 1970s, where Fox and Davis take up residence in *Desperate Characters* (1970) and *A Meaningful Life* (1971), respectively. Both authors demonstrate a borough in a state of flux, as represented by the increasing fragility of the domestic lives of their characters. The external world is a dangerous place in both novels, and incrementally encroaches on interior spaces previously considered safe and unchanging. Violence and disintegration begin to make a home inside their lovely brownstone houses, try as the protagonists might to keep the world outside from their doors. One confrontation after another occurs, buildings are evacuated and demolished piecemeal, homes are infiltrated and defiled; everything that stands for history, both personal and public, does not stand upright for long. Almost all of the authors in this book have experienced family homes becoming subject to external pressures or internal anxieties. The homes in this chapter are not always protective spaces; they can be invaded, break, or crumble.

Also instructive are Paule Marshall's novel *Brown Girl, Brownstones* (1959) and Alfred Kazin's memoir, *A Walker in the City* (1951). The area known as Bedford-Stuyvesant as described by Marshall is, like Berman's old stomping ground, reduced to rubble and, like Kazin's, transformed into something not entirely recognizable. Her own past lies in pieces and she has no way of imprinting or tracing memory here. She finds that the street is alive with individual experience, as it is in Lowell Lake's Brooklyn neighborhood. Here, memory has found its way out onto the street, where it can continue to be, as M. Christine Boyer puts it in *The City of Collective Memory*, "plural" and "alive" ([1996] 2001: 67).

In the end, the key themes with which all of these authors grapple—home, loss, memory, and urban space—represent the heart of this book, which, at its foundation, is an exploration of changing urban landscapes in twentieth-century America, the processes of renewal and destruction in these built environments, and how this impacted on the memories of those who lived in these spaces. Memory may be the only true conduit into the past, but the *process* of remembering (and indeed of forgetting) is fraught. This process is made more complex when it takes place in the modern city, a place which does not always value, and often undermines or sabotages, the conditions necessary to retain memory. Where can one go in the city for context and explanation; where can one *see* its past made manifest? If we lose our ability to "recollect forgotten experiences and retie them to conscious awareness," argues Boyer, how can we translate our own lived experiences into "meaningful contemporary forms" ([1996] 2001: 28)? "We have only to pass along the waterfront of Manhattan," she writes, taking us from the South Street Seaport to Battery Park (places which may be "both real and imaginary"), to "experience a surprising compositional effect that pulls these diverse scenes together yet sets one off against the other" (422). Walking through the city, Boyer suggests, enables us to understand it, to link it together and make it seem interconnected, continuous, and cohesive. She asks whether we are able, by traveling through it, navigating its spatial arrangements, and sifting through its detritus (as Walter Benjamin also sets out to do), to "recall, re-examine, and recontextualize" the images of the past which we come across, so that these images "awaken within us a new path to the future?" (29). I ask whether, by doing the same, we might instead be able to understand and see a path to the past with greater clarity.

1

The Garden and the Grid

D. J. Waldie and Raymond Chandler in Lakewood and Los Angeles

"Los Angeles is a city without a past" states Michael Dear (1998), arguing that its perpetual self-effacement and reinvention has disconnected it from its own history (76). Central to Marshall Berman's thesis in *All That is Solid Melts into Air* is the idea that twentieth-century modernity as made manifest in the city stands for the relentlessly new. The encroachment of urbanization often necessitates the erasure of traces of the past, with cities paving over signs of their own history in different ways. The urbanized spaces of Los Angeles seem to perfectly exhibit this sense of discontinuity between the past and the present. This disconnection leads to a feeling of absence in the place of an expected presence, as though one thing has surreptitiously replaced another. Sigmund Freud argues in his 1919 essay "The Uncanny" that this feeling marks the return of that which has been removed and/or repressed. In modern urban spaces wherein the past in physical form is continuously rearranged—demolished, rebuilt, reimagined—the sensation of the uncanny is ever-present.

Cities themselves can be uncanny (haunted, spectral) in that they are built upon a repressed or hidden landscape, evidenced in Raymond Chandler's Los Angeles-set novel, *The Big Sleep* (1939) (throughout this chapter I refer also to *Farewell, My Lovely* (1940) and *The High Window* (1942)). This is evident in Chandler's novels not only in, for example, the relationship between the Sternwood mansion and the family oil fields in *The Big Sleep*, but also in the interiors of places like Arthur Geiger's house and store and the Fulwider building in the same novel, and the Murdock family residence and the Idle Valley Club in *The High Window*. These spaces also reflect the repressed history of characters such as Carmen Sternwood (in *The Big Sleep*), Philip Marlowe (in all three novels), and Miss Davis (in *The High Window*), and their "spectacular form[s] of amnesia" (Baudrillard [1986] 2010: 10). The return of the repressed in Chandler's novels presented here is the result of the fact that cities are sedimented with histories made sporadically manifest in various ways in the built environment, persisting even when supplanted or reimagined by new urban forms. Dolores Hayden (1995) argues that the "traces of time embedded in the urban landscape of every city offer opportunities for reconnecting fragments of the [. . .] urban story" (13). For both Chandler and D. J. Waldie, the ability of the landscape, both man-made and natural, to alternately conceal and expose the past, is of paramount concern.

The ways in which we remember the past through space, through embedding or inscribing memory in space, is perfectly symbolized by Waldie through his use of the familial home as a historical site. In his semi-fictional, semi-autobiographical *Holy Land: A Suburban Memoir* (1996), Waldie depicts with delicate specificity a particular area of suburban Los Angeles County during the early to late 1950s, namely Lakewood, one of what Becky Nicolaides (2003) refers to as the "Sunbelt suburbs" constructed after the Second World War (24). Martin Dines (2015) contends that suburbs like Lakewood have long been deemed to possess a "fabricated and tamed modernity," making them spaces which are utterly removed from history "and devoid of memory" (81). But in fact, he argues, it is possible for the suburb to retain traces of history and hold memory "palimpsestically" (a term which proves significant throughout this book) (84). Similarly, despite Chandler's many depictions of a city apparently set on excising traces of its history, his novels demonstrate that the past can be physically located in those wild or pre-urban spaces of Southern California which have not quite been completely paved over, for example in the oil fields of *The Big Sleep*, and the intermittent glimpses of the ocean in *Farewell, My Lovely*.

In *Civilization and its Discontents* ([1930] 1961), Sigmund Freud compares the unconscious mind to the buried life of the modern city. Each stage or era of city life, he writes, is preserved, ready to be excavated, and thus continues to exist. The city is not only a physical place but a "psychical entity [. . .] an entity, that is to say, in which nothing that has once come into existence will have passed away and all the previous phases of development continue to exist alongside the latest one" (7). Referring to Rome, Freud notes that remnants of the ancient city still appear in the present-day, scattered in fragments across the city that has "grown up in recent centuries" (17). He continues that "much of the old is still there, but buried under modern buildings. This is how the past survives in historic places." Freud contends that when we see physical evidence of different stages of the past juxtaposed next to one another, we can finally experience spatially and tangibly these other permutations of history. He names these stages, or layers, of history in the city, "different contents" (18). In order to track the passing of time in the city and understand the ways in which, as Maurice Halbwachs ([1952] 1980) describes, it is "preserved by our physical surroundings" (140), I seek out the material changes in the landscape of the world inhabited by Chandler, Waldie, and others.

Paving the Garden

In the years between 1880 and 1932, Los Angeles grew "from a town of 10,000 people to covering roughly 29 square miles to become the country's principal western metropolis with 1.2 million people and a territory of 442 square miles" (Dear 1998: 89). As Mike Davis ([1990] 1992) points out: "Los Angeles was first and above all the creature of real-estate capitalism: the culminating speculation, in fact, of the generations of boosters and promoters who had subdivided and sold the West from the Cumberland Gap to the Pacific" (25).[1] Unlike other prominent American cities, such as New York with its adjacent harbor, Los Angeles seemed to possess no natural or locational advantages, and was merely an isolated tract of land "in the middle of the empty, semi-arid coastal plain" (Fogelson 1993: xv). It was not until the late 1800s that Los Angeles became known as "the capital city of an agricultural empire" and it was through its difficult relationship with water and the land that the city and the state of California invented itself (Starr 1985: 13). The uninhabitable landscape of Los Angeles and its peripheral land was eventually pummelled into submission, and the garden of America was cultivated and contrived. In American mythology, notes Richard Slotkin (1973), "the image of the wilderness east of the Mississippi changes from 'desert' to 'Garden' in a century and a half" (9). As Carey McWilliams ([1946] 1973) reports, the garden was "super-imposed on this semi-arid land; it is not native" (200).

Before the agricultural village that was Los Angeles could become the biggest city in the West, the problem of properly irrigating the land had to be solved. As Kevin Starr (1985) explains, Southern California is "not naturally blessed with water" (4). Providing sustainable power through water was eventually introduced through such feats of engineering as the Los Angeles Aqueduct (completed in 1913 by William Mulholland), before which "nearly 65 percent of [California's] yearly precipitation was either immediately evaporated by the sun or ran uselessly to the sea" (Starr 1990: 3). During the early 1900s, the chasm between the available supply of water and the growing population grew ever wider, leading to concerns over a possible water famine in the near future. These fears led to the formation in

1905 of a syndicate of powerful men, who slowly began to buy up land in the San Fernando Valley (the entirety of which touched the watershed of the Los Angeles River), eventually acquiring control of over 108,000 acres of land (as fictionalized in Mary Austin's 1917 novel *The Ford*). Once in possession of this land, the group proposed to the water board of the City of Los Angeles that the city should tap the waters of the Owens Valley to better irrigate the city. Ultimately, rather than bringing water to Los Angeles, it was funneled straight to the north end of the San Fernando Valley, and to the newly-acquired land that was then sold at huge profit. The Owens Valley farming community was destroyed, and the Gabrielino Indians and Spanish settlers who relied on the Owens River for food, water, and transport, were devastated. Carey McWilliams devotes much of *Southern California: An Island on the Land* ([1946] 1973) to a discussion of irrigation, providing an excellent report on the whole sordid affair.

"The drama of water," writes Kevin Starr, "would long remain the essential metaphor of the struggle in Southern California for a regional civilization" (1985: 7). The problem of irrigation resonates into the mid-twentieth century. During the 1930s city planners decided to cement over the Los Angeles River in order to put an end to a series of disastrous floods, turning the source of the city's lifeblood into a drainage ditch. Huge concrete troughs running through the city, built to control and direct the Los Angeles River, were built at the expense of the greenbelts and parks imagined by early urban planners. The mercurial and troublesome history of water in Southern California is a story that brings this history to light over and over again. In Alison Lurie's *The Nowhere City* ([1965] 1994), we are told that there has been no rain at all "for months," and by the time Paul Cattleman has flown to New England and back, it has not rained "for a year and a half" (239, 266).

The struggle to irrigate the region provides one explanation for Southern California's famous horizontal sprawl—the funneling of water from the Owens River in 1913 encouraged the molding of the city into one continuous form, connecting the various townships which required water. The grid system, another method by which this wilderness was controlled, trammeled over the erratic topography of the natural landscape in order to impose a sense of rationality, as James Howard Kunstler (1993) contends: "relentlessly straight section lines followed the compass, marching through swamps, across rivers, and over hilltops" (30). In "L.A.'s Crooked Heart," Waldie explains that it was Thomas Jefferson who first envisioned the "rational geometry penetrating forests, fording rivers and passing across prairies" which would leave in its wake a uniform series of townships all the way to the Pacific Ocean (2010b: n.p.). In *The Beer Can by the Highway*, John A. Kouwenhoven ([1961] 1988) argues that the grid system is quintessentially American, externalizing and making possible its "fluid and ever-changing unity" (44). The "gridiron pattern of the city's streets" is the same pattern which makes "almost any American town" legible, and is "the same pattern which, in the form of square townships, sections, and quarter sections, was imposed by [Jefferson's Land] Ordinance of 1785 on an almost continental scale [. . .] each man's domain clearly divided from his neighbor's" (44–5).

However, in Los Angeles these distinct domains are complicated by the fact that there are two conflicting grid systems at work, the denied co-existence of which adds to the city's spatial duplicity, incongruity, and de-centeredness. In "L.A.'s Crooked Heart," Waldie clarifies that the "north-south grid" is the manifestation of Jefferson's vision of "filling in the empty places on the blank page of the continent" (2010b: n.p.). But in downtown Los Angeles the system is different. These streets do not conform to the cartographic standards imposed by the Americans when they captured the city in 1847; "do not lead to the cardinal points of the compass but to the uncertain spaces in between," because they follow the grid *within* the American grid. This is "another, four Spanish leagues square, that conforms as best it can to the 16th century Laws of the Indies," which required "that the streets and house lots in the cities of New Spain have a 45-degree disorientation grid from true north and south." Maps and real-estate surveys of the 1870s continued to show the grid within the grid, and "House lots and streets continue to replicate its off-kilter orientation," which persisted into the nineteenth century. This duplicate system is not limited to Los Angeles alone. Samuel Stein (2019) explains that settlements and villages were planned across the Americas by indigenous nations, with "European imperialists and settler colonists [building] on these plans" and superimposing "their street grids over existing native trails" (15). In this instance, as in many others across the nation, a ghostly parallel city haunted the new one, and as this new version of the city expanded, the original grid began to look more and more like an aberration. Contemporary maps were re-drawn to show a "corrected" version of the downtown streetscape that aligns it with the national grid, straightening out the skew and maneuvering Figueroa Street so that it "appears to point due north or sometimes even east" (Waldie 2010b: n.p.). In simultaneously looking at the map and following the streets as they appear before us, Waldie remarks, we feel two separate imagined schemes crossing over each other, and it is this kind of "cartographic lie" that makes it so much harder in Los Angeles "to know where you are." History may wish for us to forget this clash, "but the streets themselves remember."

In *The History of Forgetting*, which traces the use of erasure in conceptions and (re)presentations of history in the culture of Los Angeles, Norman M. Klein (2008) notes the many ways in which Los Angeles has been transformed from a city of open farmland to one of inaccessible, introverted spaces. Instead of being used to build more verdant public spaces like parks, land was divided into an endless series of backyards, shopping malls, and theme parks. Farming, the precursor to oil as the defining industry of Los Angeles in the nineteenth century, had necessitated the construction of railroads to make it easier to transport what was grown and to ship it. The construction of the railroad in turn encouraged the promotion of land development along its new lines (for example in Pasadena, Hollywood, and Glendale). In 1876, Los Angeles was connected to the national rail network by the Southern Pacific Railroad. The first electric streetcar was used in 1887, and within three decades "the streetcar system would extend over 1600 miles and link up all the far-flung settlements in the Los Angeles basin" (Kunstler 1993: 208). Along the mainline tracks from the East sprung up several suburban enclaves "at convenient intervals." The concomitant real-estate market quickly collapsed, but, regardless, both the people who had traveled East to West (many looking for a country pile that would provide respite for respiratory complaints) and the infrastructure that had been installed to tend to the requirements of these new suburbs, remained. "At the heart of all suburban growth," notes Kenneth Jackson (1985), "is land development" (133). Waldie (2011a) explains in "How We Got This Way" that the irrigation systems that turned into suburban water companies provided "the essential ingredient to turn so much empty space into small farms and house lots" (n.p.). Mike Davis tells the tale of Harrison Gray Otis, the owner of the *Los Angeles Times*, who, during the late 1880s, allied himself with the largest landowners of the region, the transcontinental railroads, plus a coterie of various "developers, bankers and transport magnates," all of whom collectively set out to, as he puts it, "sell Los Angeles—as no city had ever been sold" ([1990] 1992: 25). Over the subsequent twenty-five years there was a huge mass migration of people seeking the panacea of California sunshine and its "open shop" (25). During the late 1800s, several semi-rural towns which had been born along the railway line (such as Pasadena and Hollywood) were incorporated. The streetcar system was consolidated by Henry E. Huntington, who named it the Pacific Electric Railroad, meanwhile buying up land scattered around the margins of the city which he tied together using this same Railroad. Other developers followed suit, filling in the gaps across Southern California. Later, the Pacific Electric Railroad was superseded by parkways, freeways, and super highways. Reyner Banham (2000) notes that these "sub-cities" were the starting point for Los Angeles' "peculiar pattern of many-centred growth" (20). The "dispersal and decentralisation of the landscape" in Los Angeles is in turn indicative of the consequential nature of the suburb to the city's environmental and spatial history (Fogelson 1993: 2).

Becoming the Grid

The word "suburb" itself has taken various forms and guises. In 1380, as Kenneth Jackson (1985) narrates in *Crabgrass Frontier*, John Wycliffe makes use of the word *suburbis*, with Geoffrey Chaucer following suit in *The Canterbury Tales* soon afterward. In North America, the suburbs began to take shape as early as 1719 in Boston, 1739 in Society Hill, Philadelphia, and 1775 in New York along Greenwich and Bloomingdale Roads in the midst of "two miles of marsh land" (Jackson 1985: 13). The "systematic growth of fringe areas at a pace more rapid than that of core cities, as a lifestyle involving a daily commute to jobs in the center" (13) began to define the suburbanization process during the nineteenth century. In California, the suburbs were "characteristically flatter, more regular, and architecturally more homogenous than some of their East Coast counterparts," due to the topography of the region, notes Jo Gill (2013: 108). In Upton Sinclair's *Oil!* ([1927] 2008), Bunny Ross and Dad drive through the peripheral towns on the outskirts of "Angel City," which consist of:

> some tens, or hundreds, or thousands of perfectly rectangular blocks, divided into perfectly rectangular lots, each containing a strictly modern bungalow [. . .] decorated with a row of red and yellow flags fluttering merrily in the breeze [. . .] an alert young man with a writing pad and a fountain-pen, [was] prepared to write you a contract of sale after two minutes conversation (21).

Early in the twentieth century, certain suburbs in Southern California, such as those south of downtown Los Angeles, retained a visible and still functioning connection to its agricultural history: "lush farmlands gradually gave way to factories and subdivisions" in the 1910s to 1920s, indicating that this "rich land had been used for sheep grazing, dairying, and farming," advises Becky Nicolaides (2002: 14). Even in 1920, Nicolaides continues, "25 percent of L.A. County's entire agricultural output was produced in this southern section [. . .] agricultural production continued to define this part of Los Angeles even as it became 'suburban.'" In *Oil!*, Bunny describes the environs of 5746 Los Robles Boulevard, which runs through a seemingly unassuming suburb a couple of miles away from "Beach City," (aka Long Beach): "you would have had to know this land of hope in order to realize that it stood in a cabbage field [. . .] The eye of hope, aided by surveyor's instruments, had determined that some day a broad boulevard would run on this line; and so there was a dirt road, and at every corner white posts set up" (Sinclair [1926] 2008: 23). Lakewood, a postwar suburban community developed by Louis Boyar, Mark Taper, and Ben Weingart from late 1949 until its completion in 1953, was part of this tradition. Joan Didion ([2003] 2004), writing about Lakewood in *Where I Was From*, tells us that just like "much of the southern end of this grid, Lakewood was until after World War Two agricultural, several thousand acres of beans and sugar beets just inland from the Signal Hill oil field" (102). Throughout the early 1950s, Waldie's home was in the process of being fabricated, forged amid the fields of lima beans: "You and I grew up in these neighborhoods when they were an interweaving of houses and fields that were soon to be filled with more houses" (Waldie 1996: 3).

Suburban narratives like Waldie's demonstrate that western history is not simply that of a Turnerian pushing back of the frontier, in search of greater space through sheer entrepreneurial spirit, but rather it is "a history of the systematic domestication, homogenization, and containment—if not outright destruction—of that open land," (Bennett 2011: 288) which has produced its own self-perpetuating grid of organized, cultivated space (as Didion's reference above to the Signal Hill oil field—by 1923, the largest in California—and its proximity to Lakewood, infers). Lakewood is notable for the speed and volume of its construction, with its developers "building tract-style housing faster, cheaper, and at a higher density than had previously been done: builders broke ground for more than 500 homes per week" (Pulido, Barraclough and Chend 2012: 172). It is part of both the history of endless development in California as a whole and of the post-war suburb specifically, becoming a model for other new communities which "seemed to develop overnight in Los Angeles County" (173) after the Second World War. After the War, millions of soldiers returned home to the United States, and were presented with the fait accompli of a ready-made home of their own. Before the War, government programs such as the Home Owners Loan Corporation, created in 1933, and the Federal Housing Administration, created in 1934, both products of Roosevelt's New Deal, served as precursors to the G. I. Bill (or the Serviceman's Readjustment Act). This parlayed post-Depression government intervention in housing into a comprehensive post-war Gosplan of sorts for returning veterans benefiting from the subsequent economic boom, including low-interest home loans with no need for a deposit and very favorable terms for new construction. Between 1948 and 1958, "11 million new suburban homes were established" (Murphy 2009: 6).

Brian Tochterman (2017) notes that developers of early post-war suburbs like Lakewood in Los Angeles County and Levittown on Long Island had also "benefited from Cold War concerns over safety and density in the atomic age and popular culture's packaging of consumption, conformity and nationalism around the 'warm hearth' of the single-family home" (6). Indeed, the mall local to Lakewood also housed a shelter to be used in case of nuclear war. In *Borderland*, John R. Stilgoe (1988) argues that the West Coast in particular felt the effects of this dread of the atomic bomb, which by the end of the 1940s "had fueled a great migration to the suburbs, to the borderlands, and to rural regions supposedly far from ground zero" (301). It was in California that "the warm, sunny land settled by so many discharged veterans educated by fire-bombed cities and by Hiroshima and Nagasaki, the flight from ground zero was fastest." In *A Single Man*, set in Los Angeles in 1962, Christopher Isherwood's narrator surveys with dismay the "dozens of new houses" being constructed on the hills outside the city, the encroachments of suburban spread spilling out "over the entire plain," eating up "the wide pastures and ranchlands and the last stretches of orange grove; it has sucked out the surrounding lakes and sapped the forests of the high mountains" ([1964] 2010: 88).

A degree of skepticism has long existed regarding not only the excesses of subdivision and development, but also the amorphous nonentity that the suburbs were deemed by some to be; incapable of retaining any kind of impression of permanence or historicity. In 1894, journalist Henry A. Beers described the new suburban areas that were being constructed as undefined and ambiguous: they existed in a liminal space as a kind of "limbo or ragged edge" (5). In a 1906 article for *Craftsman*, H. A. Caparn dismissed these suburban residential areas as "neither city no country, nor can it ever supply the place of either" (767). This attitude to the suburb persisted into the late twentieth century. In *The Geography of Nowhere*, James Howard Kunstler (1993) articulates the suburb as a place of conveyor belt aspiration capable only of producing identikit fantasies; as a "place where the dream house stood—a subdivision of many other identical dream houses" (105). It is characterized by ambivalence, being "neither the country nor the city. It was no place." Defined by its in-between-ness, its lack of inherent meaning, the suburb can perversely be seen as a kind of utopia (or ou-topos) —a literal "no place." In 2011, over a decade after the publication of *Holy Land*, Waldie continues to ask himself whether it is possible to inhabit such a place with any permanence; this is a question which encapsulates "a localization of the larger experience of California, which itself is only a portion of the immigrant experience of the

West; and the problem of the West is only an especially perplexing subset of the everlasting problem of America" (Waldie 2011b: 209). How, in "a place of presumed exile" (being Holy it is thus a garden from which one surely expects to be expelled, but also being a no place one has already been banished from the center to the margins of civilization) —a place so expansive, mimetic, new, that it is "hardly distinguishable" from other tract houses, other neighborhoods, all extending "as far as the street grid allows in a metropolis of thousands of miles of streets all just the same" —can one possibly "make a home here?" (Waldie 2011b: 209).

For Stephen M. Buhler (2000), *Holy Land* provides "a spiritual geography of Lakewood, California, a place often dismissed as soulless, as 'no-place' at all" (201). He argues that most "adopted Californians" associate the state with "a sense of displacement" rather than homeliness. Martin Dines also suggests that suburbs like Lakewood have long been aligned with a certain "blankness" due not only to their "perceived demographic and architectural uniformity" but also to what has been seen as an "absence of history" (2015: 81). Dines ultimately contends however that, contrary to arguments that the suburbs are unable to emit a sense of the past, there is evidence that "acts of remembering" are in fact "embedded in the suburban landscape" in unexpected ways. But these acts of memory are more likely, as he puts it, to "reify *absences*" (emphasis added) than make the *presence* of past lives tangible. It is in these absences, silences, and omissions, that remnants of undisclosed memory can be found and exposed.

In 1946, D. J. Waldie's parents bought the house in Lakewood in which Waldie still lives (at the time of writing), and where he wrote the book which narrates both his childhood and the life of his hometown. *Holy Land* is broken up into 316 segments, like plots of subdivided land, with Waldie incrementally moving through adjoining rooms as he carefully approaches the personal and intimate. This is akin to the careful progression from cell to cell, block to block, of the grid system. Perhaps this is what he means when he writes that he thinks he is "becoming the grid he knew" (Waldie 1996: 1). Waldie refers frequently to the grid system (touched on earlier in this chapter) according to which the spatial arrangement of Lakewood was established. This grid is "a fraction of a larger grid, anchored to one in Los Angeles," (22) making Lakewood an extension of a larger map which was first laid out in 1781 by the Spanish. He writes that it is possible to drive from the ocean to Los Angeles and remain on the same grid of streets: "Every square foot of my city has been tilled or built on and fitted into the grid" (54). As art historian Rosalind Krauss (1979) notes, "Logically speaking, the grid extends, in all directions, to infinity" (60).

Eric Avila (2004) remarks that the decision to build Lakewood on the grid system was typical for "suburban developments built on Southern California's flat terrain [. . .] The grid reflects distinct traditions of city planning, and its historical application reflects a solution to the problem of ordering undeveloped land" (2004: 45–6). Lakewood's shape and layout "epitomized the efficient organization of space that marked the development of postwar suburbia" (45). Stilgoe explains that during the mid-nineteenth century, land speculators at the edge of every major American city were throwing "an essentially urban fabric over hitherto borderland landscape," cultivating the margins so they resembled the urban spaces from which they originally sought to provide sanctuary (1988: 152). The street patterns being built on a "rectilinear" style was a reflection of the fact that urbanity was at the time "equated [. . .] with straightness." The grid represents a rejection of nineteenth-century "illegibility" in favor of more regulated space (Donald 1999: 73). In "Grids," Krauss depicts the grid as deeply modern in its function and style: "one of the important sources of this power is the way the grid is [. . .] so stridently modern to look at, seeming to have no place of refuge, no room on the face of it, for vestiges of the nineteenth century to hide" (1979: 54). (There is more to come on urban modernism in Chapter 3.) The site of Waldie's memories, in its system of intersecting grids, right angles, and straight lines, is therefore not only a reflection of his attempts to textually control and contain his memory, but is also symptomatic of *the* urban spatial arrangement of the twentieth-century city. "The ground plan of most American cities," contends urban sociologist Robert E. Park in 1967, "is a checkerboard. The unit of distance is the block" (4).

Jo Gill argues that it was the aerial photographs taken by William Garnett in the 1950s (some of which appear in *Holy Land*), which crystallized the image of the razing of land in California and the subsequent grading, trenching, and framing in order to create the suburb of Lakewood and its attendant identical houses arranged in rows, that both influenced the spatial formation of other new suburbs, and informed the literature of the period and its representations of space through time (2013: 108). Robert Fishman (2005) asserts that these images "have a special power to define the whole era" (562). In *Holy Land*, Waldie does what Reyner Banham advises his reader to do upon approaching Los Angeles, which is to read it "in the original" (2000: 5). Or more appropriately in Waldie's case, to *write* it in the original: to *become* the grid. In his discussion of the Eiffel Tower, Roland Barthes ([1979] 1997) argues that we visit the Tower in order to "perceive, comprehend, and savor a certain essence of Paris," and that this is achieved through the "panoramic vision" with which we are endowed from on high (8). This view from above gives the visitor "the world to read and not only to perceive," which enables them to "transcend sensation and to see things in their structure" in a newly intellectual manner (9). In this way the visitor deciphers the panorama of space. The Garnett photographs of Lakewood do much the same, presenting "the Olympian view" decried by Jane Jacobs (the hugely influential Greenwich Village activist and writer on postwar urban planning), of the apparently Cartesian space in which Waldie lived ([1961] 1965: 437). De Certeau ([1980] 1984) writes in similar terms, in *The Practice of Everyday Life*, of viewing "Manhattan from the 110th floor of the World Trade Center" (91). Like Barthes, he asks why one is drawn to viewing space from such vertiginous heights. In doing so, one is "lifted out of the city's grasp. One's body is no longer clasped by the streets," but rather is transformed "into a voyeur. It puts him at a distance" and it is this distance that empowers one to read the city's spatial reality like a text; "to be a solar Eye, looking down like a god" (92). Those who instead attempt to understand the city from the pavement, the "walkers," pursue the "thicks and thins of an urban 'text' they write without being able to read it" (93). The walkers write but cannot read the city, whereas the readers see but cannot negotiate with its poetic topography. The walker may not see as the reader does, but their sightless navigation still creates something—their path is a story, but it is one that is disrupted and informed by others.

In their paper "Making the Visible A Little Hard to See," Bart Eeckhout and Lesley Janssen (2014) argue that *Holy Land* is organized by two intertwined strategies: "the seemingly static grid and the ostensibly dynamic disruptions of a walking perspective" (97). Waldie, who does not drive and remains a steadfast pedestrian, writes from the same perspective.[2] He chooses to decenter the cartographic perspective imposed by the grid, creating pockets of entry and exit everywhere as he moves through it, leaving an "endlessly extendable chain of associative links" (97) in his wake. Waldie sends missives from within the grid, which is populated, peopled, not a depersonalized shell to be observed in aerial shots. From within this grid "that constitutes the pattern of his daily existence," (88) he cuts across it with his narrative, making the abstract into the lived, revealing ambiguity amid the geometry. His voice is polyphonic and plural, not hermetic and singular. For de Certeau, the walker composes a "multivalent text that inverts the totalizing scheme of the panorama-city" ([1980] 1984: 92).

He finds space for "elliptical life stories and personal psychographs," within the apparent rigidity of the grid that structures his narrative, introducing "a variety of disruptions that puncture the fiction of a self-contained narrator structurally in command" (Eeckhout and Janssen 2014: 88). However, though it is the case that the geometric textual space created by the narrator is expanded through the interspersing of personal history amid memories from the Lakewood collective, creating a kind of biographical heteroglossia, I argue that Waldie is in fact as tirelessly methodical as the grid he walks and writes from, and that his "surprising digressions" are in fact purposefully placed (92). Waldie, in conversation with Neil Campbell, discloses that walking is for him "a rhetorical or metrical organizing principle" (Waldie and Campbell 2011: 248). He is both reader and writer, and the "networks of these moving, intersecting writings," to quote de Certeau, compose a story which is "shaped out of fragments of trajectories and alterations of spaces" ([1980] 1984: 93). Just as the unnamed visitor looked down from Barthes' Eiffel Tower and de Certeau's World Trade Center, so does Waldie survey all of Lakewood's "little boxes" and consider exactly what to place in each of them (Reynolds [1962] 2000: n.p.).[3] Looking down at the city enables the visitor to rationalize space, providing a way of "conceiving and constructing space on the basis of a finite number of stable, isolatable, and interconnected properties" (Certeau (1980) 1984: 94). Viewed from above, the "Solar eye" (92) of the city connects its dots, deciding which of its elements will become part of the whole and which are to be extracted. So does the reader, empowered with this aerial authority, endeavor to write; to organize and narrativize: "On the one hand, there is a differentiation and redistribution of the parts and functions of the city [. . .] on the other there is a rejection of everything that is not capable of being dealt with in this way" (94). Such things, like "illness, death, etc." are not treated as "waste products," in the narrative of Waldie, but instead are elided, placed in a more remote box, in an act of narrative control. *Holy Land* represents a textual pulling of fragments into a whole shape (Waldie and Campbell 2011: 229).

Waldie employs a mathematically inclined language to quantify and analyze the data of his childhood in Lakewood, approaching it circuitously and through implication such that the tiniest details become hugely significant. Yet despite the sense of control emphasized by the mathematical division and subdivision of space imposed on the land by the grid, within and between those spaces there is room for chaos. In *Delirious New York* ([1978] 1994) Rem Koolhaas writes that the grid system "defines a new balance between control and de-control in which the city can be at the same time ordered and fluid, a metropolis of rigid chaos," (20) and that buildings within this system become "a stack of individual privacies" inside each of which dwells an "unstable combination of simultaneous activities" (85). Despite the sense of control emphasised by the mathematical division and subdivision of space imposed on the land by the grid, within those spaces the freedom of individual will thrives unimpeded. The internal world of such buildings obscures the "continuous changes raging inside it" (101), while the exterior of a building represents the façade of logic and control presented by urban planning and development. In *Holy Land*, characters such as Mr. H and Mrs. A recur, their stories dropped and picked up in between bouts of reportage of a more impersonal nature. The narrative of Mr. H with his surfeit of detritus in his front yard, and the innumerable letters sent by Mrs. A to the council concerning nuclear waste, secret military burial places, and the potential toppling of her house into a pit created by the Army Corps of Engineers, seep through the book surreptitiously. The grid is endless and inescapable. The grid makes land understandable. But the stories of Mr. H and Mrs. A make it clear that the grim, relentless, mathematical logic of city planners cannot altogether rid the built environment of the possibility for individual irrationality. The inability, or refusal, of such people to acquiesce to the demands of the city and toe the line, a line made sometimes literal by the borders which divide one lot from the one next door, express deviations and transgressions which cast ripples across the placid surface of the neighborhood.

Waldie, who has described Los Angeles as the "city of self-inflicted amnesia," himself embeds his own desire for control over memory and its narrative into his text (2010a: A31). We find each section of *Holy Land* sitting side by side like rooms in a house and houses in a block, connected somehow thematically and rather loosely. At first it seems that one thought slides into the next like interlinked memories gently knocking against one another. His father's death brings to mind, for example, the fact that, in Waldie's home town, a fire engine will often have a quicker response time to your house in an emergency than an ambulance, which in turn leads him to the story of a woman who set her own house alight. Incrementally it becomes evident that Waldie is placing blocks in the narrativization of his memory between the experience of pain and the remembrance of that pain. When he alternates in his remembrances between stating facts and referring circuitously to grief, he uses the rooms in his house as repositories for memory: some of these rooms provide a buffer between other rooms he does not wish to enter. "My father died behind a well-made, wooden bathroom door" (Waldie 1996: 24), writes Waldie, and this material separation is reinforced by the sequestering and demarcation of personal, painful memories within his text. The segmentation of the narrative into textual cells and silos allows him to contain things he cannot always bring himself to discuss explicitly, and on which he can shut the textual door if necessary.

A further example is provided by the two sections which stand between the disclosures that his mother died in hospital and his father died at home. These liminal sections discuss the Land Ordinance of Thomas Jefferson, written in 1785, and the sad tale of Mr. H in the present day, whose Lakewood house is taken from him when he refuses to clear his front yard and the bank forecloses on his mortgage. Section 49, in which his father's death is first mentioned, is succeeded by two sections which detail the Douglas Aircraft plant in Long Beach, and the materials from which the houses in his neighborhood are constructed. In section 55 he describes his father's death as though from a great distance ("He sat on the edge of his bed in the middle room and waited for his father to die" (28)), while in section 56 he tells the same story from the intimacy position of a first-person perspective ("I waited on the edge of my bed in the middle bedroom"). In the latter section, however, he does not mention his father's death until the final sentence. It is as though the use of "he" mitigates the pain of remembering, allowing him to tell the story as though it happened to someone else; the use of "I" on the other hand, offers no such protection. Waldie frequently writes in the second or third person when narrating both the lives of others and his own. Like Maria Wyeth, of Joan Didion's *Play It As It Lays*, who also wishes to control her own past narrative to contain her pain, when he does use the first person, it is from the position of the present, referring back to the past. For example: "*You and I grew up* in these neighborhoods"; "The house where I still live, and *where my father died*, predates the building of the rest of this city"; and "My brother and I, *who shared a room for almost twenty years*" (3, 25, 47 emphases added). These are further examples of Waldie's attempts at quarantining himself, in the form of his textual "I," from the rest of a sentence which is devoted to a painful memory.

Throughout *Holy Land*, Waldie makes reference to rooms with particular significance—symbolic spaces in which memories he does not wish to dwell on can be placed. Though each room in the house has a separate narrative lot, these spaces are in extremely close proximity to one another. There is very little separation between each room in the house, each house in the block, and each block in the grid, making each of these spaces indeterminate and conjoined. References to flimsy construction work recur throughout. Walls, posits Waldie, offer only a "thin, cement skin over absence" (42). The exteriors of the houses themselves are "little more than an inch thick," (43) making one's separation from the outside so minimal as to be almost non-existent. At one point in his narrative, Waldie states that he and his brother slept only fourteen feet away from his parents. The segmented spaces of the domestic interiors threaten to spill over into the neighboring rooms, melting into one entity. Waldie envisages feet crashing through the attic, the bathroom door knocked down, an earthquake forcing the "stucco and chicken-wire houses [. . .] off their foundations" (137). The attic stuffed with the relics of Christmases past is so structurally unsound that one "bad step will put your foot through a bedroom ceiling" (42). Such descriptions affirm Carey McWilliams' contention regarding the "impression of impermanence" exuded by Southern California (McWilliams [1946] 1973: 199).

Waldie frequently draws the reader's attention to the fragility of the manmade spaces of his neighborhood, pointing the reader toward evidence of what *Lakewood Online* tells us about the geological history of his hometown: "A lot is going on under Lakewood. Beds of water, stacked like a gravel, sand, and clay layer cake, lie beneath" ("The Lakewood Story" 2011: n.p.). "What's below my suburb," Waldie explains, is its "submerged history—the history of its making and what that led to" (Waldie and Campbell 2011: 235–6). Lakewood is topographically "a place of seasonal flooding [. . .] Submergence remains a risk," and this risk is coupled with the fact that the land is watered from below, "from the wells that draw from several underground sources, both man-made and natural" (236). In *Holy Land*, seemingly distinct spaces quickly become permeable; access for Waldie and his neighbors to a different room is only one clumsy footfall away. When it is discovered that Mr. H has dug a 300-square-feet fallout shelter beneath his garage floor, a city inspector informs the new owner that should a car actually be driven onto this floor, it would immediately collapse. The irrational behavior of Waldie's neighbors, and the pain of his own memory, cannot always be kept sequestered in separate rooms. Space is porous, and memory within it ultimately uncontainable. Just as the comportment of his neighbors continually finds a way of evading suppression and expressing itself publicly, so too does Waldie's grief, revealing itself sporadically and proving to be beyond his capacity for control of the narrative. "At some point in your story grief presents itself," he writes, as though apologizing that this is beyond his control (1996: 3). "Now, for the first time, your room is empty, not merely unoccupied." Grief is here likened to emptiness; Waldie describes his house in the present-day as "largely a void" (42). His grief is outlined very subtly in his description of the house in the wake of his bereavement: "My brother brought me back from the hospital. I spent that night in the empty house, as I continue to spend each night at home" (31). Here we find a space that was filled, but now sits uncannily empty.

Waldie consistently provides information about the measurements of rooms, the square footage taken up by houses, the distance spanned by the city which further encroaches on the land around it. Though he attempts to seal off and surround each vignette in *Holy Land* with the narration of a history which is characterized and understood much of the time through data and quantification, attempts to circumnavigate or even stop memory at the door are eventually thwarted:

> My father died behind a well-made, wooden bathroom door. It is a three-panel door. Each panel is nearly square, twenty-one inches wide by nineteen inches high. From edge to edge, the door is twenty-eight inches wide. [...] The doors in my house are abstract and ordinary. The bathroom door is now forty-seven years old. My father was sixty-nine (24–5).

Things fall apart. Death and chaos are only on the other side of a Douglas fir door.

Beneath a Raised Scar

Writing in *The Fall into Eden*, David Wyatt (1986) recalls wistfully that the California in which he grew up "was a beautiful, now vanished garden [...] a place no sooner had than lost" (xv). He contends that the way in which Californians "live in time has everything to do with the history of their experience of space" (xv–xvi). The "free land" (Bennett 2011: 285) of the West has long been "explored, mapped, surveyed, gridded, enclosed, homesteaded, fenced, plowed, railroaded, dynamited, dammed, irrigated, urbanized and suburbanized" (286). Los Angeles itself was "gridded and subdivided seven times larger than was necessary" (Starr 1997: 159), before being sold off. In Raymond Chandler's *The High Window*, Idle Valley provides an example of the subdivision of the land into geometrical pieces. As Marlowe drives through the moonlit hills he rounds a curve, beyond which "the whole valley spread out before me. A thousand white houses built up and down the hills, ten thousand lighted windows and the stars hanging down over them politely, not getting too close" (Chandler [1942] 1983: 102). This vast open space has been carved up into a sea of right angles. Here even the firmament seems within reach, toeing the rapidly diminishing line between what can and what cannot be developed. Unable to return to a mythological lost idyll, to therefore conceptualize or integrate the disappearing past into the present, according to Wyatt, Californians must exist in a perpetual present typified by the city and its symbolic and literal control over its environment. It is not just Californians who are nostalgic for their formerly verdant environment. Wyatt describes Chandler, who had lived in England for ten years from the age of seven to seventeen and who subsequently came to Los Angeles in 1912, as a "failed pastoralist, and his work can be read as an elegy for the 'Good Green Place' he had known and lost" (161). Chandler lends Marlowe his anxieties about the natural world, a man who wavers between a bleak cynicism at its degradation and concern when it obstructs his investigations. In *Farewell, My Lovely*, he describes the now polluted ocean adjacent to Bay City (i.e., Santa Monica), which can now only be perceived very faintly, "as if they had kept this much just to remind people this had once been a clean open beach where the waves came in and the wind blew and you could smell something besides hot fat and cold sweat" ([1940] 2000: 330). Paul Skenazy (1984) writes that Chandler's attitude toward nature often reflects an inherently "proagrarian" mythology (94).

The "longing for a garden," argues Wyatt, is set against the "determination to confront the world of the machine" (1986: 163). The interruption of the industrial world in the utopian ideal of pastoral life is described by Leo Marx (1964) as the *Machine in the Garden*. Whereas Marx wrote of the "counterforce" (25) represented by the locomotive, which was "associated with fire, smoke, speed, iron, and noise" (27) appearing suddenly in the woods and "shattering the harmony of the green hollow," the machine, or the counterforce, in early-twentieth-century Los Angeles, was the automobile. Where the erosion of nature was deemed necessary in order to assume control over the water supply and irrigation, it was further facilitated by the construction of the freeway system. During the early decades of the twentieth century, the Southern California freeway system was incrementally superimposed over the increasingly urbanized wilderness. In 1924 the Mulholland Highway (now Mulholland Drive) opened on the ridgeline of the Santa Monica Mountains and the Hollywood Hills; the San Francisco-Oakland Bay Bridge and the Parker Dam followed in 1936; and the Arroyo Seco Parkway after that in 1940 (the nation's first controlled limited access highway, i.e., freeway). David L. Clark (1983) explains that Los Angeles became the first city to fully adopt the car; by the 1930s "80 percent of all local trips were made in automobiles" (272). From the mid-1940s onwards, over the course of more than two decades, freeway construction flourished at the expense not just of the local flora and fauna but also of long-standing local communities.

As with the location of the various expressways built in New York City, there was a racial component to the construction of the freeway system that should be noted. In "Spatial Entitlement: Race, Displacement, and Sonic Reclamation in Postwar Los Angeles," Gaye Theresa Johnson (2014) argues that spaces can function as entities within which "to maintain both memories and practices that reinforce community knowledge and cohesiveness" (322). But this kind of meaningful space "was particularly vulnerable in postwar Los Angeles," just as it was in postwar New York. The pattern of violently conducted clearance and dislocation is a recurring one. Each generation of Mexicans in Southern California, for example, going back to the "mestizo Indians who lost their land to Anglo settlers who came to California before the Civil War, suffered humiliation, displacement, and the loss of property and status at the hands of the dominant, Anglo-American ruling class" (Laslett 2015: 131). Johnson quantifies the damage done to neighborhoods predominantly populated by people of color: "Between 1949 and 1967, 400,000 residential units were destroyed to make way for the postindustrial, suburban sensibilities that would characterize the modern U.S. city" (2014: 320). Even with the creation of the GI Bill and Federal Housing Authority Loans, there was a paucity of housing for Mexicans in particular due to zoning restrictions, which banned them and other ethnic minorities from buying houses in white communities. Not only was an insufficient number of homes being built, but certain communities were being driven out of the homes they had built for themselves. Though there was an intense need for housing during the postwar period, due to thousands of service people returning to the city, "constructing freeways took precedence over salvaging homes" (Estrada 2005: 295).

By 1957 "the construction of five freeways [...] had cut through and effectively destroyed the primarily Mexican neighborhood of Boyle Heights" (Johnson 2014: 320). The disintegration of Boyle Heights ran parallel to the displacement of another Mexican community, that of Chavez Ravine, which was notoriously demolished to make way for Dodger Stadium ("another chapter in Los Angeles' history of bulldozing as a form of social policy" (Wheeler 1996: 43)). Hundreds of families had called Chavez Ravine home for decades. In 1950, most were convinced to leave and were promised low-rent housing that would be built on the same site. However, in 1959, 300 acres of the ravine were sold to the Brooklyn Dodgers (who became the Los Angeles Dodgers in 1958) owner Walter O'Malley for the purposes of building a baseball stadium for his team. Residents who resisted the move, "were dragged from their houses and arrested as they watched their homes bulldozed in order to accommodate a higher bidder" (Estrada 2005: 288). This was re-lived by homeowners in East Los Angeles, who were also displaced when their homes were bulldozed to make way for the expansion of the freeway. In 1944 the first part of the Santa Ana Freeway opened, with the section from Soto Street to Eastman Avenue in Boyle Heights completed by 1948. Two hundred residential buildings were evacuated.[4] Ultimately freeway encroachments "account for 19 percent of East Los Angeles' land use" (Estrada 2005: 290). Just like the superimposition of the 1811 New York grid over the old, overlaying the historical trails forged by the Native American people, in this postwar era of urban redevelopment, from the spatial reality of present-day Los Angeles, "several Black and Brown neighborhoods were eviscerated, even from maps themselves, as if no one had ever lived there" (Johnson 2014: 320).

In the vein of Marshall Berman, Gil Cuadros (1994) in "My Aztlan: White Place" recalls his childhood home in City Terrace, another East Los Angeles neighborhood razed to make way for the expansion of the freeway: "I imagine the house still intact, buried under dirt and asphalt, dust and neglect. Hidden under a modern city, this is my Aztlan, a glimpse of my ancient home, my family" (55). Aztlan, explains Raúl Homero Villa, is "the nationalist-identified Chicano homeland encompassing the greater U.S. Southwest" (Villa 1999: 116). Cuadros begins his story by confessing that he is "driving down the wrong freeway back to my place," which is located in City Terrace Drive, the site of his childhood home (1994: 53). Cuadros' sense that the freeway he has chosen is somehow erroneous is echoed by author Helena Maria Viramontes (2007), also from City Terrace, who identifies in her novel *Their Dogs Came With Them* what is left behind by the bulldozers of the California Division of Highways in her East L.A. neighborhood; the "ugly bandage of cement suturing together two boulevards" which has left one character feeling that her city had become "a beast alien to her [...] she castigated herself for standing on the wrong bridge" (225). Cuadros traces the length of the San Bernardino freeway to find his parallel history, which is now only just visible via his mind's eye: "Driving the San Bernardino is the closest I get to Mecca. I was born below this freeway, in a house with a picket fence now plowed under" (1994: 54). The San Bernardino, part of the East Los Angeles Freeway System, was one in a series of freeways, constructed between 1944 and 1965, which were forged through predominantly Mexican neighborhoods in East Los Angeles. Ironically it is the path of the San Bernardino which he must now follow in order to find the site of his childhood. His point of origin is subterranean; to return there is to delve beneath the surface of the city: "I've been here before, time after time, told my mother where our old house would be buried, near the call box, under the fast lane" (54). By the end of this journey he seems to be disintegrating on a cellular level; he too is decomposing, returning to earth, hearing only the sound of cars like terrible birdsong above his shrouded head: "I can feel my body becoming tar, limbs divide, north and south. My house smells of earth and it rumbles from the traffic above. White clay sifts through the ceiling" (58).

The poet Manazar Gamboa (1996) writes in similar terms of an imagined return to his childhood home in Chavez Ravine, where he was born in 1934. He grew up in the house built by his parents, who had fled the Mexican Revolution and moved to Los Angeles in the 1920s. In his self-published epic poem, *Memories Around a Bulldozed Barrio*, he articulates his family's uprooting to make way for the baseball stadium:

> If you were to lift Dodger Stadium and its sprawling parking lots from where they now sit and replaced them with the hills, gullies, flatlands, streets, and homes that were there up to the 1950s—when they were leveled and destroyed— you would find la gente de los tres barrios traveling through their daily lives. Welcome to my barrio (n.p.).

Such descriptions of the former homes and neighborhoods of Boyle Heights and Chavez Ravine as akin to burial sites and chasms beneath the earth are reflective of the "persistent figurations of death" and the "phantom presences" which speak to "the present absences, or absent presences, of people, places, and histories that urban development often obscures or wipes out" (Villa 1999: 112–13). This imagery articulates a purposeful obfuscation in the urban spaces of Los Angeles. In his essay "How I Found Los Angeles," Waldie criticizes what he refers to as a "regime of speed" and its effects, which can be perceived, he argues, in the city's topographical erasures caused by "the rush to build a more perfect paradise" (2016: n.p.). The poet Lorna Dee Cervantes ([1981] 1982) grew up in the Mexican-American neighborhood of Sal Si Puedes on the outskirts of San Jose, which was bisected by Highway 280 in the late 1960s. Her poem "Freeway 280" evokes Leo Marx's description of the machine's unwelcome appearance, "a sudden, shocking intruder upon a fantasy of idyllic satisfaction" (Marx 1964: 29), with her formerly verdant neighborhood disappearing in the wake of the freeway's aggressive encroachments: "Las casitas near the gray cannery,/nestled amid wild abrazos of climbing roses/and man-high geraniums/are gone now. The freeway conceals it/all beneath a raised scar" (Cervantes [1981] 1982: 20). Similar erasures include the "levelling of the multi-ethnic neighborhood of Bunker Hill," which Waldie equates to the "channeling of the beds of the Los Angeles and San Gabriel rivers," which made both "nearly invisible" (Waldie 2016: n.p.).

David Wyatt recounts that if one drives south from Pasadena to Long Beach, "the freeway follows the bed of the Los Angeles River. The river is paved" (1986: xv). In Morrow Mayo's potted history of the city from the days of its conquest up to the early 1930s, he contends that this kind of excision is entirely in character: "the trees are pulled out by the roots and burned, and the ashes are scattered. In a few more years—as already in many places—the sagebrush and tumbleweed will conceal the scars from the eyes of tourists. The Angel City is covering her trail"

(1933: 244). If it is true that, in California, "every family has its paved garden," the novels of Raymond Chandler indicate that the denial or removal of such gardens creates its own enduring ghosts (Wyatt 1986: xv–xvi). The green has melted into the gray of smog and high rise, the private orchards which littered the landscape making way for a graveyard of roots and stumps. Throughout the three novels presented here, Chandler articulates the many ways in which Los Angeles is symbolic of a kind of subverted Eden, defined by its suppression and exponential disappearance.

World and Earth

In *The Detections of Totality*, Fredric Jameson (2016) finds two typologies of landscape dominate in Chandler's Southern California: the urban and the natural. Interestingly, he insists that these two landscapes coexist, "as compared to more classical cities, which *replace* the natural" (48). In Los Angeles, "both dimensions [. . .] are in play simultaneously at all times; neither is effaced by the other." However, they do remain nevertheless "two distinct languages" which frequently find themselves "juxtaposed" (50). Later Jameson refers to Heidegger's conception of art to further understand these distinct spaces. The work of art emerges, according to the latter, from "a 'rift' between what he calls World and Earth—terms we can rewrite for our own purposes as the dimensions of History and the social project on the one hand, and Nature [. . .] on the other," the latter defined as emerging from "geographical or ecological constraints" (77). Raymond Chandler's literary narratives display the ways in which Los Angeles' city dwellers live "within this tension," between these two spaces which sometimes, uneasily, intermesh.

There is the perception of a distinct lack of control when it comes to nature and the wilderness in Southern California. Its inhabitants seem not to know how to encourage or restrict its power and are "haunted by a vague and nameless fear of future disaster" which could strike their arid environs at any moment (McWilliams [1946] 1973: 199). Nathan Silver (2000) contends that the "fundamental task of architecture" is to "protect man from the tyranny of nature" (1). In Chandler's novels, this task is applied to the man-made spaces of Los Angeles and its environs, which have been built to impose order and mitigate the potentially devouring force of the external environment. In these novels there seems to be, as Jameson puts it, "a fundamental distance between human space or habitation and the Nature of Southern California; the realm of the first, and Los Angeles in general, is here marked as artificial rather than as natural" (2016: 41). In *Farewell, My Lovely*, Philip Marlowe visits the Oceanside residence of Mr. and Mrs. Grayle on Astor Drive, where the Pacific can be felt but not seen. The Grayle residence is a fortress which Marlowe has difficulty entering and exiting, losing himself amid the tall trimmed hedges. Here we find barricades that bar the entrances to the great estates (see also the Sternwood mansion). The "twelve foot walls and wrought iron gates and ornamental hedges" insulate the Grayles from the outside world (Chandler [1940] 2000: 247). Such places seem built to maintain a sense of alienation from their surroundings, through the insistence upon separation from nature. Throughout the novel, the distance between various houses and the ocean diminishes its reality to an unidentifiable sound heard across a great divide, which could be anything at all from speeding cars to a breeze coursing through trees.

Later in *Farewell*, upon re-entering the Grayle residence, Marlowe immediately forgets where he is, and after wandering down a thickly carpeted hallway for a while catches sight of the outside world briefly as though suddenly recalling a long-suppressed memory: "We turned a corner and there was more hall. A French window showed a gleam of blue water far off and I remembered almost with a shock that we were near the Pacific Ocean and that this house was on the edge of one of the canyons" (249). When Marlowe visits Montemar Vista to seek out Lindsay Marriott, he is separated from the Vista itself by a flight of concrete steps clambering up the mountain, emphasizing his alienation from this unfamiliar world which signifies to him something ironically *unnatural* (he is forced into being a pedestrian and finds himself almost overwhelmed by the effort). More steps to the Marriott residence increase the sense of detachment from the surrounding environment of the built space, which rather perversely is full of counterfeit signs of the natural, from the "knocker in the shape of a tiger's head" to the single yellow rose neutralized in a vase, and the cornflower pinned to the lapel of Marriott himself (197). Mr. Grayle also sports a signifier of nature on his person, this time in the form of a red carnation. This dead flower, detached from its original environment and purpose, is now merely decorative (a situation that finds an echo in Didion's *Play It As It Lays*: "'Actually, Nelson,' he said then, 'that lemon is not artificial. That lemon is re*con*stituted'" ([1970] 2011: 47)).

Richard Lehan (1967) posits that the city provides "a way of regulating the environment, subduing the elements and allowing a certain control over nature" (13). Despite the apparent imposition of order in the form of the grid-system and the development and subdivision of the land, nature is able to mitigate this domination. There is a certain chaos deep in its foundations, which cannot be entirely extinguished. "Built into the order of the city," writes Lehan, "was the disorder of nature; neither completely contained the other" (170). Logic and rationality, grafted onto the landscape, are frequently overpowered by such tricks as "the lack of water, the Santa Ana winds" (Wyatt 1986: 158). David L. Ulin writes that California "has always been an elemental landscape, where we don't so much master nature as coexist uneasily with it, waiting for the next fire, flood or earthquake to destabilize our lives" (2006: n.p.). Joan Didion frequently describes the physical reality of Southern California in terms of its propensity toward natural disaster. In "Los Angeles Notebook" for example she describes the "malevolent" winds, the "torrential subtropical rain," the sandstorms, the brush fires ([1965–67] 2005: 171, 172). Los Angeles ultimately became a success due to its concentration of control over water, but the knowledge that the garden is built on a flimsy foundation is hard to shake and contributes to the city's sense of superficiality. All of this could so easily be destroyed. Nothing about Southern California has come about naturally; the entire place seems to have been imported wholesale. Robert E. Park (1967) writes that the "geometrical form" that most American cities take is a sign of their inherent artificiality; the whole of Los Angeles for example, "might conceivably be taken apart and put together again, like a house of blocks" (4). Arriving at the Sternwood family pile in *The Big Sleep*, Marlowe remarks that the "whole estate looked as though it had been made about ten minutes before I rang the bell," as though the place is packed and unpacked when needed like a movie set ([1939] 2000: 48). Similarly, in *The High Window* the residences along Sunset Boulevard have "the air of being brand new," ([1942] 1983: 34) in contrast to the surrounding gardens which are "well advanced" (34).

Chandler frequently draws the reader's attention to the fragility of these man-made spaces. In *Farewell, My Lovely* the private residence of Lindsay Marriott on Cabrillo Street in Montemar Vista is a liminal space right on the edge of the Pacific Ocean. The name Montemar Vista anticipates the Mar Vista neighborhood where Katherine and Paul Cattlemen reside in Alison Lurie's *The Nowhere City*. Both are places which "Spoil-the-View" (Lurie [1965] 1994: 38). The houses along Cabrillo Street are strung along a cliff edge like precarious jewels on a sparsely populated bracelet, "hanging by their teeth and eyebrows [...] and looking as if a good sneeze would drop them down among the box lunches along the way" (Chandler [1940] 2000: 196). David Fine (1984) describes luxury homes like this, "perched on (or over) the edge of sheer cliffs" as an example of the inherent "spatial incongruity" that characterizes Los Angeles (11). The thin collection of houses presented in *Farewell* is only very tenuously part of its natural environment, clinging with white knuckles to its very edge.

Throughout Chandler's novels, it frequently appears as though the natural world is rejecting that which is built over it, like a sick body attempting to expel something undesirable from within. This is an example of the continued defilement of the pre-urban landscape (as Casey Shoop (2011) notes, nature "often appears in Chandler simply as the place to bury bodies" (227)), but also of the way in which this defilement can trigger an equal and opposite reaction from these natural spaces. Jameson's "Earth" (or "Nature") seeps frequently into Chandler's "World" (or "History") (2016: 77). In *Farewell, My Lovely*, the body of Marriott is found beyond the urban, in a remote canyon in Malibu. In *The Big Sleep* we find the natural world is depicted frequently as a burial site where dead bodies are discarded and then expunged from the earth, the wilderness a space that can both expose and hide certain repressed incidents. The body of Owen Taylor, Carmen Sternwood's old flame, is dragged out of the ocean; the hideaway house outside Realito, situated in the middle of nowhere beyond the orange groves of Pasadena, is where Mona Mars, who was presumed dead or missing, is finally found; and the body of Rusty Regan, Vivian Sternwood's husband, is buried out in the Sternwood family oil fields.

In *The Big Sleep* much of the natural world has been wrangled into a highly cultivated form. The "paved garden" belonging to the Sternwood family is another example of the overlaying of the urban atop the wilderness (Wyatt 1986: xv–xvi). Upon visiting the Sternwood compound, Marlowe takes in the immaculate lawn, the spotless garage, and the "decorative" trees trimmed to within an inch of their lives (Chandler [1939] 2000: 3). The formerly wild spaces of the pre-urban landscape have been rendered a mere ornament with which to accessorize their home, making it, like the homes of Mr. and Mrs. Grayle and Lindsay Marriott, into a kind of synthetic wonderland. Inside the Sternwood mansion an equally unsettling atmosphere awaits. As Marlowe further investigates the interior it becomes clear that the domestic spaces are as strangely lacking as the exteriors. Its internal spaces are either dilapidated or unused and items of furniture are ornamental rather than functional, making this a rather unhomely house. The eerie stillness and stagnancy of the Sternwood mansion, its manicured garden and uninhabited rooms, signify that there is something rotten at its heart—something to hide.

Marlowe weaves in and out of the house as though the inside and outside spaces are interchangeable before being introduced to General Sternwood in the greenhouse—a piece of the natural world that is maintained like a domestic space. Many places in Chandler's novels possess a certain in-between-ness: interiors can exhibit a sense of the outside, while external spaces can take on the appearance of living rooms. In Marlowe's world, "the human has absorbed the natural and now tries to create the illusion of it" (Wyatt 1986: 163). In the Sternwood greenhouse we find a synthetic indoor wilderness, full of nauseating heat and bad omens. The stalks of the plants, for example, are compared to "the newly washed fingers of dead men" (Chandler [1939] 2000: 7). The General, subsisting on brandy and heat, is kept like an exotic flower amid the orchids which emit a crudely human scent. Not only are the plants which fill this sweltering space as sweetly repugnant as a prostitute's perfume, they are also "abominable," (6) as though brought in from the pages of *The Day of the Triffids* (1951). Much like Sternwood in his greenhouse, Marlowe's client in *The High Window*, Mrs. Murdock, sits imperiously amid the dense foliage when he first meets her at her residence (a scenario deemed by Jameson to be "the feminine analogue [. . .] of General Sternwood's greenhouse" (2016: 44)). She too has created a space in which the outside and inside worlds have merged: the light is obscured by the "thick bushes" ([1942] 1983: 13) which have been allowed to infiltrate the house and the space is populated by reed patio furniture which would be better placed in the garden. Indeed, Marlowe's exit from the house illustrates how thin the line between the external and internal world of Los Angeles can be: "I went out of her office, shut the door firmly, and walked back along the empty halls through the big sunken funereal living-room and out of the front door. The sun danced on the warm lawn outside" (23). Nature it seems cannot be entirely suppressed; it can be found both within the confines of these internal spaces, and beyond only the thinnest of veneers on the other side of the Murdock walls. It is permitted to thrive in this limited and concentrated form.

Just as the exorbitant lushness of the greenhouse serves to emphasize the extremity of the General's decrepitude, so does the surreal inversion of normality with regard to both the Sternwood and the Murdock houses and gardens serve to highlight their essential strangeness. The sense that a once familiar place has become unfamiliar, that something intangible has been removed and hidden from view, provokes a sense of the uncanny, deemed by Freud in his 1919 essay to be a "particular species of the frightening" ([1919] 2003: 125). In this essay Freud embarks on an extended etymological journey through the various definitions of the word, one which is replete with several meanings. Beginning with heimlich as "belonging to the house, not strange, familiar, tame, dear and intimate, homely," he traces the word until it transforms into "something removed from the eyes of strangers, hidden, secret" which eventually is exposed

(126, 133). From its use to create a sense of warm, enclosed domesticity and the sanctity of private space, heimlich "becomes increasingly ambivalent" (134) until the domestic and familiar becomes the private and withdrawn, a space that conceals more than it reveals—a place from which hidden, unknown horrors may suddenly reveal themselves (unheimlich). Freud asserts that the "uncanny element is actually nothing new or strange, but something that was long familiar to the psyche and was estranged from it only through being repressed" (148). What has been hidden in the Sternwood's history to make their home so unheimlich? History in Southern California did not start with irrigation or the grid system, just as in Chandler's novels, the central criminal act has always already occurred before they begin. The true crime has been committed before Marlowe approaches the Sternwood place on one October morning, with "the sun not shining and a look of hard wet rain in the clearness of the foothills" (Chandler [1939] 2000: 3); indeed, before Chandler even commits pen to paper. It is beneath the surface of the narrative and not within it. All the *sturm und drang* of the novel has no real bearing on the resolution of its crime(s) which purport to be its engine. The perpetrator has fled the scene, a thief in the night. The dead body at the center has been, and remains, long gone.

"Crime in the southern California [novel] is ordinarily an act carried out in the past and hidden behind a respectable façade in the present," argues David Fine (1989/1990: 200). What particularly Californian crime might the Sternwoods be hiding? We are given a few early clues as to the roots of their wealth. Upon entering the mansion, Marlowe's eye is caught first by the stained-glass panel emblazoned across its front door representing both an attempt at antiquity (it depicts a knight and a damsel in distress) and an arch sense of irony (said damsel has conveniently placed hair—is she aware of being watched and thus covering herself up, or affecting a coy aversion to her natural state—with her so-called rescuer exhibiting signs of a hesitant inexperience rather than heroism). It is quickly established that this is a place intent upon stressing a kind of mythology, which may or may not be genuine. Even the characters in the panel appear to be acting—Marlowe's derisive eye sees that they are going through the contortions of convention rather than being genuinely adept at their roles ("I stood there and thought that if I lived in the house, I would sooner or later have to climb up there and help him. He didn't seem to be really trying" (Chandler [1939] 2000: 3). Subsequently Marlowe passes a portrait depicting "a stiffly posed job of an officer in full regimentals of about the time of the Mexican War [. . .] I thought this might be General Sternwood's grandfather" (4). Here Chandler's reference to the Mexican War touches on California's origins, "the origins of California itself in blood guilt and national aggression, in 'manifest destiny' (not a theme that unduly preoccupies Chandler)" as Jameson puts it (2016: 3).

The paving of the garden is of course not California's sole origin story. Los Angeles has both indigenous and colonial roots. Before the prelapsarian became the colonized, California was home to about one-third of all Native Americans in what is now the United States.[5] From the early sixteenth to the mid-eighteenth century, no European settlements made permanent conquest, but by 1769 the Spanish settlement had begun, with the establishment of their chain of missions and forts, continuing until Mexican independence from Spain in 1821, to the victors the spoils of the land on each occasion. The destruction of native populations began first through "the strategy of sequestering [. . .] within defined spatial borders (the reservations)" and the devastation of their land, which was "savaged and consumed in the movement west" (Weinstein 1998: 25). Vincent Brook (2013) notes that the most "fertile and productive land in California, with a rich variety of wild animal and plant life [. . .] was irreversibly damaged or vanished completely under European-style agriculture and land management" (4). California, under Mexican rule until the Mexican-American War and the Treaty of Hidalgo, was ceded to the United States in 1848, after which the Gold Rush proceeded, and an exponential rise in violence against the native people. Disease, starvation, systematic murder, and enslavement followed; between 1846 and 1870, under United States rule in particular, "California's Native American population plunged from perhaps 150,000 to 30,000" (Madley 2016: 3). In the case of the Sternwoods and their progenitors, the portrait of the original General Sternwood does not provide the answer to the question of the source of their wealth. Instead, notes Jameson, "the family's fortune comes, not from the spoils of the Mexican War [. . .] but much more recently from oil" (Jameson 2016: 33). Rather than exempt the Sternwoods from participation in the degradation of California, the fact that their name was built in the oil fields over which their family pile looms embroils them in another dirty business. The source of their crime, notes David Fine, lies "in the soil, on the land" (1991: 217). The plundering of the California landscape (before its later exaltation) pre-dates the discovery of oil, but the discovery of oil is another sordid chapter in the same story of land ownership and exploitation. Rather than the frontier of the West being expanded and cultivated by successful wilderness-tamers, the approach of the European settlers to the land, from the 1770s on, "not only radically reduced the productive land available to the nonmission Indians and corrupted beyond reclamation much that remained but within a few short generations also led to the complete 'disappearance of the Los Angeles prairie'" (Brook 2013: 4). Over

100 years later, the discovery of oil in Echo Park (the first well discovered in Los Angeles, but not in Southern California) by Edward Doheny and his partner Charles Canfield instigated a drilling boom that turned hundreds of back gardens into oil fields and Los Angeles into "the Saudi Arabia for American oil" (Klein 2008: 78). As oil belonged to the person who had first found and extracted it, regardless of the boundaries of public parks or private property, and those who owned land in the state faced few restrictions on the right to capitalize on mineral resources, an enormous amount of land was leased for the purposes of oil extraction, with row upon row of derricks dotting the landscape in crowded lots; by 1930 these had been planted ad infinitum, "like trees in a forest," as the *Los Angeles Times* described in June of that year (qtd in Elkind (2012): 82). The oil strikes of the 1920s opened up the whole of Southern California for business; it was during this decade that "Los Angeles pumped one-fifth of the world's oil" (Clark 1983: 277) while the city's population grew "from 576,000 to 1.2 million" (Wyatt 2010: 37). By 1924, Los Angeles "had 43,000 real estate agents." Early in Sinclair's *Oil!*, which expertly tracks the intersection of real estate and the oil boom, Bunny tells the story of Mr. D. H. Culver, who buys a couple of acres of land at the top of "Prospect Hill," installs an oil derrick, and proceeds to drill over 3,000 feet down into the earth. Finally, after weeks of apparently fruitless excavation, oil is struck, spewing out a "million-dollar flood of 'black gold'" ([1926] 2008: 25). Soon enough, the Hill is no longer a Hill, "no longer cabbage field or sugar-beet field, but '*the* field!'" More tracts of land are purchased, with lots "offered for sale at fabulous prices, and some of them were bought" (26). The city's relationship with oil, like its relationship with water, and with real estate, is fundamental to its history and identity. This is the world in which Marlowe's investigation takes place; a world made of black gold in which bodies are buried in a backyard laden with bobbing horse-head pumps.

Much like the way that Los Angeles was carved out of a wild, seemingly uninhabitable place, its urbanization necessitating the suppression of its agricultural past, behind every door in *The Big Sleep* lies something secret or unsavory which is repressed. The Sternwood mansion is comprised of a series of partitions, rooms within rooms and suddenly revealed entrances and exits; the Geiger bookstore is a front for a more unsavory business; Geiger's house hides a disappearing dead body and some incriminating photographs; the Fulwider Building sets the scene for the murder of Harry Crane at the hand of the obscured Camino; and the Cypress Club finds Vivian Regan frittering away her inheritance at the roulette table. It turns out to be Vivian's job to keep her family's secrets behind another such façade, as we later discover, burying the past out in the oil fields where she hopes it cannot be found. In "Raymond Chandler's City of Lies" Liahna K. Babener (1984) contends that the adulteration of the natural landscape on which Los Angeles was built is reflected in the inherent fraudulence of its urban spaces. The "buildings, roadways, and grid patterns have been perversely grafted onto an unreceptive landscape," she argues, suggesting that the city's "preoccupation with façade" is an inevitable repercussion of this imposition (110). Every building in *The Big Sleep* is a front full of false walls, hidden doors, and secret compartments.

The excision of nature and the speculation, expansion, annexation, and selling-off of the land goes to the heart of the Los Angeles identity. The subdivision of the land, which had characterized over 100 years of Southern Californian urban development, is also mimicked architecturally throughout Chandler's novels. Every dank office in *The Big Sleep*, for example, is "separated from the next; each room in the rooming house from the one next to it; each dwelling from the pavement beyond it" (Jameson 2016: 11). Throughout Chandler's fiction the polycentric nature of his city is reflected in its internal spaces, which contain multiple cells and points of entry and exit. The partitioned and secret internal spaces serve to further sequester already secluded people inside separate pockets, fragmenting the experience of the urban interior. Not only are the internal spaces that are depicted in these novels notable for the insalubrious activities which take place privately within, but also for the aura of duplicity that is galvanized by their relentless expansion, demarcation, and segmentation of space.

The façades which are so ubiquitous in Chandler's interiors are comparable to that which Norman M. Klein refers to as the "imago" (2008: 13). While the concept of the "imago" has been used in psychoanalytical circles by such practitioners and theorists as Carl Jung, Jacques Lacan, and Sigmund Freud, for the purposes of this book I follow Klein's definition of the term. In *The History of Forgetting*, Klein contends that forgetting is made possible when "one imago"—an idealized or inaccurate image— "covers over another." These imagos are "the rumour that seems haunted with memory, so satisfying that it keeps us from looking beyond it" (4). He compares such imagos to "phantom limbs" —deceptive substitutions for a tangible reality. History is frequently appropriated and cannibalized by the imago. This is evident not just here in Chandler's misleading architectural façades, but also throughout this book in, for example, Joan Didion's fabricated family tales (such as the cracked crab which both did and did not exist depending on who is asked, like a kind of Schrödinger's crab); the edited memories of Didion's Maria Wyeth and of D. J. Waldie, contained behind false textual walls;

and the reconstituted history of Lowell Lake's brownstone home, his adoption of a history that does not belong to him curdling benign nostalgia into toxic obsession. The internal spaces of *The Big Sleep* are full of such imagos in various guises, all of which replicate their duality and inauthenticity, such as the locked room in the Geiger store, the hidden door through which Eddie Mars emerges surreptitiously at the Cypress Club, and the offices in the Fulwider building which advertise the livelihoods of shysters and crooks masquerading as dentists and detectives. Every internal space, every room, serves more than one purpose. They all house both the façade and the reality on the other side.

Similar to the imago is the double, another harbinger of the uncanny, one which is brought to life when "a person may identify himself with another and so become unsure of his true self; or he may substitute the other's self for his own. The self may thus be duplicated, divided and interchanged" (Freud [1919] 2003: 142). Freud's description of catching sight of himself in the mirror captures the failure of recognition which splits the self: "the intruder was my own image, reflected in the mirror on the connecting door. I can still recall that I found his appearance thoroughly unpleasant" (162). Here, 'I' becomes 'he' and Freud disassociates his sense of self, hermetically sealed, from the 'he' who appears in the mirror before him. Before Freud's conceptualization of this experience in 1919, the preoccupation of the nineteenth century with the double was that it was "the harbinger of death, or as the shadow of the unburied dead" (Vidler 1992: 171). This splitting of the self creates both the possibility for self-expansion and for self-annihilation; the erasure of that which first existed.

The doubling and repetition which manifests itself architecturally throughout Chandler's novels is symptomatic of a city that seems to be endlessly expanding, duplicating, reinventing, and rearranging itself. The "respectable façade" which Fine identifies is made literal throughout *The Big Sleep* in its internal spaces (1989/1999: 200). An illustration of this is provided with particular clarity by Mr. A. G. Geiger's store and his home. Geiger's store, full as it is of novel smut wearing the mask of antiquity, is a space which houses the artificial. It is packed with books that are visible but cannot be touched, while the real merchandise lies hidden behind a false wall. This is a room within a room, reminiscent of the greenhouse within the Sternwood house, with the outside functioning as a screen for the real business which is conducted in the inner sanctum. The advertised purpose of Geiger's store (the selling of antique books) is displayed on its external front, while its true purpose (the selling of pornographic photography) can be found within the store behind a locked door in a separate room. The view through the windows is obscured by Chinese screens, just as the "oriental junk" and dim lighting curtail the penetration of Marlowe's gaze (Chandler [1939] 2000: 17). Once inside the store itself, Marlowe finds another space comprised of partitions and compartments, just like the Sternwood residence: "At the back there was a grained wood partition with a door in the middle of it, shut." The lone figure in the store, a long-limbed ash-blonde with a tentative smile across an easily dismantled façade, is another front, along with the mask she calls a face which slips incrementally with each line of questioning: "Her smile was tentative [. . .] She smiled bleakly [. . .] Her smile was now hanging by its teeth and eyebrows and wondering what it would hit when it dropped." The books in the store are kept in glassed-in shelves, untouchable and unidentifiable, compounding the atmosphere of secrecy and fraudulence. The store front, the glass book cases, the woman installed at the desk, are all false signifiers which speak to another function and identity, while the smut emporium behind the wall provides the real business. In this case, reality sits behind a more palatable screen. The truth is obscured, and fiction is taken for granted as fact. Though Geiger purports to sell *Rare Books and De Luxe Editions*, his products are rather more sordid than his store might wish to advertise. Geiger turns out to be a purveyor of "indescribable filth" while masquerading as a bibliophile; his books are wrapped and concealed like illicit cargo (22).

The Randall Place apartment blocks, the Cypress Club, and the Fulwider building are further examples of highly compartmentalized internal spaces in *The Big Sleep*. The first of these, which is home to Joe Brody, is punctured by holes, blanks, doorframes, and porches. A woman appears from behind a curtain that hangs over a doorway as though emerging from a portal, while Joe is killed in the open space of his front door. This is a liminal, transitional space that is neither quite domestic nor completely public and provides an exit as well as an entrance. These are architectural representations of what Ben Highmore (2005) refers to as the "perspective of spatial liminality," frequently utilized in Chandler's novels (98). For Jameson, Chandler paints a fragmentary picture of the American urban experience, one which is characterized by things falling apart. Like Joan Didion in "Slouching Towards Bethlehem," Chandler's focus is the "atomistic nature of the society" which Marlowe moves through (Jameson 2016: 11). Jameson writes that this sense of the fragmentary is "projected out onto space itself." As we see in Chandler's *High Window*, even a dentist's office has an "inner door in a wall that cut across the room" through which can be found another office with two "uncurtained" windows ([1942] 1983: 143). Back in *The Big Sleep*, inside the Fulwider Building, an unsavory residence full of the insidious grime of the city, Marlowe finds a directory within which are listed "[n]umbers with names and numbers without names" ([1939] 2000: 121). This is a place where the anonymous dwell in separate cells, identifiable only by arbitrary numbers, and where "private lives [. . .] stand side by side like closed monads" (Jameson 2016: 4). The Belfont Building in *The High Window* is described similarly. It comprises "eight storeys of nothing in particular," filled with mostly "vacant space" (Chandler [1942] 1983: 143). The Fulwider is full of compartments, one leading into the next and the next, with locked doors and unlocked doors and glass frames dividing them up. In *The Big Sleep*, the interiors of the Cypress Club, a club which makes a gesture at grandiosity but plays host to grubby activities and is named rather ironically after something verdant, natural and pure, are replete with passageways and partitions, inflicting an aura of segregation and detachment: "I checked my hat and coat and waited, listening to music and confused voices behind heavy double doors. They seemed a long way off, and not quite of the same world as the building itself" ([1939] 2000: 93). Two heavies appear from the other side of a door under the staircase to show Marlowe to the office of Eddie Mars. This inner-sanctum possesses an extra "door in the corner that had a time lock on it." After his interview here with Marlowe, Eddie makes another appearance inside the gambling room through a hidden door in the paneling. Likewise, the Idle Valley Club in *The High Window* is full of signs of dualism and deceptive surfaces, with more locked doors leading into private spaces to be found at the end of more endless corridors lined with possible exits and entries. The many fronts and partitions of the interiors of *The Big Sleep* provide examples of Norman Klein's imagos; mirages in the urban desert.

Both the phenomenological narrative of the city, concretized and visible, and the stories spun by the characters Marlowe investigates, are, as Elana Gomel (2014) explains in *Narrative Space and Time*, "riddled by omissions, evasions, and lies" and these gaps create "topographical counterparts: dark spaces, forgotten and forbidden nooks and crannies, underground lairs of the repressed" (180). In *The Big Sleep*, the interiors reflect the spatial arrangement of the urban California landscape, but also the inner world of Carmen Sternwood and the way in which she compartmentalizes memory. Depravity lurks behind both Carmen's blank stare and the Geiger store's fraudulent signage, both guarded by a thin veneer of plausible deniability and suppression. Carmen likewise superimposes false memory over authentic memory, internalizing the idea of the fake wall or duplicitous shop front (more examples of Klein's "imago" (2008: 13)), cutting off and segregating certain memories from her conscious mind. Inherently she is mimicking the compartmentalization of buildings like the

Fulwider and Randall Place apartment blocks. Carmen is present in almost every internal space in the novel, appearing in the Sternwood mansion and grounds, the Geiger house, Marlowe's apartment, and Randall Place where the ringing doorbell announces her chaotic presence like a latter-day Dionysus. This further aligns her psychological partitioning with the city's polymorphous interiors. She represents forgetting, and the damage it can do.

Haunted but Empty

When Marlowe finds Carmen at the Geiger house it seems to him that she is "not there in that room at all" as he observes her, upon awakening, sitting like a stringless puppet, immobile and expressionless (Chandler [1939] 2000: 25). Carmen, whose blankness and negligible lucidity paint her as more automaton than human, is written as the embodiment of Freud's proposition that the uncanny can also be galvanized into existence when there is "intellectual uncertainty [. . .] as to whether something is animate or inanimate, and whether the lifeless bears an excessive likeness to the living" ([1919] 2003: 140–1). She is like an uncanny doll, emitting strange disembodied noises and staring blankly: "The hissing noise came tearing out of her mouth as if she had nothing to do with it [. . .] her lips moved very slowly and carefully, as if they were artificial lips and had to be manipulated with springs" (Chandler [1939] 2000: 112). Like the novel's uncanny spaces, Carmen has suppressed something inside herself. In her case that something is expressed by her forgetful emptiness. When they meet again later in Marlowe's apartment, she claims to have no memory of the night Marlowe found her at Geiger's, "persuading herself that she didn't know" what has happened and creating her own narrative (47). "Remember what? I was sick last night. I was home," she says (46). Her memory drifts in and out, prompted by Marlowe's own reminiscences, and is as dilapidated as the Sternwood oil fields, as empty as the family pile. Carmen's mind is a place of absence in which one false memory or imago endlessly replaces another. The past is forgotten as soon as it occurs, leaving her adrift in the present.

If Carmen represents forgetting, Marlowe always has the facts. Her association with Geiger's book store, full of novel smut wearing the mask of antiquity, is a perfect allegory for her inner-vacuity. Geiger's store is a space which houses the artificial—it is full of books which are visible but cannot be touched, while the real produce, as corrupted as Carmen's mind, lies hidden behind a kind of false wall. Depravity lurks behind these surfaces, guarded by a thin veneer of denial and suppression. When Marlowe discovers Carmen in his apartment, it becomes clear that he feels she has somehow defiled something sacred. He throws her out of the room, tearing the bed to pieces "savagely" in a burst of violent need to destroy her latent presence (113). Carmen being in his space means the potential blanking out of the facts which are so sacred to him, soaking them in her vacuous, void-like aura. His sense of self is predicated on the existence of the threadbare artifacts contained in this room.

Throughout Chandler's novels, Marlowe demonstrates a certain suspicion of the outer-reaches of the borderless external landscape, exhibiting a degree of doubtfulness toward the spatial sprawl of Los Angeles' non-urban landscape and a preference for the regimented space of the gridded city he prefers to frequent. It is significant that Marlowe does not thrive outdoors, preferring the relative legibility, however misleading, of the interiors which set the scene for his investigations. In a discussion of Umberto Eco's *Travels in Hyperreality*, in which he presents an analysis of Superman's "museum of memories" (Eco 1986: 5), Ian Buchanan (2005) points out that it is "Superman's mountainous hideaway, the Fortress of Solitude, where the man-of-steel goes when he needs to be alone with his memories and 'work through' his Kryptonian otherness" (24). This fortress is "the one place where Superman can be himself, an alien whose past has been obliterated." Similarly, Marlowe is often depicted as a man with no discernible past, and very few defining characteristics other than his sardonic turn of phrase and predilection for particular brands of liquor and automobile. His uncharacteristically emotional outburst at Carmen's infiltration of his private space suggests that his sense of self is kept aside and maintained in this separate sphere. His very being is predicated on the existence of the threadbare artifacts contained therein:

> I didn't mind what she called me, what anybody called me. But this was the room I had to live in. It was all I had in the way of home. In it was everything that was mine, that had any association for me, any past, anything that took the place of a family. Not much; a few books, pictures, radio, chessmen, old letters, stuff like that. Nothing. Such as they were they had all my memories. I couldn't stand her in that room any longer (Chandler [1939] 2000: 112).

The books, pictures, and letters are less important than what they represent, and the way in which they define the space in which they exist. David Farrell Krell (1990) tells us that to memorialize, "*he mneme*," represents both "remembrance in general but also a record, memorial, or tomb" (2). Marlowe's apartment becomes a mausoleum for his past thanks to the presence of these few artifacts of memory which have the power to "reconfigure the spaces they inhabit" (West-Pavlov 2009: 24). The room in which Marlowe stores each "object of memory" is maintained as though it is an antique itself (Vidler 1992: 64).

In *The Art of Memory*, Frances Yates ([1966] 1978) explains the history of mnemotechnics, a technique mastered by the ancient Greeks to train their memory. "The first step was to imprint on the memory a series of loci or places. The commonest, though not the only, type of mnemonic place system used was the architectural type" (18). A memory is strengthened by associating it in the mind with a particular place, or locus. This has to be "easily grasped by the memory, such as a house, an intercolumnar space, a corner, an arch, or the like" (22). One must essentially choose a familiar place which can be easily visualized, such as your own home, and then walk around this place in your imagination, making note of various features and items that make each room specific. The memory locus is important because it houses the images, or signifiers, which represent a particular memory, or the things which need to be remembered. Edward S. Casey (1987) agrees that memory is undeniably tied to place, which provides a "stabilizing persistence [. . .] as a container of experiences that contributes so powerfully to its intrinsic memorability" (186).

Yates continues that the technique works best when one forms one's so-called memory palace "in a deserted and solitary place, for crowds of passing people tend to weaken the impressions. Therefore, the student intent on acquiring a sharp and well-defined set of loci will choose an unfrequented building in which to memorize places" ([1966] 1978: 23). These "deserted and solitary" places and "unfrequented buildings" sound rather similar to Klein's description of the Los Angeles landscape more generally, that is, an "empty lot where a building once stood" (2008: 4). Klein argues that such places are "haunted [. . .] but empty." For Yates these empty lots function as repositories for memory in which we may store signifiers of the past (like the unoccupied bedroom of Waldie's father in *Holy Land*), but Klein tells us that these buildings no longer exist for us to use them as repositories for memory. These now-empty lots are nothing more than spaces colonized and consumed by absence. The memory palace is a place-holder for something which is both there and not there. It marks an absent presence.

Yates' memory storehouse is also similar to Gaston Bachelard's (1969) conception in *The Poetics of Space* of the house, or our first specifically localized notion of home, as a place where one sustains one's sense of the past. It is in this place that "a great many of our memories are housed, and if the house is a bit elaborate, if it has a cellar and a garret, nooks and corridors, our memories have refuges that are all the more clearly delineated" (8). As Yates considers in

The Art of Memory, in Augustine's *Confessions* the theologian presents memory as a sequence of buildings in which memories are stored inside vast chambers. Memories appear here both in the form of tangible entities that he can recall at will, but also as objects *standing in* for memories—images, sense impressions, affections—place holders which aid him in his quest for the *original* memory. These are his "palaces of memory" where the "treasures [of] innumerable images" are housed which "forgetfulness hath not yet swallowed up and buried" (Yates [1966] 1978: 60).

If, as we have learned from Yates and Bachelard, home is where the memories are stored, Marlowe's apartment is where he has chosen to preserve his few associations with the past—seemingly arbitrary talismans like letters, books, and chess pieces which must not be disturbed. This is his memory palace, where a character like Carmen, associated with the city's capacity for erasure, is unwelcome. But despite Marlowe's desire to preserve these synecdochic objects as true representations of his past, their function is to *reproduce* the authentic thing, sentiment, or event that they represent, thus helping to jolt and preserve memory. Marlowe's memories are abridged in their object form; reduced to pieces of iconography ("treasures [of] innumerable images" (Yates [1966] 1978: 60)). As with the apparently invaluable doubloon which turns out to be a replica in *The High Window*, Chandler illustrates that it can become impossible to tell the difference between the imago and the original when the imago makes for a more convincing story.

By the end of *The High Window* for example we discover that Miss Davis' memory of her departed employer is as fake as the counterfeit gold coin created by one of the novel's many villains, Mr. Vannier, and as fake as the tale told by Mrs. Murdock's son Leslie regarding his wife's involvement in the original theft of the rare coin named the Brasher Doubloon—the reason Marlowe was hired by Mrs. Murdock in the first place and the lost point of origin of the entire case. It turns out Mrs. Murdock is in fact the guilty party with regard to her late husband's death. Just as the Doubloon is doubled by a fraudulent version of itself, and the photograph which immortalizes Mrs. Murdock's act of defenestration has been duplicated for safe-keeping, so is a slightly altered carbon copy of the memory of Miss Davis produced to counter the original. Every piece of evidence is merely a Maltese Falcon; scratch the gold and you find copper beneath.

In *The Big Sleep*, the memory palace performs two roles—that of a vault in which Marlowe can enclose himself with his memorabilia, and a house of possibly counterfeit records. Marlowe's job of course is to know the difference between the counterfeit and the authentic. His level of comfort in a fraudulent world, and his relative vulnerability when placed beyond the frontier of the urban, aligns him with the modern and thus with legibility and order. His function in life is to force others to remember and acknowledge their past crimes correctly and completely, or at least as correctly and completely as his clients allow. But he has form when it comes to complicity in maintaining the hushing up of past crimes. It seems inevitable therefore that he too is capable of dissembling and redaction. In his way, he is contributing to a more ordered world by forcing the broken pieces he sifts from the city into something coherent. In *The Big Sleep* he asks for the names of the parties involved in the blackmail plot to be suppressed (namely the Sternwoods, who, as his clients, are apparently entitled to their privacy). In *The High Window*, Miss Merle Davis, Mrs. Murdock's assistant, reveals to Marlowe under duress that the late (and original) Mr. Murdock died by falling out of a window. The death of this man is something she is, rather understandably, unable to forget, although both Marlowe and Mrs. Murdock press her to do so. The advice given to her by Marlowe is: "Forget it. Don't think about it" ([1942] 1983: 169). "People are always telling you to forget unpleasant things," she replies, "But you never do."

By the end of *The Big Sleep*, Marlowe has also fallen prey to the "false memory," as he describes it, which pervades the novel ([1939] 2000: 147). He articulates his memory as though in a trance, telling a story in a distracted, abstract way. One event leads inexorably to the next and the next like a series of slides projected onto a blank wall: "My mind drifted through waves of false memory, in which I seemed to do the same thing over and over again, go to the same places, meet the same people, say the same words to them, over and over again, and yet each time it seemed real, like something actually happening, and for the first time" (147).

"It was like that, over and over again" he says (148), as though speaking by rote. These endless recurring "waves" of duplicated memory wear away all sense of meaning associated with their recollection. When Marlowe recounts the events which occur after his discovery of Mona Mars, he articulates his memory as though it is occurring in the present, and "for the first time." Like Carmen, he is left living in the present tense; the past is nothing more than a ransacked room. Perhaps after all the big sleep is not so much a literal death as it is the death of memory, the lack of which keeps one locked in the present, with no access to the past.

Marlowe's waves of memory, as stagnant as Maria's Wyeth's deadened "red tide in the flaccid surf" (Didion [1970] 2011: 65), are reproduced like simultaneous carbon paper copies. They are detached from their "first time" (Chandler [1939] 2000: 147), their point of origin, reinforcing only their decontextualized selves, flat without affect. Like these waves, every clue discovered refers their investigator to nothing more than an endless series of other, similar, clues or McGuffins. Each crime in *The Big Sleep* replicates, covers up, or necessitates another. Every mystery is solved by the discovery of a duplicate mystery. When one body is buried in *The Big Sleep*, another is found dead and yet another disappears. Rusty Regan, an absent man, is replaced in the esteem of both the General and Carmen by Marlowe, one who is present. In turn Rusty had been preceded in Carmen's affections by Arthur Geiger, and before him by Owen Taylor. Before Geiger came along to blackmail the General, Joe Brody was at it too. The past crimes of the Sternwood family are in fact eternally present. Geiger's body which appears and disappears and then, later in the narrative, reappears, and the items of furniture which are taken, leaving empty spaces which point to where they were once situated, all speak to a sense of absent presence. Geiger himself even disappears from public consciousness. His death is not mentioned in any of the papers Marlowe reads. During or after every visit Marlowe pays throughout *The Big Sleep*, further bizarre coincidences occur. More blank envelopes are passed around, keys are lost and found, furniture is rearranged, and the body count stacks up: first Rusty and then Geiger, Owen Taylor, Joe Brody, Mona Mars, Harry Jones, and finally Lash Canino. Bodies arrive and depart, creating gaps in the narrative. Even when the location of Rusty's body is given, the body itself remains unseen, leaving a ghostly blight on any sense of narrative resolution and making the oil fields where he is buried another place of absent presence.

In Chandler's Los Angeles, the assemblage of memory (and by extension the resolution of each case) proves difficult due to the many substitutions and false signifiers that seek to take the place of the original and authentic. Marlowe's cases are full of ambiguities and vagaries, and the attempted assemblage of narrative is often more chaotic than rational. Seemingly arbitrary details are incrementally collated until they form a montage of sorts, or a continuum, expressing the whole case, which is the sum of these seemingly disparate parts. When Marlowe recounts his theory of detection to General Sternwood, he describes the evidence which is most useful but most often ignored as "something looser and vaguer" than what one might expect (151). The collection of evidence can be equated to the assemblage and establishment of past events, retroactively, through the identification and recollection of memory. Along similar lines, Krell posits that recovering a memory can be problematic, as we possess a "constellation of memories" which we cannot necessarily access through straightforward chronological thoughts in a rational order (1990: 20). The movement of recollection is "not a linear movement from starting-point to end-point but a kind of back-and-forth movement from ruling centers to adjacent, contiguous memories." The constant maneuvering back and forth and around in circles in time can cause confusion, "scattering fragments of experience in all directions or uniting them in bizarre concatenations" (21). As Barbara Tversky (2000) writes in "Remembering Spaces": "Because of the partial, incomplete, inconsistent, and multimodal nature of spatial memory, cognitive collage may be a more apt metaphor than cognitive map" (370). This way of seeing memory can be applied to the conceptualization of the physical (and metaphysical) environment of Los Angeles, which, as Edward Soja (1989) declares, "is everywhere," like an exploded star (222). Memory by Krell's measure is amorphous and expansive; beyond the "bounded space" (Krell 1990: 1) of Jameson's "History" (2016: 77). Krell describes the high wire act of recording memory as "writing on the verge of both remembrance and oblivion alike" (1990: 1). If quantifiable, measured, controlled space represents the man-made boundaries of modern urban existence, unbounded, limitless space must represent something primordial. To recollect is to observe the "edge, rim, or margin" of memory, to articulate the fence that surrounds and demarcates the internal self. "The place where memories are stored," Klein emphasizes, "has no boundaries" (2008: 13). Nature is also a "spatial construction," notes Jameson, which, "at its farthest verge [...] touches on the outer edge of Being itself" (2016: 84). To go beyond the spaces which have been settled is to be transported beyond the limits of not only the city, but of the self.

The Not-World

Driving into the foothills beyond Realito to find the missing wife of Eddie Mars in *The Big Sleep*, Chandler tells us that the ultimate destination lies "beyond" ([1939] 2000: 129). Space can be an infinite prospect outside the perimeters of the city, out in the primordial landscape of Southern California. It appears to be capable of expanding and contracting according to some will or impetus of its own. The engulfing quality of space is reflected in the enormity of the outside world against which Marlowe attempts to build a defense. The car, an inseparable component of Marlowe's life and daily routine, sets a relentless pace in its ever-onward, straight trajectory along the highways (the linear path which replicates the contemporary urban spatial form). In an apt reflection of the case itself, Marlowe's attempts to follow a straight line, build a case, collect the breadcrumbs and assemble evidence, all lead him further and further into darkness and misdirection. Away from the straight lines, drivable blocks, and quantifiable distances, he is completely lost, as though his self were somewhere detached from his body out in the amorphous blackness of the brush. Hsuan L. Hsy (2010) reports that in the work of nineteenth-century novelists such as Henry James and Edgar Allan Poe, a wary ambivalence toward the growth of the metropolitan city and its accumulating scale is frequently expressed. In the twentieth century, Chandler articulates the same sense of anxiety toward the world beyond the city, which represents a spatial indeterminacy he does not understand. This landscape, from which Marlowe feels so alienated, has made him into "an amputated leg" (Chandler [1940] 2000: 210). For Chandler it is the open space of unsettled land which represents disorder, porousness.

The external world, which borders on something primal, is a murky prospect and makes a stark contrast to the rigid geometry of the internal urban spaces of the built world that Marlowe frequents. Marlowe's trips to the hideaway house, the oil fields at the novel's conclusion, and his strange experience outside the Cypress Club, all exhibit a sense of amorphous uncertainty. The Cypress Club is a liminal place "at the far end of the town" where even the moon seems to have misplaced its exact location, losing itself "in the top layers of a beach fog" (Chandler [1939] 2000: 93). The Dickensian fog depicted in *The Big Sleep* often renders his surroundings inscrutable and indefinite. The Club appears through the mist like a murky Valhalla, its history of possessing multiple-incarnations (formerly a private summer residence, then a hotel, the club now provides speculative distractions for rich Angelenos), its obscure location behind "a thick grove of wind-twisted Monterey cypresses," its gothic architecture and its sense of "nostalgic decay," all adding to its mystique. The inclement weather further emphasizes its obscurity:

> The fog dripped from the Monterey cypresses that shadowed off into nothing towards the cliff above the ocean. You could see a scant dozen feet in any direction. I went down the porch steps and drifted off through the trees, following an indistinct path until I could hear the wash of the surf licking at the fog, low down at the bottom of the cliff. There wasn't a gleam of light anywhere. I could see a dozen trees clearly at one time, another dozen dimly, then nothing at all but the fog (100).

When Marlowe wends his way from the Cypress Club with Vivian Sternwood, the daughter of his client General Sternwood, he passes through the town of Las Olindas in his car in a kind of somnolent state, reaching finally another liminal place, this time on the waterfront of the Del Ray beach club. Here everything seems distant, as though they are retreating even further away from the reality of the city: "I turned the car and slid down a slope with a high bluff on one side, interurban tracks to the right, a low straggle of lights far off beyond the tracks, and then very far off a glitter of pier lights and a haze in the sky over a city. That way the fog was almost gone" (107). The nebulous lights form a remote constellation, with the fog seeming to lift at an indistinct point. Vivian and Marlowe kiss as the surf curls over itself languorously "like a thought trying to form itself on the edge of consciousness," much like Vivian's omissions which remain unspoken. This description of a thought in a distant inaccessible cave of the mind which cannot quite be reached and disappears as soon as one approaches it, is also rather like memory. The descriptions of the Club's external surroundings, with its fog, its inscrutable visitors with no identifiable features to mark them out, and its detachment from reality, could be applied with equal accuracy to memory itself, which is just as vague, amorphous, and potentially disturbing. In contrast to this sense of unquantifiable, infinite space, upon returning to the city an abundance of boundaries and borders such as doors, gates, and driveways appear.

The highway connects the artificial and the natural as they alternate, acting as a seam running down the landscape, making it contiguous but distinct. A neon sign is followed by an empty field, followed by an endless proliferation of stores and movie theatres followed by climbing foothills. Beyond Pasadena as the sun descends, rows of orange groves can still be seen, neat in their cultivated lines, and as Marlowe drives through the dark foothills a neon sign suddenly announces the existence of "Realito," a small town of frame houses which just as quickly fade out into an expanse of empty fields, closing in around Marlowe as he heads further into darkness; the two "distinct languages" (Jameson 2016: 50) of the natural and the urban speaking now in stereo. Jameson emphasizes that the urban is perceived as a distinct landscape, a "peculiar urban space," thanks to the contrasting "sense of the natural ecology of the Los Angeles basin itself," (50) found in the offsetting of the mountains against the plains, the ocean against the arid mass of desert, and finally the flora and fauna met by smog and neon lights.

In *The Big Sleep*, we not only visit "a quintessential selection of houses, rooms, and offices—a whole panoply of specifically urban spaces" but we "*also* live in Nature, most dramatically by keeping an eye on the weather" (Jameson 2016: 49). According to Jameson, it is the weather, as perhaps the most unavoidable manifestation of the natural world, which brings the parallel landscapes of the urban and the natural into touching distance. Much like the central murder investigation in Chandler's novels which, though often treated as beside the point, draws together the disparate threads of otherwise "essentially plotless material" (3), so does nature give meaning and context to Chandler's human world by holding together the narrative's otherwise "centrifugal tendency [. . .] to drift apart" (49) into separate episodes. The fog, the rain, the wind, provide meteorological signifiers of the natural world, and their persistent presence gives Chandler's narratives a through-line, providing a constant reminder that Los Angeles can be placed in a context which pre-dates its present incarnation; that of a "formless" place lacking the "routine and continuity" of European cities defined by the organizational framework of the past (5). Similarly, Maurice Halbwachs writes that, unlike America, "Paris and Rome [. . .] seem to have crossed the centuries without the continuity of their life having been interrupted for a single minute" (qtd in Vidler 1992: 134). American cities, which Jameson views as manifestations of "American life," are malleable, protean places "in which time is an indeterminate succession from which a few decision, explosive, irrevocable instants stand out in relief," (2016: 5) with Los Angeles "a kind of microcosm and forecast of the country as a whole" (6). By narrowing the gap between the natural and human worlds of Southern California, with the realm of the latter "marked as artificial rather than natural" (41), Chandler reunites "the indoor experiences as it were, to the atmospheric unity of the Los Angeles basin as a whole" (75–6), illuminating the presence "of some vaster absent natural unity beyond this ephemeral set of episodes" (76), concretized by the segmented urban world in its monadic landscape of "episodes" in time.

The natural alternates with the urban, the contrived, the artificial, rendered even more distinct through its being framed by such an environment. Towards the end of *The Big Sleep*, Marlowe is brought suddenly into the realm of Lash Canino and his cronies, a dash of the urban in the natural world. Canino, the human source of much of the violent crime in the novel, is another man of the city like Marlowe, a taciturn figure in the shadows without ties or commitments, acting in his own interests and according to his own code. The garden has been invaded and tarnished by the presence of men like Eddie Mars and Canino, two villains of the piece, who make it a place where wives and victims are sequestered away when necessary. The cyanide plant which marks the proximity of their hideaway expresses this toxic atmosphere. The hideaway where Eddie Mars' missing wife Mona is found is far from her usual urban haunts, beyond Pasadena, beyond the orange groves and the dark foothills, at the "outer edge of Being itself" (Jameson 2016: 84). Chandler "drowns" the location in rain, thus "restoring the watery element that is the sign of the non-human axis of matter" (86). Nature is the dominant force here. Pushed out of the insubstantial frame house in which Mona has been stowed, Marlowe finds himself again at the mercy of nature, beset by the overwhelming downpour outside. The rain proves inexhaustible and almost impenetrable, and it is here that Lash Canino meets his end. In his last moments his face is obscured by the insistent rain, and upon being shot he falls face-down into the mud, another in a long line of bodies rendered lifeless by human hand, drawn back into the earth. This place provides an opening onto the "not-World" (86), the edge of human space, and to prise open that seam is to reveal a void.

In *Farewell, My Lovely*, Marriott and Marlowe take to the car, leaving behind for a short time the streamlined geometric patterns of the grid system in favor of the nonsensical loops and arcs of the vast external landscape sprawl: "For two minutes we figure-eighted back and forth across the face of the mountain" (Chandler [1940] 2000: 205). Driving further into the darkness they traverse the foothills which lead to the Purissima Canyon, meeting first a broad paved avenue which soon dwindles into nothing more than a narrow dirt road the parameters of which are almost obscured by walls of brush. What was once a "realtor's dream" has turned into "a hangover" (206). They reach at last the seeming limit of the interference of the developers in the form of a "white painted barrier" beyond which lies only "darkness and a vague far off sea-sound" (207). Their surroundings are only tangible thanks to the smell of sage and the repeated throb of the crickets. Jameson describes the "farthest verge" (2016: 84) of the natural world, its "outer limit" (85), as a "non-space" represented by "the white wooden barrier at the end of the world" (85). In this "non-space" we find a "not-World" (86), spilling over the edge and into the void that is "non-human space."

For Jameson there is something sublime in Nature that brings it close to the semblance of death. This reflects a rather modernist attitude regarding the need for space to be formulated into a "hermetic enclosure," rather than a "domain of myth" that "prevents the full visibility of things" (Vidler 1992: 168). As Roderick Frazier Nash ([1967] 2014) contends in his landmark book *Wilderness and the American Mind*, the concept of sublimity in nature as "an aesthetic category" was formalized as something to inspire both "terror and horror" and "awe and delight" in equal measure by Edmund Burke in 1757 (45). The eighteenth-century critic Frances Reynolds moves closer still to Jameson's conceptualization of the sublime in nature as something frighteningly ambivalent, "It is a pinnacle of beatitude, bordering upon horror [. . .] It seems to stand, or rather to waver, between certainty and uncertainty, between security and destruction" (qtd in Shaw 2006: 46). As Philip Shaw (2006) affirms, true sublimity occurs in these in-between moments articulated by Reynolds; at some visible point "where the distinctions between categories [...] begin to break down," marking the "limits of human conception" (46). The experience of the sublime in nature is something close to religion or to madness, referring to things beyond our ability to quantify, perceive, and control, bringing into question our ability "to discern boundaries or spatial or temporal limitations" (78).

There is an ambiguity to the unmade space of Nature that makes it unsettling; a place in which one could dissolve all boundaries, even between self-contained being and that which is external. The "rational grids and spatial orders" (Vidler 1992: 172) imposed upon urban space are a defense against this uncertainty. French philosopher Roger Caillois depicts space as something which is "perceived and represented [...] a double dihedral changing at every moment in size and position: a dihedral of action whose horizontal plane is formed by the ground and the vertical plane by the man himself who walks" (qtd in Vidler 1992: 173). Krell writes in similar terms when he describes the quantification of space as "both the vertical measure and the horizontal measure, the boundary marker and the greensward within" (1990: 2). If we are no longer distinct from space, no longer able to measure its distance through time or footsteps or rational thought, unable to define its scale and its limits, we are *inside* space. "To these dispossessed souls," Caillois continues, "space seems to be a devouring force. Space pursues them, encircles them, digests them [...] It ends by replacing them" (qtd in Vidler 1992: 174). The experience of space as a void that absorbs and consumes, as an absence, an obscure non-place which resists the scrutinizing eyes of the surveyor, as foothills which spill out beyond the "white painted barrier," is deeply unnerving. The threshold that marks the borders of our constructed world of "History and the social project" (Jameson 2016: 77) is a buffer against unknown horrors of *not* being in space. But like the highway taken by Marlowe to bridge two realms, perhaps these liminal spaces in between can be their own kind of spatial concept, rather than a non-space, which "mark the seam between a prehistoric nature" and the constructed world of humans.

At the end of *The Big Sleep* Marlowe finds the preternaturally youthful Carmen outside the Sternwood mansion. She is placed halfway between the railings which surround her home and the wilderness beyond in a space of ambivalence in which she equivocates between civilization and chaos. Marlowe accompanies her down to the field; a neglected place where the land is littered with debris and the noise of the city recedes into memory. Here, Carmen returns to a somewhat primordial state: "Aged, deteriorated, become animal, and not a nice animal" (Chandler [1939] 2000: 156). No longer a fatuous figure, her broken façade reveals a woman near disintegration, her memory as spoiled as the Sternwood oil field. He accompanies her further, down to the old oil wells, driving through the deserted gardens and out of the gates until they reach a "narrow dirt track," (154) an unassuming path to a very dirty history: "The wells were no longer pumping. There was a pile of rusted pipe, a loading platform that sagged at one end, half a dozen empty oil drums lying in a ragged pile. There was the stagnant, oil-scummed water of an old sump iridescent in the sunlight" (155).

Anthony Vidler argues that memory in the modern city experiences "dislocation" (1992: 181). This is made literal in the case of the relationship that the Sternwoods have with their oil fields, which provide an example of the suppression of the past made manifest in the external landscape. They live in a house that keeps them at a distance from these fields and thus have physically removed themselves from their own past. Yet the windows of the house look out on this past, providing a constant, but distant, reminder of the place which gave them everything they have. As Fine writes, the Sternwoods are one of several antagonists in Chandler's fiction who inhabit "respectable facades that insulate and isolate them from the acts they have committed in the flatlands. To live above the city is to live away from past crimes" (1991: 216). When Marlowe gazes beyond the surrounding gardens of the Sternwood mansion to the oil fields which established them, he is looking at the place where the past dwells: "The Sternwoods, having moved up the hill, could no longer smell the stale sump water or the oil, but they could still look out of their front windows and see what had made them rich. If they wanted to. I don't suppose they would want to" (Chandler [1939] 2000: 15–16).

Here is where their money was made, bled out of the earth, the remnants of industry strewn about like bloody handprints at a crime scene. Having first contaminated the environment, plans are now afoot to turn it into some sort of verdant playground. Invented memories take the place of those willfully forgotten; a once fertile terrain becomes a wasteland to be turned later into a park, further paving over signifiers of the city's past. Aptly, Rusty's body lies buried somewhere in this urban graveyard, murdered at the hands of Carmen in another example of the suppression of a family secret. As Wyatt observes: "Carmen's love lies buried in the sump; the site of the family's success is also the grave of its crimes" (1986: 166). The site of the murder is, of course, its most imperative component, for the family's fortunes were made in the same place which has cemented their corruption. Similarly, in *The High Window*, Leslie Murdock is responsible for the missing doubloon after all, just as he is responsible for the death of Vannier, and just as his mother is the perpetrator of the eight-year-old crime which is the original sin that lies beneath the surface of the novel. As with the Sternwoods, all of the crimes committed within these domestic interiors can be laid at the feet of the Murdock family itself. The "aristocratic 'degeneracy,'" as William Marling (2010) puts it, of families like the Sternwoods and the Murdocks, incriminates everyone (115). David Fine contends that General Sternwood, while "not himself a criminal, has nonetheless made his fortune by exploiting the oil reserves beneath the city" (1989/1990: 200). The oil fields are the city's ultimate confidence trick, a "family secret" writ large. "Family," in this case, takes the form and temperature of an entire state. These reserves from which the family so purposefully distance themselves may be depleted but are still functioning, serving as "reminders of the primeval power bubbling beneath the city's surface" (Bryson 2010: 172).

The natural landscape of the oil fields represents the past in *The Big Sleep*—a place which has been plundered, abandoned, and turned into a dumping ground for crimes which must be denied and purposefully forgotten. With the Sternwoods' past a place removed from sight, a faraway land that they have turned their backs on, their present becomes a constantly uncanny experience. Vidler writes that the expectation of a presence "which turns out to be haunted by absence instead" seems to operate "as a parable of the dislocation of memory in the modern city" (1992: 181). If the past is forcibly detached and removed from the present, this creates a kind of black hole in the present where memory used to be. In this way an absence takes the place of a presence. Vivian repeatedly relies upon her sister's capacity to empty herself of memory in order to maintain the wall of silence that surrounds her family: "I thought she might even forget it herself, I've heard they do forget what happens in those fits. Maybe she has forgotten it" (Chandler [1939] 2000: 163). She believes that Carmen has forgotten her crime completely. Carmen's memory of the past is instead dislocated—excised and discarded in the oil fields, leaving a gap in her mind where it used to reside. Marlowe proposes a solution that both protects the family and solves Carmen's problem. She must be taken away and sequestered inside a place where she can continue to forget, as though this forcible detachment from the past, a continuation of her present detachment, will resolve her psychological ailments.

The behavior of the Sternwoods replicates on a small scale the effect of urbanization on the natural landscape of Southern California. The desertion of the oil fields in *The Big Sleep*, and at the opposite end of the scale the extreme cultivation of the land surrounding the Sternwood mansion, speaks to the incremental degradation of, and withdrawal from, the natural landscape on which Southern California has been built. This is repeated in Joan Didion's *Play*

It As It Lays, in which the natural world outside Maria Wyeth's hotel rooms and beyond the confines of her car is a foul, corrupted wasteland, from the eerily placid water to the fly-riddled kelp to the yellow haze from an oil fire that hangs in the air. On one of the few occasions where Maria finds herself close to nature she observes the "oil scum on the sand and a red tide in the flaccid surf and mounds of kelp at the waterline. The kelp hummed with flies" ([1970] 2011: 65).

In *The Big Sleep*, bodies are disposed of in the oil fields just as the detritus of the city is dumped into the concrete river bed; the oil fields providing a waste disposal site for unwanted bodies just as the Los Angeles River has been repurposed as a concretized water conveyance system.[6] We encounter always "the presence of graves beneath the bright sunlight" (Jameson 2016: 87). In Chandler's novels we find evidence that to build over or repress the natural landscape is to pave over the past. The failure to acknowledge the processes of modernity detaches the city from its most essential, primordial self, and makes it a place where the uncanny sets up permanent residence. Carmen personifies the dangers involved in repressing personal memory and living in a perpetual present where the past is erased as soon as it occurs. Her psychological damage is writ large on the uncanny urban landscape of Chandler's Los Angeles, which has become a machine in the garden of Southern California. The uncanny is a constant reminder that the city's shadow self, buried somewhere in the wilderness, endures. As Lorna Dee Cervantes writes in "Freeway 280," traces reveal themselves with time; the land itself remembers: "wild mustard remembers, old gardens/come back stronger than they were" (Cervantes [1981] 1982: 21).

2

The Imago City
Joan Didion, Hisaye Yamamoto, and Alison Lurie in Los Angeles and Sacramento

Three decades after the publication of *The Big Sleep*, Joan Didion articulates in her essay "Slouching Towards Bethlehem" (1967) the same fears that Fredric Jameson writes of regarding the "atomistic nature" of Los Angeles society which materializes spatially in the city's external sprawl and internal fragmentation (Jameson 2016: 11). Indeed, Didion, who thinks of history in terms of its manifestation in particular places, uses the same language as Jameson, referring to the "atomization" of the world she sees around her in Southern California (Didion [1967d] 2005: 98). For her, the transience of the young people she interviews, the incompletion and banality of their language, the absence of temporal structure, and the general sense of drift and emptiness, all speak to the similar sense of fracture Chandler articulates in spatial and architectural terms.

In Didion's *Play It As It Lays* (1970), Hisaye Yamamoto's "Wilshire Bus" (1950), and Alison Lurie's *The Nowhere City* (1965), signs of the past are rendered obscure, hidden, scattered, scrubbed clean or torn down, abandoned to the rearview mirror of a city intent on moving forward; a city seemingly defined by what David Fine (1984) describes as its "spatial disarray" and "temporal confusion" (12). Fine's "spatial disarray," like Dolores Hayden's (1995) "spatial conflict," (9) gives expression to the way in which urban renewal in cities like New York and Los Angeles can disrupt the connection, as visible in the physical landscape of a city, between the past and the present. At first glance, in Los Angeles it seems that the past does not count and is not accounted for, because the city makes the very concept of time passing conspicuous in its absence. Yet the past has been built to last in unexpected ways. It is not entirely buried or absent, but instead secreted and awaiting excavation.

Didion's "Slouching" depicts the lives of those who, continuing the tradition of the crossing story of America's early "pioneers" (on which, more later), moved west to the Haight-Ashbury district of San Francisco during the late 1960s as part of the wave of enormous social changes crashing over the country. During this period university campus rebellions against the government spread from its nucleus in Berkeley, near San Francisco. Hugh Brogan ([1985] 2001) remarks that the "sixties youth movement," of which the people Didion speaks to in "Slouching" were a part, "discovered just how racialist and brutal parts of the country were," resulting in an increasing "[a]lienation from conventional society and its pieties" (657–8). From the assassinations of President Kennedy, Martin Luther King, Robert F. Kennedy, and Malcolm X, to the war in Vietnam, the Watts Riots, President Nixon and Watergate, Charles Manson and the murder of a pregnant Sharon Tate, the pill, the Jimi Hendrix Experience, Patty Hearst, Neil Armstrong's giant leap, and civil rights protestors, the women's rights movement and anti-war demonstrators echoing each other's calls for revolution—the list of social and political earthquakes which occurred during this time seems endless.

Leonard Wilcox (1984) reasons that the historical context for Didion's writing on Haight-Ashbury is what defines it. This was a period characterized by "The simultaneous sense of exile from and paralysis by the past, the breakup of an old order, a loss of a sense of historical coherence" (69). He continues that, for Didion, "the counterculture phenomenon is the final symbol of the fall from an intact historical world into a chaos of historical discontinuity." Lacking the historical context within which to place their own narrative, the people of Haight-Ashbury with whom Didion speaks all lack a point of origin. Didion writes of "misplaced children and abandoned houses"; of disappearances and reappearances ([1967d] 2005: 72). Her notebook is confiscated by the police. Phone numbers are given out and not called. Whole afternoons drift by with little activity to account for the expenditure of time, and characters enter and exit the narrative to answer phones or go to the hospital with pneumonia or chicken pox. Interviewees fail to remember where they came from: "I ask where he comes from. 'Here,' he says. I mean before here. 'San Jose, Chula Vista, I dunno'" (74). They forget how long they have been in San Francisco: "Vicki [. . .] has been here 'for a while'" (85). They "do not believe in words" (99), repeating stock phrases ("the trip," "media poisoning," "the flash," and "groovy" [92, 93, 87, 100]), and peppering vague explanations with equivocations ("kind of," "sort of," and "dunno," (93, 76, 77)). Katherine Usher Henderson (1981) contends that people "need words to integrate their past into their present" (104). The collapse of language is echoed by the failure to integrate the past into the present. The days are a "continual happening," Didion writes ([1967d] 2005: 79), worrying that they "do not seem to be getting to the point," a statement that seems to be a description endemic to the text (81). Everything circumnavigates "the point," as though there is a black hole at the center of the narrative. The "center cannot hold," perhaps because there is no center to speak of (Yeats [1920] 1994: 158). We are continuously returned to the sense that something is missing or that the world has exploded and been pieced back together incorrectly. What is missing at the heart of the city in this period for Didion is the institutional memory that used to provide a center of gravity, a thread of continuity.

In "Slouching," the point of origin (family, geography, home, language) that Didion seeks, which used to provide some sort of historical context within which she and her subject could be situated, no longer exists. The bridge that would have taken the people of San Francisco back toward a legible past has crumbled, leaving Didion with no way back to a history she can understand or find comfort in. Didion signals that the mid-twentieth century in America represented an era when things demonstrably fell apart and old narratives relied upon to create a larger national identity were by necessity unpicked. Her consistent challenge of authority (in terms of narrative control, formal genre conventions, accepted historical and familial fact) and its evident failures resonates throughout her work. Using *Play It As It Lays* (1970) and *Where I Was From* (2003), I analyze Didion's treatment of, respectively, fiction and nonfiction narratives, unpacking the way in which she resists the notion of their mutually exclusive nature and instead seeks to use them both almost interchangeably, in order to express a sense of loss—the loss of authority, or a particular center of gravity. This failure or lack echoes through both *Play It* and *Where I*, resonating in Maria Wyeth's unreliable narrative voice in the former and Didion's own in the latter. She continuously undermines the possibility of a powerful and unified authorial voice within the text or single organizing principle outside the text, drawing our attention to the absence where such an authority or center of gravity should be.

Rather than shore up the sense of power America sought to project in the postwar era, throughout her work Didion undermines it through her blurring of the lines between fiction and nonfiction, being an unreliable narrator herself, and telling stories of failed attempts to control narrative and contain history. Throughout Didion's 1984 novel *Democracy*, she plays at being both author, narrator, and character (beginning Chapter 2 with the allusive words "Call me the author" ([1984] 1995: 16)), resisting the idea of a hermetically sealed and uniquely positioned author-as-fountainhead, instead spilling her various narrative selves out across her pages and inserting them into the story itself. Instead of exemplifying the symbiosis of narrative forms into a single authoritative voice, Didion pushes against the possibility that such reconciliation is possible and articulates instead a sense of atomization born of this failure. This kind of "counternarrative of insecurity" (Steigman 2012: 113) is found in her use of querulous, mutable narrative voice(s), as we see in both *Where I* and *Play It*. *Democracy* is concerned with the *absence* of the central principle denoted by its title, rather than its successful perpetuation. Indeed, her work is more often about loss; essentially, the loss of a central authority. Alan Nadel (1995) asserts that the problem that is presented by *Democracy*, for example, is that "the methods for writing 'truthfully,' in fiction, journalism, or history, are not techniques for establishing adequate authority but rather techniques for masking the *absence of that authority*" (279, emphasis added).

Throughout *Where I*, Didion looks for an authoritative version of the past in her California of the mind, trying to find it in the homes of relatives, in family heirlooms, and in the myths told about the land itself.[1] She asks herself, and the reader in turn, how we remember the past in space; how we make it real. She thinks through the stories that have led her to conceive of her own personal history in a particular way—the myths which have controlled her own self-narrative. The first California myth she gently deconstructs is the sanctity and value of the land, which she traces from consecrated space to commodity; the next is the crossing story, propagated by unreliable narrators and blindly romanticized. Both myths prove to be structurally unsound, leaving her grappling with a history that is more slippery than she first imagined. California always seems to be "somewhere else," she writes in "Notes from a Native Daughter" ([1965] 2005: 137), repeating the phrase spoken by both Maria and her mother in *Play It As It Lays*. Traveling there is "a longer and in many ways a more difficult trip" than one might imagine, "one of those trips on which the destination flickers chimerically on the horizon, ever receding, ever diminishing."

Didion articulates her slow realization that the indisputable authority of her family lore, as rendered synonymous with the myths of the Californian frontier and the preciousness of its landscape, is not sustainable under questioning (as I chronicle in Chapter 1). Similarly, in *Play It*, it is impossible to trace one single authoritative version of any aspect of the story. With the exception of the first and some of the closing chapters, for most of the novel Maria is deprived of a first-person narrative. Indeed, she seems to sit outside her own narrative, becoming "she" rather than "I" and being talked about rather than leading her own story. Throughout the rest of the book she exists only in the removed reflections of others, with the story moved forward by her friend Helene, her ex-husband Carter, and a remote narrative voice. A similar problem is embedded in the multiple narratives referred to in *Where I*. In the telling and re-telling of crossing stories through multiple narratives, Didion argues, there exists a "problem with point of view: the actual observer, or camera-eye, is often hard to locate" ([2003] 2004: 30). She uses the example of a story told by Josephus Adamson Cornwall, who in turn is repeating the tale told by Nancy Hardin Cornwall, who was herself not a witness to the events. We are left to contend with second- or third-hand information, with re-iterations of stories purporting to be truths from multiple perspectives, passed down the family line like heirlooms. Through such fractured narrative voices, Didion takes the myth of American authority and reveals its fragile timbre.

Joan Didion's California of the Mind

Where I Was From, a study in authorial fabrication and myth-making, tracks the author's own genealogical history through the nineteenth century and her reflections on this familial inheritance in the more recent mid-twentieth-century past. Throughout *Where I*, in which she recounts her family's Sacramento history, Didion turns toward the pastoral, looking to the landscape to find herself and a continuity with her past that she cannot find elsewhere: "Flying to Monterey. I had a sharp apprehension of the many times before when I had [...] 'come back,' flown west, followed the sun, each time experiencing a lightening of spirit as the land below opened up [...] *home, there, where I was from, me,* California" (204). She asks herself a series of questions as she watches the unfolding landscape below: "*who will look out for me now, who will remember me as I was, who will know what happens to me now, where will I be from*," the answer to each rhetorical question, the same. *California* will remember her as she was; *California* will be where she is always from.

Didion's place of birth, Sacramento, the Central Valley capital city of California State, began its life as a single fort alone on the prairie, cut off from the entire continent by the Sierra Nevada. The discovery of gold in its foothills put Sacramento on the map, and before long its settlers, descended from farmers who had been moving west across the frontier for 200 years, came and cultivated it with myopic determination.[2] In many ways Sacramento proves to be the *urtext* of all her work. For Didion, "Sacramento is California," ([1965] 2005: 138) a synecdoche that represents the whole, meaning that her hometown and her home state are often written as though they are interchangeable. In Sacramento, as in California, the land, above all else, is the defining quality. "There is [...] no reality other than land," she explains in her 1965 essay "Notes from a Native

Daughter" ([1965] 2005: 146). She wistfully describes her memories of running over "the same flat fields that our great-great-grandfather had found virgin and had planted" as a child, and swimming "the same rivers we had swum for a century." It is hard, she qualifies, to "*find* California now," yet she seeks what may be ephemeral in the Sierras and the Donner Pass and the "wide rivers" (141, 142). This, she emphasizes, is the *idea* of California which is eternal—the idea of the garden, its cultivation and its propagation, and the accompanying idea of the frontier which must be endlessly pushed back to maximize its potential. Richard Lehan (1998) writes that the frontier signified "the line at which two powers met in the Old World and open space and opportunity in the New. In America, encountering the frontier meant encountering the wilderness" (167). The vision of America as an agrarian idyll, with the fruits of the earth the only pure, viable form of commerce and industry, can be traced back to Thomas Jefferson, who believed in the republic, the utopia of the land and individual toil, and whose idea of the frontier "dominated American intellectual debate for two hundred years" (168). The evolution of the New World into an urban, industrial landscape of competing compromise may have been inevitable, but Jefferson's ideals became the ideals of later generations nostalgic for this prelapsarian place.

Didion quotes Josiah Royce, born in 1855 in Grass Valley, near Sacramento, who wrote of the "familiar sacred stories" told regarding the "pilgrimage" undertaken to settle in California ([2003] 2004: 29). Nothing else has quite the same value; even the crossing story, which is another idea about California that continues to drive its identity and is rooted in its land: "When they could not think what else to do they moved another thousand miles, set out another garden [. . .] The past could be jettisoned, children buried and parents left behind, but seeds got carried" (7). In *Inventing the Dream*, Kevin Starr (1985) argues that "The land conferred identity and stability upon a rather haphazard, genetically diverse band of colonists" (16). Didion looks to the landscape of Sacramento to find herself; to establish some kind of continuity with her past that she cannot find elsewhere.

Didion confides in *Where I Was From* that California is so ingrained within her that, when living in New York in the late 1950s, she felt the need to recreate it in the form of *Run River*, her 1963 novel about life on the Sacramento River. The intention of *Run River* "was to return me to a California I wished had been there to keep me" ([2003] 2004: 170). Later she comes to the realization that this California had likely never "been there" at all, except in her mind's eye. Assessing the novel forty years after its publication, Didion finds within it a strange resistance to the changes experienced by California during the time in which the novel is set. It seems the young author was herself not immune to the self-mythologizing bent of her state. Despite her growing understanding of the impetus to constantly expand, subdivide, and sell the land, an impetus which ultimately she sees as an endemic and defining characteristic of California, her past self, as expressed in *Run River*, believed there was a divide between the California of old, and the postwar boosterism and boom of the later California. At moments like these Didion could be appended to the thesis of George L. Henderson ([1998] 2003), who categorizes certain purveyors of Californian fiction, like Frank Norris and Mary Austin, as authors of "rural realism." These are writers "bred on sentiment and local color, [who] might gravitate to 'pastoral' California, and, intending to romanticize its marginality, find that the rural was the very picture of everything that was contemporary and modern about the Far West" (xv). Over the course of *Where I*, it dawns on Didion that the inextricable coupling of person and place in the telling of history may have blinded her to the reality of the place in which she grew up. The "weakness for the speculative venture" expressed by California's endless real-estate sales spree is mirrored in Didion's own self-narrative, in itself another kind of speculative venture (Didion [2003] 2004: 167).

"The creation of the entirely artificial environment that is now the Sacramento Valley was not achieved at one stroke, nor is it complete to this day," Didion writes in *Where I Was From* (22). Her description of this "artificial" landscape—something constantly in the process of reinventing and expanding itself—is equally applicable to California storytelling as it is to the repurposing of the land. She argues elsewhere that after the Second World War, Sacramento "woke to the fact that the outside world was moving in, fast and hard" and began to lose sight of its character ([1965] 2005: 138). In allowing such changes to happen, Sacramento has "lost its *raison d'etre*" without realizing it (146). It has parted company with the past to which it thinks it clings. People have been "selling their rights-of-way and living on the proceeds." Land formerly cultivated to grow green hops is now called Larchmont Riviera, the Whitney ranch has become Sunset City, the agricultural history of Gilroy is turned into the Bonfante Gardens. The Didion family were themselves not exempt from this California tradition of selling off their heritage: "Occasionally, late at night, my father and brother and I would talk about buying out the interests of our cousins in what we still called 'the hill ranch' [. . .] My mother had no interest in keeping the hill ranch, or in fact any California land" ([2003] 2004: 14). In her short story, "Sunset," published in 1956, her heroine returns to her childhood home in the Sacramento Valley which no longer stands: "All the land had been sold and subdivided [. . .]

and even the house in which she had lived her first sixteen years had been turned into a day nursery" (21). All are merely "one more enthusiastic fall into a familiar California error, that of selling the future of the place we lived to the highest bidder" ([2003] 2004: 184). This is another systematic erasure of all previous "traces of custom and community" to create California anew and pretend it had been ever thus (173). Like D. J. Waldie, she perceives that she comes from a place "of presumed exile," one which forces her to ask in myriad ways the same question Waldie must ask himself, "which is how to make a home here?" (Waldie 2011: 209). Robert Bennett (2011) notes that the Jeffersonian reverence for the frontier, later famously exalted by Frederick Jackson Turner in his 1894 essay "The Significance of the Frontier in American History" as responsible for the cementation of a specifically American identity and character, idealized its western front as a place "populated by rugged individualists who develop democratic sensibilities as they test their mettle against a vast, untamed natural landscape" (Bennett 2011: 283). In recent years the idea of the western frontier has been reconceptualized; it is now "defined less by the existence of free land than by its disappearance" (285).

Throughout *Where I Was From*, Didion itemizes the extensive list of enterprising people and companies which have laid claim to the land in California, and have made money from its cultivation, subdivision, and acquisition. California has been said to have given way "first to industrial parks and subdivisions and then to strip malls and meth labs" (177). As outlined in Chapter 1, land in California has perennially been subdivided and developed for the purposes of farming, irrigation, and oil speculation (violently displacing its previous inhabitants an apparently necessary evil), sold off to the aerospace and defense industry, used for housing and country club complexes, or to make way for the further expansion of the freeway. Land is no longer land alone; it is real estate.[3] In fact, as outlined in Chapter 1, it was the local entrepreneurs who, in building the railroad through the state, opened it up to extensive settlement, creating a conveniently located, immense swathe of subdivided land to be cultivated and irrigated, bought and sold. As Morrow Mayo writes in 1933 about Los Angeles, this has long been the case: land is "and has been since 1888, a commodity; something to be advertised and sold to the people of the United States like automobiles, cigarettes, and mouth washes" (319). There was no point in the history of California when land was not for sale. Equally there was no point it seems at which land was not subject to the *myth* that it was not for sale, a myth which draws a line in history before and after which land was and then was not sacrosanct. "*In what way does the Holy Land resemble the*

Sacramento Valley?" Didion repeats as she has learned to do by rote. The answer is always the same: "*In the type and diversity of its agricultural products*" ([1965] 2005: 139).

Historian Steven Avella (2013) argues that Sacramento ultimately chose to betray its own image as cultivators of California's garden. He writes that the Sacramento and American Rivers, which merge and flow together through California's state capital, proved both a blessing and a curse, having wrought havoc in the form of terrible floods while also nourishing this earthly paradise. Originally the new city's land had been "platted and gridded for easy sale," but after the floods of 1862 residents chose to "raise the city grade" above the cresting level of the rivers, "rather than abandon what had been chosen in haste" (5). Avella contends that the very creation of the city was "an act of defiance against nature." That it continued to survive is a testament to California's ability to suppress its own nature while simultaneously maintaining its image as the guardians of that very same nature. In 2011, after powerful Santa Ana winds destroyed thousands of trees across the state, *Los Angeles Times* journalist Gale Holland (2011) derided the traumatized reaction as "nostalgic, a futile gesture to hold on to a lost California Eden that perhaps never existed," arguing that anything verdant in California is there for commercial purposes only: "The reality is that our urban forest is an artificial landscape created to serve agriculture and development interests" (n.p.). The garden always represented an idea of California's history, which is, in turn, a way of seeing oneself as an agent and participant of that history.[4] This is the story, to paraphrase Didion, that Californians tell themselves in order to live. "Discussion of how California has 'changed' [. . .] tends locally to define the more ideal California as that which existed at whatever past point the speaker first saw it" ([2003] 2004: 174–5).

Ultimately, in confronting her own misapprehensions, she confronts the grand narratives of America's self-mythologization, charting her realization of the "blinkering effect" of California's "dreamtime" on her: "it would be some years before I recognized that certain aspects of 'Our California Heritage' did not add up" ([2003] 2004): 17). "A good deal about California," she repeats drily, "does not, on its own preferred terms, add up" (19). Later in the same text she recalls a visit in the early 1970s with her mother and young daughter Quintana to Old Sacramento. Upon beginning to explain to Quintana that everything around her was imbued with the history of California, Didion realizes that Old Sacramento, which has redeveloped its sidewalks "to give the effect of 1850," represents a mythologized vision of Sacramento's past form: "a theme, a decorative effect" ([2003] 2004: 219). "Later it seemed to me," she writes, that this had been the moment when all of it—the crossing, the redemption [...] the rivers I had written to replace the rivers I had left [...] the two hundred years of clearings in Virginia and Kentucky and Tennessee and then the break, the dream of America, the entire enchantment under which I had lived my life— began to seem remote (219–20).

Not immune from waxing a little nostalgic herself, Didion laments in 1965 that "All that is constant about the California of my childhood is the rate at which it disappears" ([1965] 2005: 140). Small details she notes regarding the discontinuities visible in her hometown on each return express her gradual realization of a particular kind of grief: "there is no longer a veranda at the Senator Hotel—it was turned into an airline ticket office" (141). Her "sentimental journeys" to and from Sacramento compound Marshall Berman's notion that to live in the modern world is to expose oneself constantly to grief. Here we can relate her text explicitly to Berman's writing on the Bronx—his narrative of gradual destruction and the accompanying sense of his own childhood disintegrating before his eyes. However, arguably it is this very rate of disappearance, to paraphrase Didion, which allows Berman to measure his own change and his own distance from the site of his youth. Though he watches his neighborhood become a building-site and vows revenge against the man he holds responsible, he later admits that this deconstruction only hastened his inevitable departure; the end of his childhood is, in a way, heralded and made tangible by the flattening of tenement buildings and neighborhood stores. Berman's own maturation is reflected in the evolution of the city around him. He too can measure his own changes, but he can measure them against absence and difference.

At the family graveyard, Didion observes the newly vandalized site, its monuments broken and overturned on the grass. Her journeys home are fraught with this sense of exponential decay and impending expiration, and her idyllic reveries of the garden of her childhood are surreptitiously laced with foreboding in the form of the sinkholes and the rivers in which many incautious children were drowned; the three-week-long spring after which the "brilliant ephemeral green" of the fields would diminish into arid yellowed stalks; the sight of rattlesnakes sunning themselves on the rocks ([1965] 2005: 139). On the subject of snakes, she recollects in *Where I* that:

> If my grandfather spotted a rattlesnake while driving, he would stop his car and go into the brush after it. To do less, he advised me more than once, was to endanger whoever later entered the brush, and so violate what he called "the code of the West." New people, I was told, did not understand their

responsibility to kill rattlesnakes. [They did not understand] the physical reality of the place (95–6).

Similarly, despite the fact that in *Play It* Maria has moved away from Nevada to New York and then to Los Angeles, she sees these snakes, which were an ever-present part of her childhood out in the desert of Silver Wells, everywhere. When Maria confesses that "I never ask about snakes," the implication is that she is attempting to ignore her past until it goes away of its own accord ([1970] 2011: 3). But on the same page Didion's authorial voice makes clear that to ignore the snake is fatal: "two honeymooners, natives of Detroit, found dead in their Scout camper near Boca Raton, a coral snake still coiled in the thermal blanket" (3). One of Maria's recollections finds snakes taking the place of sustenance on her plate when she attempts to eat: "She had known that there was no rattlesnake on her plate but once the image had seized her there was no eating the food" (60). This memory leads her to thoughts of her mother's demise in her car, and she tortures herself with imagined scenarios of her thwarted attempts to speak to her on the day she died. Snakes imbue the environment with dread and death and the promise that the past remains to pick off future possibilities. At the end of the novel, Maria speaks of one of the lessons her father taught her as a child: "overturning a rock was apt to reveal a rattlesnake" (200). One must, as Maria is instructed in *Play It*, be vigilant about one's hostile environment, an environment which is frequently rendered synonymous with personal history. By tying the snake to California, Didion is not only relaying the reality of her own lived experience, but is also rendering her home state analogous to a reptile which perpetually reinvents itself. The snake is an apt avatar for California in terms of its ability to continuously shed the skin of its own self, its own history, while broadly retaining the outline of its original form.

Narratives that present history in a certain way in order to maintain a certain sense of the past as a rationale for American national identity in the present, such as an America defined by its love of the land and its rugged individualism, are called into question. The myth of the eternal, life-giving, unchanging landscape which underpins the story of California is not the only fabrication Didion unpicks in order to come to a true understanding of her own history. As she explores her own past expressions of California's pioneer history, her text becomes imbued with a sense of things falling apart, even the myths around which a nation could coalesce. In *Where I Was From*, she refers frequently to the crossing story of America's early pioneers—those who traveled westward from the 1840s to claim and cultivate unsettled land. (Though of course much, if not all, of the California they sought to claim had already been settled and inhabited by Native Americans.) California became home to travelers who were "reborn in the wilderness," with the crossing a literal and metaphorical journey of relinquishment and sacrifice ([2003] 2004: 29). Ultimately what was left behind was one's old life, one's old skin, making the decision to embark upon such a journey "a kind of death, involving the total abandonment of all previous life" (29). Indeed, it was this "moment of leaving" which is presented as the most potent aspect of the crossing story; the "death that must precede the rebirth" a prerequisite for the reward that is California (30). The crossing story is one not only of new life, but of the death of one's previous history; another West Coast grand narrative concerned, underneath it all, with shedding one's skin or selling off some aspect of one's history for mercenary purposes. Didion asks herself what, in fact, was the purpose of the original journey west? Was it really a "noble odyssey," or was it instead a "mean scrambling for survival, a blind flight" (35)?

The mythic narrative of the crossing story insists upon the former, but she scratches at the surface tenaciously until she reveals some darker truths beneath the polish. A fragment of a letter written by Virginia Reed, a Donner Party child who survived the crossing into California, is repeated throughout the book by Didion like a sinister mantra: "*Remember, never take no cutoffs and hurry along as fast as you can*" (75). This fragment becomes a refrain imbued with an increasing sense of horror. The Donner-Reed party, memorialized in the Pass and Donner Summit Road and Donner Memorial State Park, was one such group of early settlers, comprised of about eighty people who left Missouri in 1846.[5] Throughout *Where I*, Didion compulsively repeats the somber words of Virginia Reed, who made the 2,500-mile journey to California in the early 1800s, as though trying to heed a warning she had never before allowed herself to hear. Their decision to take a shortcut, the Hastings Cut-off ("never take no cutoffs"), was fatal, and in determining to cross the Sierra Nevada mountain range to reach their final destination they became subject to such harsh winter conditions that only just over half survived the crossing, many of whom did so having resorted to cannibalism to sustain themselves. During the journey west undertaken by Didion's "great-great-great-great-great" grandparents, the Scott Hardins, they traveled part of the way with members of the Donner-Reed party, binding her family history to that of a group defined by madness, starvation, and cannibalism (3). Why had they moved in the first place? To push back the frontier, grapple with snakes, partake in their manifest destiny? Or has California in fact attracted "the hunter-gatherers of the frontier rather than its cultivators" (24)? In any event, the frontier was a place of violence, where these "Proto-planners," as Samuel Stein christens the pioneers, enabled "the country's murderous westward expansion" (2019: 15). "What exactly was our heritage?" Didion asks uneasily, at the beginning of her memoir not truly wishing to know the answer ([2003] 2004: 160). But in hovering over her family's history, and the intertwined history of her home state, Didion cannot help but pick at the scab.

In an interview with Hilton Als (2006) for *The Paris Review*, Didion explains that she initially did not want to write a personal account of her California history because she was not yet ready to reconcile her new-found understanding of the place with the nostalgia and romanticism imbued by her parents: "I didn't want to figure out California because whatever I figured out would be different from the California my mother and father had told me about. I didn't want to engage that" (Didion 2006: n.p.). Jason Mosser ([2011] 2012) suggests that Didion "interprets her experience textually, that is, as a series of stories" (197). Storytelling in California seems almost as old as the land itself. For example, despite the fact that Southern California was responsible for reprehensible behavior toward the Native Americans, Carey McWilliams ([1946] 1973) insists that a certain mythology has been spun concerning "the well-being of the natives under Mission rule" (70). Notwithstanding the mistreatment of Native Americans under Spanish, Mexican, and American rule in the region, history in its re-telling is often replaced with a fantasy notion of halcyon days. The land itself, it seems, asks for this purifying treatment: "The newness of the land itself seems [. . .] to have demanded, the evocation of a mythology which could give people a sense of continuity" (71). Helen Hunt Jackson, a writer and poet who visited California in the late 1800s, became one of the most vocal proponents of this myth-making. During her frequent stays in the region she became increasingly enamored of the Spanish Missions which littered the Southern California landscape in varying states of dilapidation, taking it upon herself to write a novel describing, in hyperbolically romantic terms, the "Mission legend" of the land (79). According to McWilliams ([1946] 1973), Jackson's novel, *Ramona*, published in 1884, was based loosely on research she had conducted into the area on behalf of *Century* magazine. However, her interest in the facts quickly dissipated in the face of a desire to create a rosier myth out of the ashes of a more unsavory historical truth, and the novel became responsible in its way for the perpetuation of mythology over historical accuracy.

Didion's forefathers likewise told themselves stories to justify and validate *how* they chose to live; to legitimize and even romanticize in history the fateful decision to push back the frontier. What proportion of these stories are "merely imagined or improvised," and indeed how much of this institutional memory is "no true memory at all but only the traces of someone else's memory, stories handed down on the family network" ([1965] 2005: 141)? In *The Past is a Foreign Country*, David Lowenthal (1985) writes about the problematics of memory, nostalgia, and collective narratives of the past, arguing that the recollections of other people "occlude and often masquerade as our own" and that in the "process of knitting our own discontinuous recollections into narratives, we revise personal components to fit the collectively remembered past" (196). Didion asserts that it was through narratives like that of the Cornwall family that "the crossing stories became elevated to a kind of single master odyssey, its stations of veneration fixed" ([2003] 2004: 31). She implies that there is a certain difficulty in reporting the truth of a place so swathed in its own mythology, and so intent upon indoctrinating its inhabitants with a sense of the infallibility of that mythology. She points out, as one example of this tendency toward mythomania, the irony of Collis P. Huntington's decision to commission a painting (Albert Bierstadt's *Donner Lake from the Summit* (1873)) depicting the traversing of the Donner Pass by Central Pacific Railroad. Didion calls the painting "a wilful revision to this point of the locale" (75). Here, again, we see the California narrative at work. Bierstadt's painting illustrates the vista of the Donner Pass as romantic, even sublime. In thus representing this part of the land and wiping the slate clean of any remnants of the bloody history which previously stained it, the history of California becomes likewise ennobled and romantic. But the truth is that those who were slowed by sickness or age were sometimes abandoned to the wilderness; children of other parties who were discovered, orphaned, on the journey, were left behind. The crossing story, the version of history told and re-told through the generations, denies that such tragedy exists.

"How much of it actually happened? Did any of it?" Didion asks herself in "On Keeping a Notebook" ([1966a] 2005: 108), providing an example of the way in which she frequently destabilizes even her own authority as author. Mosser observes in *The Participatory Journalism* that "Autobiographical narratives are sometimes unreliable, unverifiable, even fictional" ([2011] 2012: 7). For Didion's purposes, both fiction and nonfiction are equally useful because they are equally, and appropriately, unreliable methods for bearing witness during this period. In "Failed Cultural Narratives," Alan Nadel (1992) points out that, "in foregrounding herself in both the role of journalist and of novelist [. . .] Didion also foregrounds the conflict between the two roles" (104). However, at the same time, "Didion knows" that the fiction crafted by the novelist requires the same effort at internal narrative coherence as a work of nonfiction. Both are problematized by the fact that "information never arrives in a pure form; rather, it comes framed by a series of inventions and imaginings [. . .] selective observations and more selective memories, render reportage as much the filter of fictions as fiction is the invention of reportage." In this way, authorship itself can become "one more fiction."

In both *Play It* and *Where I*, the separating line between fiction and nonfiction is fragile. One must consider that Didion is associated with the New Journalism, detailed by Tom Wolfe in a 1972 article for *New York Magazine*, in which he writes that this genre established that "it just might be possible to write journalism that would [. . .] read like a novel" (1972: 4). As fellow new journalist Hunter S. Thompson explains in *Fear and Loathing: On the Campaign Trail '72*: "there is no way to know the truth—except to be there" ([1973] 2012: 180). For this new band of nonfiction writers, the idea behind their new journalistic modus operandi "was to give the full objective description, plus something that readers had always had to go to novels and short stories for: namely, the subjective or emotional life of the characters" (Wolfe 1972: 10). The work of the new journalists involved obscuring the categorical distinctions that separated them from the novelist. I argue that Didion goes beyond this sense of interchangeability between apparently oppositional narrative genres, and moves into an essential de-centered diffuseness and multiplicity in her narrative voice(s) that speaks to the impossibility that fact and fiction can even be separated in the first place. The scrubbing out of the line between fiction and nonfiction—leading to, respectively, "the subjective" and "the objective," as outlined by Tom Wolfe, becoming synonymous (Wolfe 1972: 10)—is another way in which Didion deconstructs the myth of authority. Didion frequently articulates the inevitability of fiction creeping into its opposite number in order to connect the narrative dots and present the story in an authoritative way. In her 1966 piece for *Holiday* magazine, "On Keeping a Notebook," Didion recalls the cracked crab eaten the day her father returned from Detroit in 1945. Later she admits that it is unlikely that cracked crab was in fact eaten that day, writing that it is "easy to deceive oneself" about the reality behind any memory ([1966a] 2005: 108). In the same piece, she accepts that "it is precisely that fictitious crab that makes me see the afternoon all over again" (109). Just as Waldie remarks of *Holy Land* that nothing in the book is fictional, "except to say that all memories are" (Waldie and Campbell 2011: 230), Didion's cracked crab "might as well" have existed, and though Didion admits that she is capable of telling "what some would call lies" (or, when she feels kinder toward herself, "embroidery, worked into the day's pattern to lend verisimilitude"), she finds its necessity inevitable in terms of the creation of a coherent narrative ([1996a] 2005: 109).

In *Where I*, the form taken by Didion's reminiscences, that of a purposeful excision and control of the narrative, is a specific kind of storytelling, or "embroidery," as she puts it, through which she seeks to (re)define the past ([2003] 2004: 3).[6] Didion uses textual fabrication to stitch her own decoration through and over the preexisting text, further embellishing the family biography. This sense of placing layer upon layer connects her textual fabrications to the idea of the palimpsest, which in physical form dates back to the seventh century during which parchment was reused by overwriting the previous text inscribed upon it with new text using chemical methods. Sarah Dillon (2007a) explains in her essay "Palimpsesting" that "although the first writing on the vellum seemed to have been eradicated after treatment, it was often imperfectly erased. Its ghostly trace then reappeared in the following centuries" (2007a: 29). Taking inspiration from the work of Thomas De Quincey, who detailed the concept in his 1845 essay "The Palimpsest," Dillon explains that the famous essayist understood the mind itself as a palimpsest, in which ideas, images and feelings have impressed themselves. While "each succession has seemed to bury all that went before [. . .] in reality not one has been extinguished" (Dillon 2005: 243). Dillon defines the concept of the palimpsest therefore as "an involuted phenomenon where otherwise unrelated texts are involved and entangled, intricately interwoven, interrupting and inhabiting each other" (2007b: 4). Even writing about the palimpsest becomes palimpsestic, she notes, in that "any new text about the palimpsest erases, superimposes itself upon, and yet is still haunted by, the other texts in the palimpsest's history" (9). Andreas Huyssen (2003) meanwhile reasons that the idea of the palimpsest can be both literary in the way Dillon describes, and also "fruitfully used to discuss configurations of urban spaces and their unfolding in time" (7).

In "The Third Meaning," Roland Barthes ([1970] 1977) writes in similar terms that a text possessing multiple interpretations of a narrative, possesses "a multilayer of meanings which always lets the previous meaning continue, as in a geological formation" (58). Didion likewise makes her family's stories just like these "geological formation[s]," stitching her own decoration through and over the preexisting text. Didion's narratives unpick old threads and create new cavities. This is also reflected in her descriptions of the Californian landscape, portrayed as full of dangerous breaches in the form of devouring sinkholes and rapid rivers and houses leaning perilously close to the ocean, all of which create chasms in its veneer, replicated in the narrative lacunae of each of her texts which are likewise perforated with gaps and omissions in the stories told by her subjects, both fictional and nonfictional. Didion is as much a product of her environment as Carmen Sternwood, Maria Wyeth, or D. J. Waldie. They all reorganize and resuscitate history, to paraphrase M. Christine Boyer ([1996] 2001), creating a "fictional space" where it can live in fabricated form (66). Didion begins *Where I* by stating that what she tells us "may be true or it may be, in a local oral tradition inclined to stories that turn on decisive gestures, embroidery" ([2003] 2004: 3), arguing that "Conflicting details must be resolved, reworked into a plausible whole" (30). Like Maria, whose memory of events we must question throughout *Play It* ("I try not to think of dead things and plumbing. I try not to hear the air conditioner in that bedroom in Encino. I try not to live in Silver Wells or in New York or with Carter" ([1970] 2011: 9–10)), Didion presents herself to the reader in her nonfiction as an unreliable or amnesiac narrator. In both texts, Didion sets the scene for the presence, and perhaps the inevitability, of fabrication. In this way, she demonstrates that history, presenting itself as nonfiction, is as subject to the conventions of storytelling as fiction, and therefore equally at the mercy of the storyteller.

How much of Didion's Sacramento ever existed, outside of family stories told and re-told? Perhaps it comes into view only when juxtaposed against an empirical reality, appearing like the "gap between two [. . .] beats," to quote Vladimir Nabokov (1969). It is "the Tender Interval" that exists for a moment in between fiction and non (538).[7] In both *Where I Was From* and the *Slouching* essays she articulates this gap in terms of a sense of loss; the idea of a recognizable past and a way back into it is the collapsed star at the center of her work. The central organizing principle of each text is, ironically, the absence of center. Memory is found within the absences that suggest something is missing; in the distance between what she sees and what she feels she should see.

"Perhaps in retrospect this has been a story not about Sacramento at all, but about the things we lose" she realizes, understanding now that the "real past" is never entirely real in the first place ([1965] 2005: 147). If a "sense of Chekhovian loss" is built into the very foundations of Sacramento-as-California, perhaps the rate of its disappearance is entirely characteristic and to be expected (138). What is Didion actually mourning, asks Katherine Usher Henderson, "the old Sacramento or her own irretrievable childhood" (1981: 111)? The past of California pre-dates her own, but it is *her* California for which she mourns; the disappearance of her own past. Didion closes "Notes from a Native Daughter" with the final lines from "Spring and Fall" by Gerard Manley Hopkins: "*It is*

Margaret you mourn for" ([1965] 2005: 147). She knows that we mourn ourselves, seen in the places we once knew and to which we can no longer travel.

Didion comes in the end to an understanding about the impossibility of a backward glance in California; an understanding that, as "a child of the crossing story," she should know by heart ([2003] 2004: 217). Each return home becomes a form of perpetual leaving. For those who attempted the long crossing west, "Sentiment, like grief and dissent, cost time. A hesitation, a moment spent looking back, and the grail was forfeited" (32). As in *Play It As It Lays*, Didion teaches us that this is an archetypal California mantra: "Never discuss. Cut" ([1970] 2011: 203).

Damnatio Memoriae In L.A.: *Play It As It Lays*

In *Play It*, our ostensible heroine Maria Wyeth describes herself as "a radical surgeon of my own life. Never discuss. Cut. In that way I resemble the only man in Los Angeles County who does clean work," referring to the man who performs the abortion which so traumatizes her for the course of her remaining narrative (Didion [1970] 2001: 203). Such an equation speaks to the novel's preoccupation with removal and erasure. Maria may boast at the novel's conclusion that she has superior skills of excision, but this ability is belied by the novel as a whole, which is full of seeping wounds both real and imaginary, physical and emotional: holes in domestic interiors that gape and emit strange, accusatory noises; random acts of frenzied behavior; snakes hidden beneath rocks; and houses falling into the ocean. Neither Maria nor her environment truly embodies the imperative to never discuss, but only to cut. Maria herself, far from being an acolyte of the clean work she purports to be capable of, bleeds profusely across the pages of the novel. Her past haunts her at every turn, making unpredictable appearances in various guises and consuming her thoughts in the form of fantasy, dream, nightmare, and delusion. As Waldie articulates in a 2016 essay, "I write about Los Angeles where, despite our desire for forgetfulness, the back-and-forth of past and present persists" (2016: n.p.). Los Angeles seems to reflect and duplicate Maria's own desire to forget. But as Didion herself articulates in *Where I*, the California mantra of "Westward ho!," of continuous expansion, is a part of her inheritance she becomes compelled to deconstruct.

At the opening of *Play It*, Maria is insistent upon living "in the now," expressing from the start her desire for a firmer connection to her present in lieu of the past (Didion [1970] 2011: 8). A further emphasis of this desire comes in the absence of first-person narrative. It is only when we turn to the present-day at the beginning and toward the end of the novel that the first person is used, implying that Maria herself only exists, or only wishes to exist, in the present tense of the preliminary and final chapters. Only by existing willfully in what Leonard Wilcox (1984) describes as a "fatalistic yielding to an eternal present" (72) can Maria Wyeth bear to return to the past, and even then she must "stick to certain facts" in order to maintain that illusion of control (Didion [1970] 2011: 8). It seems that it is only in the blinding light of Los Angeles, from her prone poolside position, that Maria is able to exist in her preferred present. For her, thinking about the past "leads nowhere," and thinking about the future gives her occasion to dream, not to plan (7). Silver Wells now exists only as a dreamscape or imagined place where the past is played out on an empty stage. "An underground nuclear device was detonated where Silver Wells, Nevada, her childhood home, had once been, and Maria got up before dawn to feel the blast. She felt nothing" (204).

In present-day Los Angeles, Maria is insistent upon seeing "no one I used to know," as though by barring particular people who carry remnants of the past from her, she can exclude them entirely from her story ([1970] 2011: 10). She does not wish to think about *as it was*, an incantatory phrase repeated throughout the novel in much the same way that "*hurry along as fast as you can*" is repeated throughout *Where I* ([2003] 2004: 75). Maria describes her father as her opposite; he had always lived ahead of himself ("he was a man always twenty years before his time" ([1970] 2011: 6)), but now only exists in her past, as fragments or impressions of moments she does not wish to fully extrapolate. For her father, more of a "pioneer," the future was the point. This was something to anticipate as being better than the past, simply because it had to be: "I was raised to believe that what came in on the next roll would always be better than what came in on the last. I no longer believe that, but I am telling you how it was" (5). Wyeth family friend Benny Austin insists that, conversely, what matters is the past: "I'm speaking about *then*, Maria. *As it was*" (6). Later in the novel even benign figures like Benny, who is too closely associated with her past, her home, and her dead parents, become people to avoid. When she sees him in Las Vegas she finds herself paralyzed by an inability to acknowledge his presence: "She could not go back to the tables because Benny Austin was out there. Somehow she had never expected to see Benny Austin again: in her mind he was always in her father's pickup, or standing with her mother and father on the tarmac at McCarran waving at the wrong window" (147–8).

In *Where I*, Didion explains that, when writing her novel *Run River*, she had been of the opinion that "California '*as it was*' [. . .] got bulldozed out of existence" in the postwar boom years ([2003] 2004: 170–1, emphasis added). It is notable that "as it was" is a refrain found in both *Play It* and *Where I*, and used in reference to places both literal, in the form of the California Joan Didion herself knew that she feels has changed beyond recognition, and metaphorical, in terms of the past which Maria Wyeth does not wish to contemplate. In *Play It*, the passing of time after a sojourn into childhood in the early part of the novel is not quantified for the reader and instead is categorized merely as "bad" or unmemorable: "I am not sure what year it was because I have this problem with *as it was*, but after a while I had a bad time" ([1970] 2011: 9). Despite her efforts, the missing *as it was* remains at the center of her narrative.

Her mother is one past subject she does not wish to think about, but turns over in her mind torturously regardless. After the abortion, Maria thinks of her: "Silver Wells was with her again. She wanted to see her mother"; as is typical of Didion, place becomes synonymous with person ([1970] 2011: 86). When she visits a Silverlake hypnotist who claims that her worries can be traced back to her mother's womb, Maria sees only visions of driving along Sunset when she places herself in his apparently healing hands. "You're lying in water and it's warm and you hear your mother's voice" her hypnotist insists, but Maria can hear no such thing, and the repeated emphasis of the word "lying" infuses the scene with the suggestion of fraudulence (124). As Mark Royden Winchell (1980) writes, her "ties with her past have been so irrevocably severed that she is unable to 'go back' even under hypnosis" (130). When she sees nothing, the hypnotist blames her own resistance to the process of remembering, claiming that she "couldn't open enough doors to get back" (Didion [1970] 2011: 143). In the opinion of the hypnotist, Maria cannot find an opening through which she may return to some primordial state of being. His statement is significant for its invocation of voids in space—doors are ambivalent holes in walls, creating hyphenate spaces which provide ways in and out, entries and exits, and both link spaces and separate them, subdividing interiors.

All internal spaces in *Play It* are porous, flimsy, and often disturbing. When forced to exist inside various pseudo-domestic settings, Maria is filled with a nameless, creeping horror. Each interior is troubling in a distinctive way: the too "immaculate" motel room in Oxnard which, upon leaving, she straightens out "as if to erase any sign of herself," the bedroom blanched white and cream in Encino where she has her abortion, and in which she "had left the point," the Vegas interior painted purple in which she recalls that she had been told by her mother that "purple rooms could send people into irreversible insanity," and the apartment on Fountain Avenue with the unnervingly slow-draining shower ([1970] 2011: 132, 135, 165). The open mouths of sink plugs and shower drains threaten to unleash some torrent of subterranean discharge, and she dreams of "gray water bubbling up in every sink" (96–7), certain in the knowledge that the pipes contain "hacked pieces of human flesh" (97). Every interior which should emit a sense of the familiar and the impregnable, becomes instead a potential crime scene at which her sense of guilt is exposed and made manifest in the pipes bursting with the detritus of human waste, threatening to overwhelm the borders of each space inside which she attempts to take shelter. Likewise, in *Where I Was From* and "Slouching Towards Bethlehem" unpleasant and uncomfortable memories push against their cages, manifesting themselves spatially in the form of uncanny hotel suites which disturb rather than provide comfort; family homes which house runaway teenagers for whom home is no-place; rooms into which the narrator is barred entry for fear of encountering ghosts; and ancestral houses filled with an excess of mementos left to disintegrate inside cupboard drawers. I am reminded of a passage from "The Uncanny" in which Freud ([1919] 2003) recounts a conversation that illuminated for him the trajectory of heimlich as it moved toward unheimlich: "I have the same impression with them as I have with a buried spring or a dried-up pond. You can't walk over them without constantly feeling that water might reappear.' 'We call that uncanny'" (129). Though she may not wish to "think of dead things and plumbing," Maria regardless finds that evasion and redaction will only get her so far, and is confronted with remnants of her past manifesting themselves in these uncanny physical ways (Didion [1970] 2011: 9–10).

Unable to cope with the reality of the present, Maria frequently slips into dream-like reminiscences that may or may not be true replications of the past. During her abortion, she recreates a fantasy of the past, constructed upon the foundation of a single image, and focusing on small details to pull herself into this image: "if she could concentrate for one more minute on that shed, on whether this minute twenty years later the heat still shimmered off its roof, those were two minutes during which she was not entirely party to what was happening in this bedroom in Encino" (81). She remembers herself as a child, captured in the image of herself reading a book about contending with rattlesnake bites on the steps of the house in Silver Wells. She explicitly excludes her father from these thoughts, as though his inclusion would somehow blight the purity of the memory: "her father was not in this picture, keep him out of it."

Through Maria's propensity for narrative excisions, we find that she is ambiguous on the subject of whether gaps in her narrative are a sign of control or of a contrivance to remove certain defective or unwanted memories from the pack. Maria conceptualizes the past as a sequence of scenes or pictures, assembling a series of static moments into a narrative of her choosing. This is her attempt at instituting order amid the chaos of de-contextualized fragments of time: "After BZ's death there was a time when I played and replayed these scenes and others like them, composed them as if for the camera, trying to find some order, a pattern. I found none" (14). Her slideshow of scenes contain a number of faulty slides blighted by age, their pictures partly obscured, some missing completely, others displayed out of their correct order. Where is the time in between? What do the missing slides show? There are fingerprints on the negative, holes in the narrative. As touched upon in Chapter 1, Klein (2008) discusses the use of erasure in conceptions and (re)presentations of history in Los Angeles culture with particular reference to the concept of the "imago." This is a heightened iconographic image of someone (usually a parent) which he defines as "an idealised face left over from childhood—a photograph, the color of mother's dress on the day she took ill (the photological trace)" (3–4). These imagos, so convincing that they prevent us from seeing their true fraudulence, do not stray so far from reality as to draw attention to their fictive nature. Thus, such images or visions can easily replace an authentic, but less palpable or even perhaps less desirable, memory. Klein writes of the internal diversionary tactics through which we forget the past, of "the quiet instant where one imago covers over another" (13). Even if the examples noted here from *Play It* do represent authentic visions from the past, we know from Maria's narration that this is not the complete picture. She attempts to internalize her mantra to "Never discuss. Cut" through cutting out parts of her own history in order to create a less painful narrative (Didion [1970] 2011: 203). She attempts to replace the original with the imago, claiming that hers is the authoritative version.

Crossing Nothing to Go Nowhere: The Freeway Experience

In *Play It*, Maria decides that if she cannot live in her own edited version of the past, the white noise of the present is the state in which she wishes to permanently reside. In Los Angeles, it becomes "essential" to Maria that "she be on the freeway by ten o'clock. Not somewhere on Hollywood Boulevard, not on her way to the freeway, but actually on the freeway" (Didion [1970] 2011: 15).

By ten o'clock she must be in the present, not on her way to the present, but actually there, driving forward within it: "If she was not she lost the day's rhythm, its precariously imposed momentum." David J. Alworth (2016) notes in *Site Reading* that Maria "experiences the freeway as a special site" (86). *Site Reading* itself, devoted to the unpacking of particular sites and settings in narrative prose fiction, argues that, rather than the settings of fiction providing a "fixed container for the characters that are presumed to define [its] social world," the specific sites within which these novels are situated are instead "determinants of sociality" which exercise "a kind of agency with and through their human and non-human constituents" (2). Alworth refers to Henri Lefebvre (1991) who asserts in *The Production of Space* that such "social relations" only become concretized when made manifest in space; in the physical environment in which these relations take place (404). Therefore, Alworth continues, sites are not merely the stage upon which characters play out their narrative dramas, but are themselves mediators engaging in "active participation," capable of transforming and modifying meaning themselves, not just providing the setting for this to take place (Alworth 2016: 11). What does the site of the freeway therefore tell us about Maria's West Coast world? How does it translate meaning in the novel?

In her 1976 essay "Bureaucrats," Didion describes the "freeway experience" as "the only secular communion Los Angeles has" ([1976] 1995: 252). This is an assertion supported by David Brodsky (1981) in *L.A. Freeway: An Appreciative Essay*, in which he argues that "Driving the freeway is absolutely central to the experience of living in Los Angeles, and any anthropologist studying our city would head for the nearest onramp," continuing that the freeway is "a concrete testament to who we are [. . .] the backbone of southern California. They rank with the mountains and the rivers in influencing the organization of a changing city, and uncontestably they are the single most important feature of the man-made landscape" (2). Mike Davis ([1998] 2000) articulates California's autophilia, describing the construction and later expansion of one of the state's most famous and scenic roads, Highway 126, as "a primal scene—the familiar tremor heralding an eruption of growth that will wipe away human and natural history" (91). What does the freeway symbolize for Maria? The stasis of a permanent present, the way of the future, or the evasion of the past? Maria's self-imposed metronomic existence recalls Lefebvre's discussion of rhythm, time, and movement through space in *Rhythmanalysis* (1992). Lefebvre argues that in order to properly understand the internal logic of urban spaces, one must first attempt to observe and sense their rhythms. Rhythm, he writes, consists of the linear (the pendulum back and forth of the quotidian) and the cyclical (longer and more circuitous movements). In order to internalize this rhythm, to "abandon oneself" to it, one must assume a position of ambivalence, by which he means one must somehow be suspended between the twin poles of internal and external space: "it is therefore necessary to situate oneself simultaneously inside and outside" (Lefebvre [1992] 2004: 27). This reflects Didion's ambivalent narrative voice, which allows her to be both outside and inside the narrative, even when that narrative is as personal as a family memoir.

Lefebvre recommends a balcony or window, as this perspective offers an empirical view which allows one, from on high, to appreciate the rhythmic patterns made manifest in the urban sprawl which lies below. While Maria is not looking *down* at the world around her, but *out*, she does "abandon herself" to rhythm, and she is both inside (the car) and outside (on the freeway). Elsewhere, in "Bureaucrats," Didion explains that "participation" in this experience "requires a total surrender, a concentration so intense as to seem a kind of narcosis, a rapture-of-the-freeway. The mind goes clean. The rhythm takes over" (1976: 252). In *Play It*, though Maria claims to be "a radical surgeon of my own life" ([1970] 2011: 203), it becomes apparent from her relived memories of her mother's death, her inability to reunite with figures from her parents' past, her regret over her abortion and her perpetual return visits to the daughter from whom she has been separated, that this statement merely signifies her ability to divest herself of any semblance of agency and amputate the shadow that is her own history. And though the freeway purports to be a space in which individual autonomy rules, it requires, as Reyner Banham (2000), points out, "the almost total surrender of personal freedom for most of the journey" (217). Maria gives herself over to the control and rule of a higher power; her route languorously cyclical and repetitive and seemingly endless.

Banham contends that the "freedom of movement" in the city is its "prime symbolic attribute" (18). The appropriate way to approach Los Angeles, he suggests, is not in a straight, sequential line, but via a circular motion. As though mimicking the highways and freeways which loop and interweave their way through the city, chronology is not linear, but spherical. The essential fact, he notes, about Los Angeles is that it has "grown almost simultaneously all over," thereby making "all its parts equal and equally accessible from all other parts at once" (18). It seems to begin again, but only repeats and renews itself. The automobile is therefore the perfect expression (or symptom) of both the city's unique spatial structure and its attitude to history. If Los Angeles is a city that moves forward, collecting additions to its "extraordinary mixture" as it progresses, the only way of looking back is to glance quickly into the rear-view mirror of one's insular cell (6). There is no other way of looking backward in a city which one can only navigate by taking to the road and driving onwards, like a crossing story that never ends. Alworth (2016) argues that in this "era of automobility" depicted in *Play It*, "the road manifests a particular kind of flux—a movement of bodies and machines, of mechanical centaurs, through a space designed specifically for speed" (95). Speed and mobility require and necessitate forward momentum, and thus "since it is manifestly dangerous to face backward while at the steering wheel, the common metaphor of history as the rear-view mirror of civilization seems necessary, as well as apt, in any study of Los Angeles" (Banham 2000: 6). In the era of the freeway, it seems, history in Los Angeles is always behind you, never pantheistic or contextual, and can only be seen in fleeting, smudged glimpses as one leaves it further and further behind.

However, for Leonard Wilcox, Maria's "daily runs on the freeway" (1984: 72) are symbolic of more than just the desire to escape the past; for him they are in fact "a debased version of the journey west, a parody of the effort to find new passages in a land beyond history" (72–3). Ironically, by taking these drives, rather than evading history, Maria is reliving it. This is Maria's crossing story, but instead of continuing in order to settle, Maria continues for the sake of continuing. Maria is a prime example of Katherine Usher Henderson's assertion that all of Didion's heroines "inherit the legacy of the frontier experience" (1981: vii). When she remembers the last time she saw her mother, she recalls her father speaking of opening a diner adjacent to the freeway, an idea to which her mother objected: "'*Not* on 95,' Francine Wyeth said. '*Somewhere else*'" (Didion [1970] 2011: 87). In her own endless circling of the freeway, Maria does not actually get *somewhere else*, instead going through the motions of forward momentum without moving beyond this insular, labyrinthine space.

When writing in *Where I* about the small town of Gilroy, Didion tracks its journey from farm town to commuter town, with the only sign of its previous agricultural history available in the reconstituted and contained form of the "ninety-million-dollar theme park" that was the Bonfante Gardens ([2003] 2004: 174). Didion describes each of Gilroy's iterations as "a hologram that dematerialises as I drive through it" (174–5). According to this assertion, driving can render the past as a harmless mirage on the other side of your window; you can speed through the land and ignore the presence of history on the way to *somewhere else*. Vidler (1992) states that in a city stripped of memory, one wanders "across already vanished thresholds that leave only traces of their former status as places. Amid the ruins [. . .] we cross nothing to go nowhere" (185). Arguably this city is much like the one Didion describes; one which encourages people to drive endlessly without needing to stop or look back. The freeway, notes David Fine (2004) in similar terms, offers "endless mobility without destination" (2004: 248). For Maria, the lack of conclusion, the ability to continue on and on without reaching any finite point, *is* the point and the lure of the freeway. In fact, she wants to leave the point *somewhere else*. For her, the mindless rhythm of the road is a form of erasure, and rather than sharpening her perception (as per *Rhythmanalysis*), instead it numbs her. Only when she stops is her mind once again filled with those images "of Les Goodwin in New York and Carter out there on the desert with BZ and Helene and the irrevocability of what seemed already to have happened, but she never thought about that on the freeway" (Didion [1970] 2011: 18). From the safety of her car, she is spared the pain of remembrance; in her mind there are "no beginnings or endings, no point beyond itself" (69).

Jennifer Brady (1984) writes that Maria's obsession with driving the freeway represents an "attempt to find refuge from thought and memory" (52). The freeway is a place she associates consciously with the freedom of forgetting. Maria's intention is to put as much distance as possible between herself and the events of the past. By the end of the first month succeeding the breakdown of her marriage, she has quantified this necessary distance into a total of 7,000 miles. Jean Baudrillard ([1986] 2010) writes in *America* that the speed of travel made possible by the car represents the "Triumph of forgetting over memory, an uncultivated, amnesiac intoxication" (7). Driving itself is deemed "a spectacular form of amnesia," and the journey embarked upon on the road is, simultaneously, one of "excessive, pitiless distance" (10) and of "immobility, concealed beneath the very intensification of their mobility" (7). How far can we persist on this "journey which is no longer a journey," Baudrillard asks, one which aims only for "the point of no return"? Maria's wish is to remain immobile, suspended in time. On the freeway one can only function in the present, and if she can only find a way to live indefinitely in that present, she does not have to look back.

Maria's desperation to face forward, to pursue the frontier's endlessly deferred end, is a recurring trait echoed in other nonfiction Californian tales. "Never discuss. Cut" ([1970] 2011: 203), is an echo of Virginia Reed's counsel to "never look back at all" (Didion [2003] 2004): 199). Historical precedent in California seems to encourage the notion that it is possible for one to escape history there, or to escape oneself, by choosing to, as David Fine (1991) puts it, "move to the better neighborhood, take to the hills, or travel across the landscape and enjoy, for a time, a state of amnesia. Ultimately, though, the road ends or turns back on its beginnings" (218). Maria finds that, ultimately, she cannot move any further into forgetting; history, it turns out, "is not so easily outstepped" (218). From the very beginning of *Play It*, Didion makes clear that the past is something we can never be rid of. We see this in the sheer effort exerted continually by our protagonist to block, repress, cut-out, or move away from the physical sites of unwanted memories. Most of all, we see this in Maria's historical antecedents. In the end, the attempt to control and curtail her own historical narrative so exhausts her that she lies near-catatonic by the swimming pool, talked about by others who now control her story, but terminally silent herself.

The narration of the past evident in both *Play It* and *Where I*, represents more of an exclusion or curtailment of reality from official accounts. The former uses compartmentalization, repression, and redaction, the latter state-wide myths and ancestral stories. Both are forms of narrative control, and both leave a sense of loss and absence in their wake. By a consistent demonstration that fiction can easily present itself as fact, Didion intentionally undermines both her own authority and by extension that of the nation, as an unreliable narrator writ large. We all tell ourselves stories in order to live, and she proves herself and her home state from whence perhaps this impulse came, as no exception.[8] Snakes are as fixed an element of California's mythology as the crossing story and the land itself. All are concerned equally with the threat of fatality, and the possibility of renewal. The snake sheds its skin but does not really change; the crossing story is more fixated on rebirth than death; the garden is what is offered to those who are willing to abandon other histories. The freeway, too, now says something about "who we are" (Brodsky 1981: 2), and it can be added to this list of mythic motifs. It is something reiterative and renewing, repeating its own looping patterns, eating its own tail, reliving old stories and giving them new names, over and over again.

Glassworld: Hisaye Yamamoto's "Wilshire Bus"

Throughout the fifteen short stories of *Seventeen Syllables and Other Stories*, the Japanese-American author Hisaye Yamamoto ([1950] 1998) examines postwar life and provides "a new angle on the common literary image of Los Angeles as a 'nowhere city,' a place one 'can't be from'" (Wheeler 1996: 19). Alison Lurie, whose novel *The Nowhere City* finds fertile terrain in the exploration of this ambivalent city of lack, explicates the city from an outsider's point of view in a similar manner (as do so many other authors associated with Los Angeles who are in fact not from Los Angeles: the city of newcomers). However, Yamamoto's alienation is far more tangible, having been "displaced and rendered alien not by private despair but by forces of racism beyond her control" (20). In Yamamoto's short story, "Wilshire Bus," published in 1950, we find Esther, a Japanese-American woman, traveling by bus along Wilshire Boulevard to see her husband in hospital.

Wilshire Boulevard itself was originally created by the Tongva Native American tribe as a "pathway from the Indian Village Yang Na [. . .] to the Pacific Ocean" (Rasmussen 1989: n.p.) for whom it provided a route by which they could bring back tar from the La Brea pits, arguably making it the city's first highway. The same path was later used by Spanish colonialists, and wended its way through "the original pueblo of Los Angeles and five of the original Spanish land grants, or ranchos" ("Birth of the Boulevard" n.p.). Kevin Starr (2009) calls it "a sixteen-mile spatial repository of Los Angeles history and aspiration, a chromosomatic strip of the past, the present, and the unfolding future of the city" (176). Reyner Banham (2000) notes that the freeway system is "the third or fourth transportation diagram drawn on a map that is a deep palimpsest of earlier methods of moving about the basin" (57). Its existence as a palimpsestic pathway that both follows and overwrites its own past is symptomatic of the development of urban space in Southern California, and also represents a grand cross-section of the architectural and spatial history of Los Angeles. If one travels along the Boulevard, which crosses 206 streets on its way to the Pacific, one will encounter "architectural remnants of every phase of Los Angeles development, more or less in sequence" (Starr 2009: 176). Indeed, westward expansion has been "paced by Wilshire Boulevard" since the early twentieth century, when the city began to expand "westward to the sea from the 1920s onward" (175).

Banham argues that the motor age of Los Angeles did not begin until 1927, when work had begun on "the first real monument of the Motor Age: Miracle Mile on Wilshire Boulevard" (66). Wilshire Boulevard represented "the creation of years of ad hoc subdivisions" from the space created to make MacArthur Park in 1895 which stretched west of the Boulevard by a quarter of a mile, to its progression through Beverly Hills in 1906, its extension to Santa Monica in 1919, and its eastward movement downtown in 1934. By the 1950s Wilshire was part of "a network of automotive boulevards" which "defined the form of the city" (Starr 2009: 175).

In "Wilshire Bus," Yamamoto ([1950] 1998) notes that Wiltshire Boulevard, like the city it serves, "begins somewhere," exhibits a "few digressions" and "goes straight out to the edge of the Pacific Ocean" (34). Its journey through this centrifugal city is cyclical, endless; we are not privy even to Esther's embarkation, her own beginnings obscured.[9] Though she is mobile, she is subject to the whims of others on the bus, stopping and starting according to their desires, stationary as a commuter who must sit and wait for her point of disembarkation to appear, rather than drive decisively toward or away from it, as Maria Wyeth or Philip Marlowe are able to do. Esther is similar to Maria in one respect, in that the autonomy of both is subjugated to the road. Like Maria as she drives around the freeway, Esther's bus journey goes "back and forth along the Boulevard," but "never reaches either end" (Wheeler 1996: 42). The city has no finite point at which it can be seen to physically conclude, instead expanding ever outwards, mutating into something "more pastoral" before spilling out into the ocean itself (Yamamoto [1950] 1998: 34).

As Esther peers through the window, she surveys the scene, describing the "recent stark architecture which favors a great deal of glass" (34). In a 1928 article for the *Architectural Record*, Frank Lloyd Wright ([1928] 2008) decreed that "the greatest difference eventually between ancient and modern buildings will be due to our modern machine-made glass. Glass, in any wide utilitarian sense, is new [...] our modern world is drifting towards structures of glass and steel" (137). For the famed architect, glass had the ability to make external structures disappear into the air and turn themselves inside out, making private space highly visible, and public space resplendent with amplified and "bewildering vistas and avenues" (138). The modern city would be full of this material, making it "imperishable! Buildings—shimmering fabrics—woven of rich glass [. . .] Such a city would clean itself in the rain, would know no fire alarms—nor any glooms" (140). The nineteenth century, writes Isobel Armstrong (2008) in *Victorian Glassworlds*, was "the era of public glass," a material which created urban environments in its own image (1). Armstrong describes the "scopic culture" that emerged from that century and the proliferation of glass in buildings both domestic and commercial (3). Writing in 1933, Walter Benjamin quotes the modernist author and architectural theorist Paul Scheerbart who declared "a good twenty years ago" that "a 'culture of glass'" would "transform humanity utterly" (Benjamin [1933] 1999: 734).

By the twentieth century there had emerged an "unhappy recent trend," according to the Federal Writers' Project, of the "'moderne' façade, which utilizes polished steel, chromium, curved glass, mirrors, glass blocks, and concrete" (*Los Angeles: A Guide to the City and Its Environs* 1941: 109). Glass windows in particular had become desirable consumer goods by the early decades of the twentieth century, and a symbol of ambivalence, "uniquely positioned both inside and outside and thus subject to the rule of two realms"

(Isenstadt 2006: 146). The window internalizes the "tension between being both present and absent, there and not there" (156), between the internal/domestic and external/public world, that came with the use of glass in modern buildings, allowing the outside in and projecting the inside out—all of which makes it the perfect manifestation of the city's uncanny or spectral nature. The conflation of the internal and external, literally the homely and the unhomely, was made manifest in the glass building, so much a part of its environment that it became indistinguishable, near-transparent against its background.

Glass was not simply appreciated for its capacity to increase light and maximize the capacity of the view, it was also heralded for its ability to expand space. Glass reconfigures spatial boundaries, making the built environment capricious and reflexive, its walls reformulating themselves like liquid mercury. Nothing stays the same. To move through such an environment is to find oneself in a mise-en-abyme in which one is reflected over and over again, broken into fragments, somehow both within space and outside its enclosure. This is internalized by Esther, who sits surrounded by reflective surfaces. The glass that surrounds her, both in the form of the bus windows through which she peers at the outside world, and in the buildings that line the stretch of Boulevard along which she travels, imbues the scene with a sense of ambivalence. This kind of material, notes Walter Benjamin, creates space "in which it is hard to leave traces" (recalling Derrida's theory of the trace) ([1933] 1999: 734). What traces are made visible during Esther's journey? Beneath the "manifest" plotline of Esther's journey to visit her husband in hospital and the racial abuse she both witnesses and suffers while on her way, we find the "buried" story of wartime imprisonment (Yogi 1989: 179).

The bus at first seems to offer safe passage, but instead Esther finds herself trapped in a no-place which is neither public nor private, stationary nor ambulant, watching the newly developed city appear and disappear through the window, unable to touch its reality. The window, much like history's (re)presentation in Los Angeles, gives her only brief glimpses of the city's unvarnished past. The pane of glass offers only an obscured vision, removing her from a lived experienced of its built environment and preventing immediate access. She is hermetically sealed instead inside a terrible re-enactment of a not-so-distant history from which she cannot seem to escape, but which the city itself shows no signs of. Instead it reflects back only a veneer of itself in duplicate and her own face in its placid surfaces, surveying her from a panoptic position, a series of the same "closed monads" found in Chandler's world of private, inaccessible interiors (Jameson 2016: 4).

Throughout the story, Esther's gaze changes from an act of pleasure projected outwards ("she took vicarious pleasure in gazing out"), to a self-contained performance ("Esther, pretending to look out the window") that transforms the look into a façade behind which she can bury her pain ("Esther stared out the window with eyes that did not see") (Yamamoto [1950] 1998: 34, 36, 37). However, the agency of her gaze is undermined by its "vicarious" nature (she is removed from actively participating in that which she surveys), and limited by the danger of its being met by those who consider looking to be an audacious assertion of self by someone who should only be looked *at* ("Esther felt her giving him a quick but thorough examination before she turned around. 'So you don't like it?' the man inquired [. . .] 'why don't you go back where you came from?'" (35)). She, too, fixes her gaze upon others, distinguishing the "considerable mass of people" from the "elderly Oriental man and his wife" who was "probably Chinese" (35). Though she expresses a degree of solidarity with the couple, smiling a greeting which is ignored, she nevertheless feels initially "quite detached" from the racist abuse they endure, seeing herself as "in the present case immune," feeling only the "tenseness in the body of the women beside her" and not within herself (36).

Like the buildings of the city themselves, the facades of which reflect out but never in, revealing nothing but a glassy blankness, she describes her silence in this moment as a "grave sin of omission" (34). There are things which are never spoken of, internalized as pain and leaving no trace on the outside ("which caused her acute discomfort for a long time afterwards whenever something reminded her of it"). She insulates her past from the rest of her thought process through parenthesis, for example, "on her way home from work. (This was not long after she had returned to Los Angeles from the concentration camp in Arkansas and had been lucky enough to get a clerical job with the Community Chest)," and in the same way intimates a shared history with others: "Esther turned her head to smile a greeting (well, here we are, Orientals together on a bus)," referring to her own past without warning, a sudden pothole in the smooth flatness (36, 35). "She found herself wondering whether the man meant her in his exclusion order or whether she was identifiably Japanese" (36). Here Yamamoto broaches the subject of the Civilian Exclusion Order number 69, which was issued on May 12, 1942, in the wake of Pearl Harbour. Japanese-Americans in California were forced to leave their homes to be "interned in concentration camps scattered across the country" (Laslett 2015: 131). Yamamoto herself was interned with her family in Poston, Arizona, during the Second World War. This violent form of dislocation in the past manifests itself suddenly in Esther's memory of "an elderly

Oriental man" who she remembers had been standing on "a concrete island at Seventh and Broadway" (Yamamoto (1950) 1998: 36). He appears in her mind as though in the middle of an ocean, jolting her like a sudden dip in an otherwise smooth concrete surface, like the "lump" that Yamamoto herself feels in her "subconscious" when watching a documentary about "the camp experience" of which she rarely speaks (Yamamoto 1976: 11). She remembers her shock at seeing that the man was wearing a badge that stated "I AM KOREAN," having been readying herself to smile at him "benignly as a fellow Oriental" (Yamamoto [1950] 1998: 36). She is reminded brutally of her own alienation, her own sense of self as separate, dislocated. Her memories are not contiguous with the fabric of the city in which she lives, rather they are like an island that has been forcibly detached from the mainland.

Now looking again through the window, she sees the landscape outside the confines of the bus as insubstantial, melting into air, reflecting her feeling that she herself cannot find purchase in this environment which does not enable her to leave traces of herself, her history, within it. As the bus makes its way along the Boulevard she feels a "sickening sensation of there being in the world nothing solid she could put her finger on, nothing solid she could come to grips with, nothing solid she could sink her teeth into, nothing solid" (37). Like Marshall Berman, she feels her world is more ghostly than tangible, reflecting back her own precariousness within it. This fragility is of course emphasized by the origins of the Boulevard along which she habitually travels, which speak to the city's proclivity for historical effacement and superimposition. To quote Sarah Dillon, this palimpsestic city's "perpetual openness to new inscription ensures that this history will constantly be rewritten" (2007b: 9). Wilshire Boulevard stands as a reminder that there are other stories about itself which the city would rather render obscure.

An Eternal, Dizzying Present: *The Nowhere City*

Paul and Katherine Cattleman are at odds from the start of Alison Lurie's *The Nowhere City*. Her two central protagonists, temporary emigrants from the East who reside for a short but life-changing period of time in the West, approach the foreign terrain of Los Angeles from two opposing points of view. Initially, where Harvard historian Paul feels curiosity, his wife, research assistant Katherine, feels revulsion, seeing only a flagrant inauthenticity and willful surreality where Paul sees "limitless freedom and opportunity" (Lurie [1965] 1994: 231). Paul admits his vision is based on a mythological view of the frontier: "it had come to him straight out of American history: 'Go West, Young Man'" (231). Katherine, conversely, is fearful of the *newness* that surrounds her; the fact that everything seems "'so exaggerated, so unnatural'" (11).

Despite his professional commitment to the past, Harvard historian Paul Cattleman is fascinated by his adopted city's ability to imagine itself as the urban wave of the future. Like Reyner Banham in *Los Angeles: The Architecture of Four Ecologies*, Paul sets out to "read Los Angeles in the original" (2000: 5) or to submit to, rather than fight, the tide which pulls him out to sea. Thus, he goes about diligently exploring this future-scape, for if "he wanted to find out how it felt to live in the future, wasn't that almost his duty?" (Lurie [1965] 1994: 6). There has long been a tradition of writing about Los Angeles which paints it as a city somehow speaking to us from some future space. In agreement with Katherine's sense that she has left a meaningful life defined by continuity behind her in the East, Fine writes that the past "is left behind, in the East; the future lies before us, in the West" (1991: 209). In fact, what Paul learns is that the Los Angeles of *The Nowhere City* is a place where the future is deferred. He finds himself living in a seemingly permanent present, where time merely duplicates repetitively. In turn, what at first seems to Katherine the most awful impediment to her acceptance of the city, that is, its apparent fraudulence and lack of consequence, ultimately becomes the reason why she grows to accept it and to find her place within it. As Richard Lehan (1967) puts it, they both, in different ways, "fall into a hole in time" (449).

"Los Angeles is so far away from everywhere and everything here is so peculiar; it's as if it weren't real," Katherine observes (Lurie [1965] 1994: 200). If it isn't quite real, then surely nothing that happens here counts. In the end, the diametrically opposed positions of husband and wife are reversed, and Paul comes around to Katherine's initial diagnosis of the city: "there was no past or future—only an eternal dizzying present" (267). But their new roles are not so easily assumed, and neither Katherine nor Paul are quite right in their assumptions about Los Angeles.

Upon first arriving in the city, Katherine, removed from the rote and the familiar, struggles to adapt to what she sees as total de-contextualization. Los Angeles refuses to situate itself within the context of chronology ("a dozen architectural styles were represented in painted stucco"), within a cyclical seasonal framework ("I don't like lilies or whatever they are growing at this time of year, or peaches"), or even within a familiar time-zone ("'What time is it really?' she asked. 'It feels dreadfully late'" (4, 11, 12)). The notion of things being somehow out of time or displaced recurs with frequency throughout the novel. "I don't like the sun shining all the time in November," complains Katherine, "and the grass growing. Its unnatural, it's as if we were all shut up in some horrible big greenhouse away from the real world and the real seasons" (38). The fruit is "over-ripe" or "out of season" (55, 44). The complete absence "of seasons that conform to those of the East or Midwest," argues David Fine (1984), "signals the disappearance of time itself" (12). Without the juxtaposition of the winter and the summer, the old and the new, there is no sense of repetition and renewal. Without sequence, there is no sense of consequence. Alison Lurie explains that the novel is structured around the missing "moods and forms" which define life on the East Coast and are missing on the West, in her experience: "there are no seasons in Los Angeles [. . .] there is no day or night [. . .] there are no days of the week [. . .] there is no past or future. It is sort of an eternal present" (Lurie "Alison Lurie: The Nowhen City": n.p.).

Everything here is very slightly out of context or somehow ill-fitting. Los Angeles residents look "out of place [. . .] much too small for the roads and buildings" (Lurie [1965] 1994: 231). The animals Katherine sees at the Putty mansion have "the air of creatures who have been forcibly torn from their natural habitat" (58), as do the paintings by the Old Masters which line the walls of the millionaire's abode. The *unnaturalness* of Los Angeles, its ludicrous incongruity and failure to observe or even care about notions of correct time or seasonal weather or realistically sized fruit, strike fear into Katherine's rigid notions of what is appropriate, at least when compared to what is deemed normal on the East Coast. The Cattlemans' Victorian furniture, inherited from Katherine's parents, looks incongruous in the blinding brightness of the bare Mar Vista bedroom. The wooden fruit carved into the mahogany bed frame is a dead weight next to the superfluity of peaches and golden flowers splayed across various surfaces. Katherine's desire to hold on to her sense of East Coast history is evident in her itemization of each piece of furniture. The past is for her a static image that she does not at this point wish to change, much like her inflexible idea of who she is as a person under the watchful eye of this vision of inescapable history. Her family heirlooms are taken out of plain sight and sequestered in the garage: "Gradually, over the past few months, the garage had filled up with ghosts" (130). Such homely objects are literally, as Freud puts it, "removed from the eyes of strangers, hidden," becoming signs of an ambivalent attitude to a once-cherished heritage ([1919] 2003: 133). Here the old is replaced by the new and the past is neatly displaced: "it just didn't look right here" (Lurie [1965] 1994: 129).

Katherine is accustomed to deriving meaning from the passing of time in a sequential, structured manner. But Los Angeles lacks "the dimension of time" (267) and the absence of seasons or inclement weather means that "everything runs together" (144). Even the stores do not adhere to normal opening hours. Day and night become almost interchangeable, and mealtimes are not strictly observed in uniformity: "You go to a restaurant for dinner and you see people sitting at the next table eating breakfast. Everything's all mixed up and wrong" (144). For Dr. Einsam, Katherine's boss, the absence of a schedule imposed by appropriate timings for all activities means he is free to create his own sense of temporal structure: "A place like this, Los Angeles, actually it's a great opportunity" (148). Between midnight and 4:00 a.m., it transpires, Los Angeles experiences its "best time"; even Venice Beach, discovers Paul, "came alive" at night (148, 105). Paul is equally aware of the fact that "out here it was so easy to lose track of time" (208). Time also seems to have its own logic in the Los Angeles of *The Big Sleep*. The entire book spans only a period of five days, which seems absurd, as though Philip Marlowe has become a kind of Southern Californian Rip Van Winkle. "This is Marlowe" he says to Norris over the telephone, "Remember me? I met you about a hundred years ago—or was it yesterday?" as though the two are interchangeable (Chandler [1939] 2000: 84). Perhaps in Chandler's Los Angeles, they are.

Time seems to work differently here, with the five days of *The Big Sleep*'s time-span furling and un-furling endlessly and erratically, and memory proving to be equally fitful. In "Slouching Towards Bethlehem," published two years after *The Nowhere City*, Joan Didion describes a similar sense of unquantifiable time. "Time passes and I lose the thread," ([1967d] 2005: 80) she writes, her words echoing Katherine's anxiety about losing her thread in the labyrinth, as though she is Theseus without Ariadne. Katherine's sense of time in Los Angeles is defined by suspension and anticipation; the movement of the present into the past is endlessly deferred, and even the time of day is an irrelevance. In an interview Lurie describes Los Angeles as "really the nowhere city and the *nowhen* city" (Lurie "Alison Lurie: The Nowhen City": n.p. emphasis added). What is repressed here does not seem to be individual memory so much as persistent signs of tangible city history. Katherine's attitude in the earlier stages of the novel is reflective of a longing for history, but her historical context is dislocated, her family's furniture removed to the garage. How can one possibly situate oneself within any kind of space/time continuum when space is constantly expanding and time apparently does not exist?

For Katherine, the enormous spinning doughnut she sees immediately upon her arrival atop a roadside stand is a synecdoche for the city as a whole:

"a great big advertisement for nothing" (Lurie [1965] 1994: 38).¹⁰ This "big empty hole" echoes Didion's fear that, in Southern California, the center cannot hold, because in fact there *is* no center. For her this means, fatally, that history has been forgotten and its lessons neglected. Perhaps it is more accurate to say that *absence* is the center. For both, the absence most keenly felt is that of a tangible sense of time passing, without which life is for both a frightening, empty prospect. The void at the center of the doughnut finds resonance through this book as a heightened symbol of lack. It is the "negative path" (Vidler 1992: 180) forged by the obliteration of Berman's entire Bronx neighborhood; it is Didion's descriptions of the absence of history in Haight-Ashbury and the intentional omissions in Maria Wyeth's narrative; it is the gradual disappearance of the familiar Sacramento landscape in "Notes from a Native Daughter" and in *Where I Was From*; the abandoned oil fields and eerily vacant Sternwood mansion in *The Big Sleep*; the heartache of Waldie's empty rooms in *Holy Land*.

Alongside the temporal derangement which resides in Los Angeles is its counterpart: a sense of spatial disorder. Despite the imposition of the grid system, the seemingly endless pushing back of the real-estate frontier has led to a sense of disordered sprawl. Just as the two grid systems (outlined in Chapter 1) distort the legibility of the downtown Los Angeles streetscape, creating a disorienting tilt that is inherently duplicative, so does the city's geometric subdivision bleeding its edges out into a more fluid expansion create a conflict between rational and irrational space. Richard S. Weinstein (1998) defines the topographic development in Southern California during the early twentieth century as increasingly "ad hoc" and characterized by a "lack of hierarchical organization" (34). The disorganized sprawl of Los Angeles as it expands throughout Southern California creates pockets of misinterpreted and misused space—the "Vacant lots, parking lots, irrational left-over spaces" which in turn encourage a sense of "porosity, flux, and impermanence" (35). In *The Dream Endures*, Kevin Starr (1997) describes Los Angeles in the 1930s and 1940s as an "eclectic, even a hodgepodge city," full of a "sometimes phantasmagoric variety of streetscapes" (157). James Howard Kunstler points to the "fantasy aesthetic" of the Los Angeles movie set as the originator of the fact that "Angelenos became accustomed to outlandish buildings springing up in their communities, buildings that had no physical continuity with their surroundings" (1993: 209, 210).¹¹ Paul sees all this for himself when he looks at the modern houses which are built as signifiers of a past never personally experienced by their inhabitants, these reconstituted versions of history becoming ludicrously anachronistic when taken out of the context of place and time. The "Louisiana plantation house," for example, and the "movie executive's castle," which is "glaringly Colonial" (Lurie [1965] 1994: 232–3). Here we find the city's aversion to linear chronology, it's a-temporality, made visible in the built environment.

In *Postmodern Geographies* Edward Soja (1989) contends that Los Angeles has long defied "conventional categorical description of the urban, of what is a city" (245). Indeed, it has "deconstruct[ed] the urban into a confusing collage of signs" which signify only the imaginary and outlandish. David Fine (1984) writes that in the landscape of Southern California there is a sense of constant juxtaposition, disruption, and contrast, which he calls "spatial incongruity" (11). Los Angeles, Weinstein (1998) argues, is not able to physically represent traces of its past because it is continually in the process of erasing "previous urbanisms," thus rupturing the possibility of temporal and spatial continuity (76). In *The Nowhere City*, Lurie presents a space in which urban and pre-urban landscapes are alternately riddled with marks of disrepair or cosmetic enhancement. She notes the incessant disruption of continuous construction within the built environment of the city, the "dust of excavation" that hangs in the air, the "groans of trucks hauling dirt up and down the hills" and the "great ugly hill[s] of bare earth" that are interspersed between houses that will soon be pulled down ([1965] 1994: 13, 14, 270). Wherever Paul sets his gaze he sees "the red and orange iron skeletons of tall buildings rising above the palms," and hears the ominous "bang, bang, of construction and demolition" (13, 14). This is a sound that echoes the spectacle created by the construction of the Cross-Bronx Expressway, a similarity that becomes more emphatic when it is revealed that many of the houses in Paul's own neighborhood are being torn down to make way for the extension of the freeway. During this mid-1960s period, Interstate 405 would have been hacking its way both north and south through California.[12] As discussed in more detail in Chapter 3 in the context of Robert Moses and New York, the movement toward recasting urban spaces in a more modernist light reverberated in a disconnection between past and present in pursuit of the future. This evidently also applies to postwar construction in the Greater Los Angeles area, where the value of progress was greater than that of preservation and, to quote Spiro Kostof (1991), "the concern for context became an irrelevancy" (90). Lewis Mumford (1968) writes in *The Urban Prospect* that continually choosing the new and rejecting the old in too extreme a fashion "is bad for continuity and stability in life" (93). Progress should be, he argues, "cumulative" rather than violent, but it seems that not much has changed since nineteenth-century attitudes toward urban (de)construction sought to destroy "every vestige of the past, without preserving any links in form or visible structure between past and future" (125).

At the beginning of his stay in Los Angeles, Paul frequently expresses his admiration for the city's commitment to living in the now: "Thank Christ he had decided to come to Los Angeles, where people were really alive and things happened right now as well as in the past" (Lurie [1965] 1994: 107). But its ability to transform and recalibrate itself begins to have negative connotations for him. In due course Paul discovers that despite having been hired to write the history of the Nutting Corporation, his employers care very little for the fruits of his academic labors: "They didn't care about the past: they were only interested in the present and the immediate future" (49). His research, without the proper context within which to situate it outside of the "piles of paper" given to him which contain insufficient data, becomes nothing more than "flakes of paint fallen on to his desk [...] broken, meaningless messages" (156). There is no sense of connection or continuity that links these messages together. Reduced to "disordered layers of paper," Paul's work lacks a sense of accumulation. Rather, these scraps and flakes reduce the past to the parts of its sum: "nothing remained but these scattered notes and scraps" (158). Presenting his findings to an uninterested executive, Paul realizes that what he is contributing to is the sense of lack which permeates the city: "it was the expensive manufacture of nothing [...] no result—no product." Paul imagines the machinery of the Corporation devouring his research— "Had it already eaten his history?" — his papers reduced to nothing more than "unwanted and obsolete materials" which are processed and pulverized (159). History at the Corporation becomes a disparate collection of scattered scraps which, without a sense of continuity, mean nothing at all. "Paul's history turns out to be 'Nutting' in every sense" comments Judie Newman (2000) drily (47). Anyway, "what does it matter," asks Paul's colleague, "It's all in the past" (Lurie [1965] 1994: 231). Ultimately Paul finds value in history, defining himself in the end, above all, as a historian. But history, in academic, theoretical terms, has little explicit value or currency here.

Katherine in turn is ultimately able to move beyond her own history, but this is achieved through a rejection and inversion of all and any signs of her past. While she ultimately embraces the "eternal present and disordered spatial (dis) organization," her husband returns East, having hit his limit "in the antihistorical city" (Fine 2004: 245). By the time Paul has been back to his Cambridge coterie, re-establishing himself as a dyed-in-the-wool East Coast historian, and subsequently returned to collect his wife, Katherine has come to see Los Angeles as her permanent residence of choice. "Welcome home" reads her note to him, not "Welcome back" (Lurie [1965] 1994: 271). She changes her name to Kay, her brown hair to ash blonde, and her soft New England tone to a California twang. It is the act of ridding herself of signs of her previous history (she even bestows her inherited furniture upon Paul to take with him back East), in addition to her insistence on constructing a self-narrative which befits her new identity (her hair "wasn't dyed, she had insisted, only bleached by the sun" (275)) that most aligns her with the Los Angeles attitude. "Kay" here gives us more "embroidery," as Didion would say, to refashion her own story. In Los Angeles it is possible to push back the frontier even of one's own identity.

But are such alterations permanent? Are all of the city's previous forms likewise permanently obscured? At Venice Beach, Paul wanders around what botanist Abbot Kinney had in 1905 planned as a resort town ("I wonder what this place used to be'" (105)). Kinney had set his sights in the early 1900s on a stretch of beach twenty-five miles outside Los Angeles. He envisioned, of all things, a replica of Venice with its accompanying network of canals, gondolas, marble palaces, and gold basilicas. Unfortunately, nature could not quite be sufficiently corralled into behaving itself for the masses, and the canals became home to, as historian Morrow Mayo describes, "the perfume of dying kelp and dead fish" (1933: 207). By 1933 only remnants of Kinney's dream remained: "Nailed to a telephone pole near the fallen 'Ponte di Rialto' there is a crude wooden sign, a pine board awkwardly lettered, which some romanticist no doubt made and put up tenderly with his own hands. Bravely and sadly it reads: 'The Grand Canal'" (209–10). The streets of Venice, which once made for a "fashionable seaside resort," have by 1965 sunk into disrepair. The transformation of Venice Beach from transplanted resort replica to rundown beachside neighborhood populated, according to Paul, by "Bums and cripples and criminals" suggests that the past *is* able to persist, but only by taking a rather different form: "The ruins of its earlier glory [. . .] still stood: the long arcades, the graceful balconies, arches, and pilasters of coloured stucco. But it was all in the last stages of desecration" (Lurie [1965] 1994: 85).

At the end of *The Nowhere City* Paul briefly returns to his home in Mar Vista, watching as the bulldozers raze the remaining buildings to the ground and level the lots. Katherine's early exclamation that it should be re-named "Spoil-the-View, California" becomes rather prescient in retrospect (38). He imagines that "everything that had once been across the street was there still, buried beneath the dirt: the flowering bushes, the stucco walls and tiled roofs, the kitchen tables, the lemon trees, the children on their tricycles" (271). Though it may not always be possible to excavate canals, kitchen tables, or tricycles, the novel implies that remnants of history *are* visible in the Los Angeles landscape. Paul, though seemingly adept at casting himself as a futurist, is still a historian at heart, seeing evidence of the past everywhere in a city he thought existed purely as a facsimile of the future: "he saw parallels between Los Angeles and his 'own' period of English history, the late sixteenth century" (7). He goes back further than that—looking at the Santa Monica mountain range visible from actress Glory Green's pool Paul sees the prehistoric jungle that used to be in the vicinity, replete with "ferns twenty feet tall and giant carnivorous reptiles" (238). As Mumford (1940) maintains, "in the city, time becomes visible" (3). In *The Nowhere City*, the natural wilderness upon which apartment buildings and oil wells now stand was once the stomping ground of the tyrannosaurus and the brontosaurus, whose battles are now "petrified in rock for tourists" (Lurie [1965] 1994: 13). The mountainous land visible from Mulholland Drive, which was once home to "flowers and brush" is now a construction site comprised of "flat rectangular lots [. . .] marked out with stick and string and red rags" (162).

Toward the end of the novel, across the street from Paul's house, the buildings sit empty and dark. While the flora and fauna have quickly overrun the derelict buildings, the houses themselves prove structurally unsound and disintegrate with little provocation: "devil-grass cracked the sidewalks, and vines, some flowering profusely, poured over the ruins" (204). The plaster "crack[s] under his feet" as he walks through the rubble, the cement crumbles beneath his weight, and although they have been only empty for a short period of time, "the little stucco villas and castles had already begun to come apart" (205). The stucco houses on the Cattlemans' block in Mar Vista, which are short-term architectural "experiments," exhibit "cracks [. . .] in the flimsy pink and green plaster walls" and are removed in their entirety like chess pieces plucked from a board and taken out of the game: "the chateau slowly turned the corner on to Sepulveda Boulevard [. . .] and disappeared forever" (5, 205, 206).

The flimsy craftsmanship of the Mar Vista houses anticipates Didion's apocalyptic visions of houses crumbling into the sea in *Play It As It Lays*, the fragile rooms of Waldie's Lakewood house in *Holy Land*, and recalls Chandler's descriptions of cliff-edge abodes living next to potential catastrophe, not to mention Berman's Baudelairean walks through the rubble of the Bronx. Nothing man-made seems to last very long in Los Angeles or in these other examples of fabricated urban and suburban spaces; indeed nothing is built with the idea of lasting in mind. The grass that surrounds the row of vacant houses on Paul's old street is "half a foot high" when Katherine first shows her employer Dr. Einsam her home; the houses are at that point "deserted" but not yet dilapidated (132).

By the time she is in the midst of her affair with him, and her husband is at the nadir of his own extra-marital relationship, the area is a "swath of desolate jungle two blocks wide" which resembles the "prehistoric jungle" populated by dinosaurs and inordinately large ferns described by Paul as the original Los Angeles landscape (204).

It seems feasible that such a past could return, pterodactyls aside, while the present crumbles, literally in some cases, under the slightest disruption. In this city, time is made visible through signs of abandonment, like Kinney's lost Venice and the roads which take residents on an unwitting tour of the city's neglected history, razed to lie beneath new construction or buried beneath the refuse of the city: "Olympic Boulevard, along which Paul was now driving, rose up between the two sections of the Twentieth Century Fox lot, where oil derricks and the plaster-and-lath towers of disused movie sets showed fleetingly above the trees" (231). Here history is found secreted in the land itself, and in what lies beneath it. Just as the continuing presence of the oil beneath the surface of Chandler's Los Angeles reminds us that its primordial history has not been entirely excised, in Lurie's Los Angeles we seem at first to find a decayed, deadened natural environment. Yet it is an environment that is capable of claiming back its spaces now covered over by the landscape of modernity like AstroTurf over grass seeds. Though Alison Lurie implies that in Los Angeles history is reduced to "notes and scraps," her novel is full of signs that it does nonetheless endure (158). In *The Nowhere City* we are presented with an "ambivalent Eden" (Newman 2000: 47) in which the past is located in unexpected places: it is a piece of land bulldozed into a space for more development, a dirt road ending in a pile of trash, a garage full of disused, cloaked furniture, or the constant struggle to irrigate the unevenly parched land. A little excavation in this city reveals the deep marks of history.

3

The Suture
Marshall Berman and Robert Moses in the Bronx

In a 1954 address before the National Education Association in Madison Square Garden, city planner par excellence Robert Moses said of his plans for New York: "our objective is honest. We aim to rebuild New York, saving what is still durable, what is salvageable and what is genuinely historical, and substituting progress for obsolescence. We don't believe big cities are dated. At any rate New York is not" ("The City of New York"). In Flushing Meadows-Corona Park in Queens, which Moses created out of the literal ashes that constituted the Corona Ash Dumps in order to provide a home for the 1939–40 World's Fair, the Unisphere—a 140-foot-tall stainless-steel facsimile of Earth built for the subsequent World's Fair in 1964–5—dominates the landscape. Standing on the site of the now-destroyed Perisphere, another Moses construction built twenty-five years earlier (in 1939), the Unisphere is an enormous testament to the cycle of creation and erasure that characterized Moses' tenure. Writing of Moses and his impact on New York City in *The Power Broker*, his Pulitzer-prize-winning biography, Robert Caro (1974) refers the reader to the epitaph on the tomb of Sir Christopher Wren: *si monumentum requiris, circumspice* ("if you would seek his monument, look around") (508).

As an archetypal modern city, New York is simultaneously a site of progression, renewal, and destruction. To quote Michel de Certeau ([1980] 1984) in *The Practice of Everyday Life*, this is a city which "invents itself, from hour to hour" (91). Architecture critic Ada Louise Huxtable writes of the way in which the city paves over itself in its quest for newness, stating that, in New York, neighborhoods tend to "fall like dominoes" (1997: 14). The very nature of the city is, she argues, "to destroy, build and change" ([1968] 2008: 224). The landscape of a city like New York is remade many times over, and that remaking leads to the disorientation of locational, material history. Those who live within this cycle must somehow reconcile themselves to the requirements of the modern city for forward movement and evolution, while concurrently attempting to root themselves in what the late academic, philosopher, and author Marshall Berman ([1982] 2010) describes as "a stable and coherent personal and social past" (35). In *The Collective Memory*, Maurice Halbwachs ([1952] 1980) argues that "memory unfolds within a spatial framework" (140). What are the consequences of discovering a conflict within this spatial framework between the individual's conception of the past (memory) and what the city concretizes and externalizes with regard to the past (history)? This potential schism is what Dolores Hayden (1995) refers to as the experience of "spatial conflict," (9) which can be applied to the capacity for urban redevelopment to obliterate the collective memory that formerly rendered a particular pocket of the city familiar. The onward momentum of urban renewal, Berman argues, "destroys both the physical and social landscapes of our past, and our emotional links with those lost worlds" ([1982] 2010: 35). This chapter examines several articles and essays by Berman, with a particular focus on the final section, "In the Forest of Symbols: Some Notes on Modernism in New York," from his autobiographical and polemical opus *All That is Solid Melts into Air* (1982). I explore the relationship between memory and history, and the ways in which both manifest themselves in New York City, particularly in the Bronx, the borough in which Berman was born in 1940. Throughout his work, Berman analyzes the issues inherent in living in the city in the second half of the twentieth century, in particular explaining the impact of Robert Moses (presented here as Berman's antagonist, and vice versa) both on urban development in the Bronx and on the possibility of maintaining a connection to the past as embedded in the physical landscape.

The Modern and Robert Moses

Robert Moses held numerous positions of public office in the city from 1924 to 1968, but his influence and reach extended far beyond the traditional remit of his duties. He began his career in New York at the Municipal Research Bureau in 1913, and by 1922 had expanded into an astonishing number of departments, ultimately encompassing parks, construction, highways, and public housing. He looms large over many of the most colossal constructions and public spaces in the city, such as the Triborough and Verrazano-Narrows Bridges, the West Side Highway, Riverside Park, Jones Beach, Co-op City, and most of the parkways out on Long Island. In his obituary the *New York Times* recorded that by the time he had departed his post as head of the state park system, "the state had 2,567,256 acres. He built 658 playgrounds in New York City, 416 miles of parkways, and 13 bridges" (Goldberger 1981: n.p.). I have been incredibly fortunate to have been able to speak to several people whose paths had crossed professionally with Moses over the years; they gave me some insight into the man himself. In the 1960s, Gilbert Tauber worked for the New York Convention and Visitors Bureau and had a chance to observe Moses on several occasions during preparations for the 1964–5 World's Fair. Gil was at the table when Moses presided over a meeting of around fifty people, including prominent executives in the travel and hotel industries, concerning hotel accommodations for the Fair. The deference shown to him at that meeting, says Gil, was extraordinary. During the meeting he observed the interactions around the table, telling me: "I could compare him to, in some of his facial expressions and gestures, Vito Corleone. But I think Vito Corleone had a warm side to him" (2015: n.p.). Professor David Bruce Allen, who as a representative for the Building Contractors Association sat in on meetings with the Long Island Planning Commission, describes the man as "imperious and impervious to everything that was around him, and even though he was an elderly man he was clearly the most impressive person in the room," (2017: n.p.) while Professor Lee Koppelman tells me about a letter he received from Moses that started "Dear Nincompoop," when he worked for the Suffolk County Planning Commission (2015: n.p.).

In *All That is Solid*, Berman writes that to oppose the work of Moses was to "oppose history, progress, modernity itself" ([1982] 2010: 294). Caro quotes an anonymous official who worked for one borough president who got in the way of Moses' progress by daring to raise objections to his plans. Moses would send voluminous amounts of telegrams contesting such interventions, repeating the claim that they were "holding up work, [they] were holding up progress" (1974: 749). What does Berman mean when he refers to modernity in this context? "To be modern," he contends, is to "live a life of paradox and contradiction." In essence, it is "a mode of vital experience" ([1982] 2010: 15); one which is characterized by the simultaneous promise of adventure, growth, and transformation, and the threat of annihilation. Berman takes his cues about modernity from *The Communist Manifesto*, in which Karl Marx and Friedrich Engels ([1848] 1992) describe the shock of the new inherent during the period of nineteenth-century modernization characterized, in their words, by the constant "revolutionizing of production, uninterrupted disturbance of all social conditions, everlasting uncertainty and agitation" (6).[1] Throughout this chapter I in turn take my cues about modernity from Berman, and am guided by what he writes on this—what it does and does not mean to him. The "paradox and contradiction," which Berman writes of lies in the simultaneous fear and pursuit of the new that defines modernity ([1982] 2010: 13). Modernity concerns itself with both a fascination for the future and simultaneously with a sense of lineage; with referent points from which one travels, suggesting a point of origin. One travels onward from this line with an acute awareness of what is lost the further from the point of origin one moves. This gives its expression a sense of impending loss and an anxiety about potential fragmentation.

In *The Architectural Uncanny*, Anthony Vidler (1992) contends that it is not just the *regulation* of a sense of history in the urban environment that has been a key modernist aim, but *escaping* it completely. If only houses, for example, were not "haunted by the weight of tradition and the imbrications of generations of family drama, if no cranny was left for the storage of the bric-a-brac once deposited in damp cellars and musty attics," then people would be liberated from the anchor of memory, which was deemed an "unhealthy preoccupation" (64). He writes that these attitudes stem from "the conventional wisdom of modern urbanism" (168); this wisdom dictated that one must "flood dark space with light" and open it up to "vision and occupation." In *Imagining the Modern City*, James Donald (1999) argues that modernist urban planners saw modernity as "a state of mind to do with accommodating newness" (54). This accommodation of a "new social order" apparently made the "absolute repression of all traces of history, memory and desire from the city" a necessity (84). Modernity, like Enlightenment thinking, aims to "eradicate the domain of myth, suspicion, tyranny and, above all, the irrational" (73). The desire to remove the irrational became a "mechanism of governmental power," one which feared "the illegibility of men and things." This move towards greater transparency and order symbolized a rejection of the built environment of the late-eighteenth-century city, which Michel Foucault (1980) argues was defined by its "stone walls, darkness, hideouts and dungeons" (154).

Of course, the landscape of the city had been molded and remade long before Moses took its stage as a kind of twentieth-century Ozymandias. Berman describes Moses as coming from a long line of public figures with similar concerns about the urban environment, all of whom were "moved at once by a will to change—to transform both themselves and their world—and by a terror of disorientation and disintegration, of life falling apart" ([1982] 2010: 13). In order to prevent this annihilation, this "falling apart," Moses felt it necessary to break open the city's "darkened spaces" and let in the light of modern planning (Donald 1999: 73). In this respect he was very much in the tradition of other renowned arbiters of modernity in the city who made a permanent mark on their respective urban landscapes. For example, during the 1850s Baron Haussmann, as obsessed with slum clearance and urban renewal in nineteenth-century Paris as Robert Moses was in twentieth-century New York, sought to re-create his city as one of the great open spaces, filtering out any undesirable elements.[2] In so doing, he displaced vast numbers of people and built expansive boulevards.[3] Ben Highmore (2005) writes in *Cityscapes* that, in the nineteenth century, there was a perception among "social explorers" that the "rapidly expanding and modernizing city was an unreadable environment," continuing that to "make urban culture intelligible and legible meant policing it" (6). It therefore became necessary to plan "a regulated form of modernization." The need to ensure material order as a bulwark against social chaos can be seen in, for example, the "rational grids and spatial orders" imposed upon the urban spaces of a city like New York (Vidler 1992: 172). Rosalind Krauss writes that the leveling effect of the grid intends to smooth over anything unsystematic: "In the flatness that results from its coordinates, the grid is the means of crowding out the dimensions of the real and replacing them with the lateral spread of a single surface [. . .] the grid is a way of abrogating the claims of natural objects to have an order particular to themselves" (50). The grid system was to be a defense against the otherwise uncertain, unquantifiable (and already inhabited) landscape of the city.

Max Page (1999) reports in *The Creative Destruction of Manhattan* that it is now "almost impossible, except in a few places in the larger parks of the city, to be visually reminded that the island of Manhattan was one of the richest natural environments in North America" (179). Samuel Stein (2019) writes in *Capital City* that New York was built on land belonging to the Lenape people, "as a series of scattered settlements emerging from lower Manhattan. By 1811, city leaders had imposed a rigid street grid pattern and a standardized set of twenty-five-by-one hundred-foot lots" (16). Hills were leveled, ponds were drained, streams were funneled into pipes, trees were felled and forests were razed, and by the end of the nineteenth century, New York's original natural landscape had been suppressed "beneath the straight streets of the city's 1811 grid plan" and segregated into park land, removing it from the "lives of citizens in order to make way for the accelerating spin of destruction and rebuilding" (Page 1999: 177-9). Central Park, ironically "not a natural development," was likewise superimposed over "the barrens of mid-Manhattan" using "dynamite, drainage machinery, tons of imported topsoil, nursery-bred plantations, and the efforts of several thousand laborers during the 1850s and 1860s" (Scobey 2002: 17). This vast space, thus tamed and controlled, came to represent "the possibility of a public sphere that was at once popular and refined, disciplined and open" (21). As the late nineteenth century became the early twentieth, New York experienced its most important period of growth and development thus far. The 1916 Zoning Resolution, which, like the grid, aimed to "rationalize the landscape" (8), created area districts which determined the purpose of space; subjected the city to three types of regulation according to three types of use; put into practice certain height restrictions; and excluded certain types of development which may have "caused (or exacerbated) the decline in land values" (Revell 1992: 32).

Randall Mason (2009) reports in *The Once and Future New York* that one consequence of the barrage of changes during this period was an increased impetus to strengthen ties to the past as made manifest in the urban landscape: "The faster the pace of modernization, the more intensely were connections to the past sought" (xxiii). The periodic urge to preserve evidence of the city's past was galvanized by, as described by Anne Friedberg (1993), "the threat of the 'modern' and the shock of the new" (188). The desire to protect certain monuments, buildings, and even neighborhoods from New York's propensity for redevelopment began to emerge in earnest during the late 1890s, when the idea of preservation was "asserted as a key urbanistic strategy—creating places that represented stability and continuity with a noble past, providing a cultural counterweight to the often chaotic growth of the metropolis" (x). Henry James ([1907] 1994), for whom the discovery that the house in which he was born had been replaced by a shirt factory was a trauma from which he could not quite recover, wrote in *The American Scene*: "the effect for me, in Washington Place, was of having been amputated of half my history" (71). James provides an example of what Bryan Waterman (2010) describes as the "nostalgic strain in New York writing," (233) which he argues is "rooted not just in the fear that the old city will pass away unnoticed, but that it already passed away before one arrived." During the mid-nineteenth-century building boom, to which James was responding when he gasped at the sight of the altered city, the *New-York Mirror* likewise reported with great sorrow in 1853 that Manhattan is a "modern city of ruins" (qtd in Burrows and Wallace 1999: 695). D. J. Waldie (2016) notes that in 1905 the historian and writer Henry Adams wondered about the possibility for preserving history in writing "at a time when [he] felt the past slipping away with ever greater velocity and the imaginations he observed had become weary of remembering except as an excuse for nostalgia," continuing that Adams regarded with melancholy "what he called 'the acceleration of history' at the turn of the 20th century" (Waldie 2016: n.p.). In *Naked City*, Sharon Zukin ([2009] 2010) affirms that such responses to the changing city as those of James, the *Mirror*, and Adams, "drew an aura of regret around the landscape of memory" (10).

An acute awareness of the rapid disappearance of the city's historic buildings, which provided examples of the city's past in physical form, again came to the fore in the second half of the twentieth century, during which the large-scale construction that could be found everywhere in New York was "of necessity, accompanied by large-scale destruction—often of architecturally significant buildings" (Stern, Mellins and Fishman 1997: 8). In 1963, Ada Louise Huxtable wrote in the *New York Times* that "we will probably be judged not by the monuments we build but by the ones we have destroyed" (n.p.). Six years later, John S. Pyke, Jr. (1969) articulates this awareness when he reports that "there is not a single building which dates back to the seventeenth century and only nine that date back to the eighteenth century. The relentless destruction and construction of buildings in New York City has been sporadically interrupted by attempts to preserve the visible evidence of the City's heritage" (15). During this period, particularly post-1963 and the destruction of Pennsylvania Station (with Jane Jacobs one of the picketers), "many New Yorkers began to fully recognize the architectural richness of their own city as well as the need to preserve it." David Lowenthal and Marcus Binney (1981) state in *Our Past Before Us: Why Do We Save It?* that "preservation stems from a three-fold awareness of the past: that it was unlike the present, that it is crucial to our sense of identity, and that its tangible remnants are rapidly disappearing" (17). The city's remedy was the New York City Landmarks Law, enacted in 1965 alongside the creation of a permanent New York City Landmarks Preservation Commission (both preceded the National Historic Preservation Act of 1966), which designates landmark sites and historic districts. Architectural historian and writer, Frances Morrone, observes that the buildings which have been classified thus by the Commission are, in the minds of the organization, "a kind of palimpsest of its neighbourhoods' history," (2016: n.p.) with designated spaces marking the spots where the past has pushed through the surface of the present.

Robert Moses sought to create order out of chaos, rendering the amorphous irrationality of New York's urban spaces into what he saw as something of a cleaner logic. In the pursuit of this aim, he oversaw the creation of what is today one of the world's greatest examples of the modern metropolis. In order to do so, he first had to destroy what had preceded it. Did he succeed? Of course, not everything in New York has disappeared, and furthermore it is difficult to argue that everything that stood in Moses' path to progress was destroyed, particularly when he was as responsible for building as he was for bulldozing, and indeed when several of his projects did not come to fruition. Two examples of projects which did not come to pass are the proposal to extend Manhattan's Fifth Avenue through Washington Square Park in 1955, and another to extend all ten lanes of Interstate 78 from the Holland Tunnel to the Manhattan and Williamsburg Bridges in the form of the Lower Manhattan Expressway during the early 1960s—a plan which would have destroyed the neighborhood of SoHo, now designated a Historic District by the Landmarks Preservation Commission.[4]

Anthony Vidler contends that modernizing figures wish to "forget the old city, its old monuments, its traditional significance" (179). For Robert Moses, forgetting the old city translated as an attempt at its erasure, one haunted house at a time. In his eyes the mental and physical health of the city was contingent upon the excision of particular components of its historical legacy. While in his position as Chairman of the Committee on Slum Clearance (a title he assumed from 1949 to 1960), Moses described the remaining neighborhood blocks yet to be cleared as "cancerous growths" which were "just as bad as those which have been removed." The entirety of this "malignancy" as he called it, "must be surgically cut out" (Statement by Robert Moses: 2). Moses' metaphorical surgery left behind a great number of suture wounds. One memo written by Moses to one of his closest colleagues, George Spargo, perfectly summarizes his attitude to the material presence of history in the city he was reshaping. Moses writes of a neighborhood church in the "Park Row project," soon to be demolished: "I don't see how this church can possibly be saved." Perhaps, he concedes, "some plaque or memorial in or on one of the new buildings or in a small park giving briefly the history of the church and indicating that it stood there, might solve the problem" (Memo to Mr Spargo: n.p.). These are the traces Moses left behind—*here is where the city used to be.*

Robert Caro posits that the exact impact of Moses on the city is hard to quantify with any real certainty: "It is impossible to say that New York would have been a better city if Robert Moses had never lived. It is possible to say only that it would have been a different city" (1974: 21).[5] For the purposes of this chapter, and this book, the point is not the relative success or failure of Moses' plans, or the ability to measure the dimensions of his destruction.[6] The point is to attempt to gather and quantify the psychological fallout from what he *did* manage to excise from the physical landscape and the collective memory of its inhabitants.

Mosesization: Title I and the Interstate Highway System

Moses' plans for the city were facilitated in the second half of the twentieth century by the economic boom that followed the end of the Second World War in the United States, which saw a surge in new construction that transformed cities like New York. Robert A. M. Stern, Thomas Mellins, and David Fishman explain in *New York 1960* that during this period, "the city's role within the surrounding region, and its relationship to the nation as a whole, underwent redefinition, entire precincts of the city itself were virtually rebuilt [...] the waning Classicism of the nineteenth century gave way almost completely to the Modernism that had been making significant in-roads in America since the 1930s" (8–9). Berman argues that the "whole fabric of America" was reconstructed in the postwar period, and views the Federal Aid Highway Act and Federal Housing Administration, both grasped with two hands and put to work by Moses, as the "motive forces in this reconstruction" (*New York: A Documentary Film* 1999: n.p.). "The policies of slum clearance and 'urban renewal,'" notes Spiro Kostof (1991), "seemed determined to finish the work of the bombs" (90).

New York's endless cycle of renewal was given an extra push by the American Housing Act of 1949, the increased authorization given to the Federal Housing Administration (first created in 1934 as part of the New Deal), and the Federal Aid Highway Act of 1956, which brought to life the Interstate Highway System. All of these factors paved the way for slum clearance and highway construction, two operations that often went hand in hand. Both the Housing Act and Interstate Highway System represented the forward thrust demanded by modernity, but also the incoherence and destruction which seem its permanent partner. The New York City Housing Association was put in charge of constructing public housing on a huge scale for those who could not afford the costs of private accommodation. This was in order to both mitigate the exodus to the suburbs and combat the decaying state of the American city. Sharon Zukin writes in *Naked City* ([2009] 2010) that during this postwar period of acute urban crisis which began in earnest during the 1960s, "American cities were routinely described as hopeless victims of a fatal disease" (5). Title I of the Housing Act, which permitted the federal government to give grants to the appropriate local public bodies for the purpose of urban regeneration, was one of the programs which served as a driving force for many of Moses' plans for the city. By 1960, under his leadership, "New York had been allocated more Title I money than any other American city—$65.8 million, which was twice as much as the second-place city, Chicago" (*Affordable New York*). But the construction of new housing necessitated the demolishing of old housing stock, otherwise known as slum clearance, for which municipal governments received federal funding. In 1953 more funding was set aside for the redevelopment of these areas, in other words for urban renewal projects, and also "for interstate highway arterials," both of which "projected the postwar vision of a modern, decentralized, and segregated utopia" (Tochterman 2017: 4). Caro reports that in order to "clear the land for these improvements," Moses "evicted the city's people, not thousands of them or tens of thousands but hundreds of thousands, from their homes and tore the homes down" (1974: 7). During the same period, the city saw the rise of iconic and monumental structures such as the Lincoln Center for the Performing Arts, the Verrazano-Narrows Bridge, and the Cross-Bronx Expressway. In each case, something had to be torn down and communities had to be dispersed in order for the new constructions to rise.

Even before these mid-twentieth-century upheavals, the so-called City Beautiful movement of the late nineteenth century was responsible for projects which were "often built on centrally located land inhabited by poor people, immigrants and African Americans" (Stein 2019: 16). This tradition is traceable back to the superimposition of Broadway, the main exception to the grid's geometry, "over a pre-existing Native American trail" (16). Moses did not deviate from this tradition. Between 1962 and 1966 the new Lincoln Center was built over what Moses called "the worst slum in New York" (1977: n.p.) but what Berman defines as "formerly the largely black and Hispanic neighborhood of San Juan Hill" (Message to Brian Berger 2007b: n.p.). In 1964, the reporter Gay Talese would write in *The Bridge* about the former inhabitants of Bay Ridge, a neighborhood in the south-west corner of Brooklyn, whose homes were torn down to make way for the Verrazano-Narrows Bridge in 1959: "One day in the early spring of 1964, Eugene and Roy took a nostalgic journey back to their old neighborhood [. . .] and revisited the land upon which their old home had stood. Now all was flattened and smoothed by concrete—it was buried by the highway leading to the bridge" ([1964] 2003: 122). Talese describes the feelings of the locals who saw their neighborhood of 800 buildings and 7,000 people, leveled: "They saw the coming bridge not as a sign of progress, but as a symbol of destruction" (21).

Planners like Moses, who saw themselves as merely "efficient, scientific, apolitical experts" who "knew better than those whose spaces were being planned" (Stein 2019: 22), were complicit in systems which shut out immigrants, the poor, and people of color from the usual financial and residential avenues to stability in the city. Negligence and disinvestment in urban space was galvanized by a conveyor belt of practices connected to urban renewal and slum clearance, such as: planned shrinkage (proposed by Roger Starr (Commissioner of Housing Preservation and Development under Mayor Beame in the 1970s) in 1976, this was the deliberate withdrawal of city services to devastated neighborhoods); benign neglect (first floated by New York senator Daniel Patrick Moynihan in a 1970 memo to Nixon which subsequently went public, becoming "a rallying cry to justify reductions in social services to the inner cities" (Chang 2006: 14)); redlining (the practice whereby the "investment community withdraws funds and 'redlines' the neighborhood," which as a general rule is lived in by people of color, the poor, and/or immigrants (Jensen 1979: 70)); eminent domain (the power of government to claim private property and adapt it for public use); and the expansion of the suburb.

In *Manhattan Projects*, Samuel Zipp (2010) posits that the "spatial transformation" (7) that occurred as a result of these exercises in urban planning was a signifier of the "embrace of modernity" which Moses himself clearly exhibited: "Slum clearance scoured away the old cityscape and its traditional, sedimented urban patterns. Then, the clean, progressive rationality of the towers and plazas rose over the ruins. City blocks were literally uprooted, broken down, and reconstructed in geometric arrangements that produced a new, unfamiliar sense of order and a remade experience of urban space" (9). Hundreds of thousands of people were displaced when longstanding working-class neighborhoods were destroyed and replaced by highways and high rises. The Bronx itself began to burn.

The landscape of the Bronx was, by the late 1950s, morphing into "gigantic, twisted, grotesque ruins," thanks to a hellish combination of New York's deepening fiscal crisis, the slashing of its social services, and de-industrialization, all of which hit the poorest parts of the city the hardest and created more problems for New York City housing (Berman 2007a: 15). This enforced urban austerity was imposed first by President Nixon and then President Ford, who declared that he would veto any bill that sought a federal bailout of New York City, inspiring the famous *New York Daily News* headline of October 30, 1975: "Ford to City: 'Drop Dead.'"[7]

In *All That is Solid*, Marshall Berman ([1982] 2010) argues that "Thousands of urban neighborhoods were obliterated by this new order; what happened to my Bronx was only the largest and most dramatic instance of something that was happening all over" (307). Berman's telling of the story of Moses's impact on the Bronx is a cautionary tale of the capacity of modernizing sensibilities to decimate. In "Slouching Towards Bethlehem," Joan Didion repeats W. B. Yeats' warning that "Things fall apart; the centre cannot hold" (Yeats [1920] 1994: 158). The language used by Berman throughout *All That is Solid* (not least in his choice of Marx's famous estimation as his book title), and indeed all of his work on the Bronx, suggests that there is resonance in this very prospect—that any solidity and cohesion he might have known has since proven transient. Not only has much of what he knew disappeared, but the entirety of his neighborhood has been opened up and stretched out beyond its capacity. The "malignancy," as Moses would have referred to it, of this now-dead space has been "cut out," but so have its surrounding areas also been completely divested of history (Moses 1957b: 2).

Ironically, the fear that things may fall apart led in this case to real disintegration. Moses' plan to unblock the darkened corners of the city's historical spaces caused the displacement and dispersal of great swathes of people, leading inexorably to a permanently altered cityscape and leaving the psycho-geographical scars which are so deeply felt and articulated by Berman. Moses the modernizer, who "hack[ed] his expressway world through the cities, obliterating every trace of the life that was there before," had cracked wide open what had been intact (Berman (1982) 2010: 331).[8] This falling apart left in its wake traces and signs of a past which used to exist in the spaces now occupied by ruins and rubble. This brings to mind Ben Highmore's description of ruins as evidence of an environment "where the past continually impinges on the present," signaling "the trauma of history" (2005: 4).

The Bronx, particularly the South Bronx, produced in the postwar decades the very worst ramifications of programs like the Federal Aid Highway Act and the American Housing Act when put to work together in densely built-up, highly populated urban areas. It became, as Berman puts it, "an international code word for our epoch's accumulated urban nightmares" ([1982] 2010: 290). The "South Bronx" has come into particular disrepute as a symbol of the very worst aspects of the borough, becoming more a synecdoche than a locatable place. Robert Jensen (1979) states that from the late 1960s the term was used "in the context of fires, destruction and rubble" (13). Gilbert Tauber said to me that "After the Cross-Bronx Expressway was built, everything south of the Cross-Bronx was the South Bronx. When I was younger the South Bronx was everything south of 149th. It seemed that the South Bronx began some blocks south of wherever you were" (2015: n.p.).[9] Berman, who grew up in the South Bronx neighborhood of Tremont during the 1940s and 1950s, found himself immersed in a period of great change in the borough, thanks to the myriad ways in which these postwar federal programs were utilized by Robert Moses.

Alongside Title I of the Housing Act, the multi-billion-dollar Interstate Highway System of the 1950s was also championed by Moses in order to push through his vision of the modern city. Via these acts, Moses and his team created a system that brought to life such paeans to "Automonumentality" as the Bruckner Expressway, the Major Deegan Expressway, and the Cross-Bronx Expressway

(Koolhaas [1978] 1994: 100). Lee Zimmerman (1999) argues that in this postwar period there was a "massive reshaping of the environment around the needs of the automobile" to the detriment of the cities, like New York, which were denied essential financial resources as a consequence and thereby "drained of what might have kept them vital" (567). In *All That is Solid* Berman bemoans the fact that the Interstate Highway System encouraged drivers to fall into a seamless flow which could quite feasibly take them from one coast to the other "without encountering any traffic lights at all" (330). Writing about the ways in which the Los Angeles freeway has led to the subdivision of that city, encouraging a sense of "extraordinary isolation" that he argues is now a defining characteristic, Norman M. Klein contends that the "habit" of forward momentum without the structure of a backward glance is "well fixed, like the freeway to work. One literally passes through to arrive, but rarely stops" (2008: 85). There seems to be no sense of before or after in a city like this, just movement. This is the ultimate symbolic endpoint of the roadscapes, parkways, highways, and bridges created by Moses and his team—an intertwined system of transit through the metropolis, creating momentum and losing any quantifiable sense of time or space. This is precisely what Jane Jacobs decried in *The Death and Life of Great American Cities* when she wrote of "promenades that go from no place to nowhere and have no promenaders; expressways that eviscerate great cities" ([1961] 1965: 14). In the rubble of the modern city, stripped of its significance, there is no link between the past and the present; no crossing that can bridge the two, and no way to cast a backward glance. Deprived of this connection, this sense of tangible evolution, both the past and the present become meaningless—become this "nowhere," or no place, which we cross into.

Nicknamed "Heartbreak Highway" before it was even built (Tierney 1994: n.p.), the Cross-Bronx was one of the most controversial of Moses' projects and is the subject, indeed, the organizing principle, of the final chapter of *All That is Solid*. This project combined the dual purposes of the Interstate Highway System and the Housing Act, that is, to both clear out and rebuild over "slum housing" *and* to be part of a great "tapestry of expressways" which would connect the New York metropolitan area and beyond (Rosenblum 2009a: 208).[10] Construction for the Cross-Bronx, a "six-lane-wide, seven-mile-long concrete and steel monster," began in 1948. As its name suggests, it cuts directly through and bisects the borough it is named after. It would ultimately cross "113 streets and avenues," writes *New York Post* journalist George J. Marlin (2010), and necessitate the dispersal of "40,000 middle-class households" (n.p.). John J. Egan reports in a 1958 article titled "Trojan Horse in our Cities": "When the superhighway is rammed through such a neighborhood, it takes with it more than the buildings it demolishes for its right of way" (n.p.). It was rammed through residential neighborhoods along what had been the Grand Boulevard and Concourse, and though the apartment houses which sat directly on the Concourse were not immediately impacted (the Cross-Bronx passed beneath the Boulevard itself), "deeply rooted communities on either side of the Grand Concourse were literally ground underfoot" (Rosenblum 2009a: 8).

The Grand Concourse, which runs for four-and-a-half miles through the West Bronx to Manhattan, was completed in its original form in 1909. Berman, who grew up a few blocks east of the Concourse, describes it as "our borough's closest thing to a Parisian boulevard" ([1982] 2010: 295). In its heyday it symbolized, in the words of Constance Rosenblum (2009a), "a true street of dreams" (6). But ultimately it became, over time, "one of the most potent symbols of urban disintegration" (11). Its demolition served to heighten its symbolic significance. This transformation provides a symbol of the architectural sleight of hand demonstrated by Moses and made acutely manifest in the Bronx. It seemed as though one day the Grand Concourse and its neighborhood "were intact," and the next they were both "shattered like fragile crystal" (7).

In the constantly fraught state in which Moses worked, residents could not plan for the future, nor could they attach themselves to the past; upon their removal, their place of origin became lost in memory. "This used to be," write journalists Gene Gleason and Fred J. Cook (1959), in one of several investigative pieces about the impact of Moses and the slum clearance program, "a city composed of a wide variety of solid, established neighborhoods [. . .] One after another, they've been torn up, destroyed, scattered to the winds" (Gleason and Cook 1959: n.p.). Of his own family's relocation Berman writes with quiet desolation, noting that the buildings which were demolished were "barely as old as I was," but regardless, when he returned from camp that autumn, "they were gone, even the rubble was gone. Soon our family, too, would go" (1973: n.p.).[11] In 1959 Samuel A. Spiegel, Assemblyman from the Fourth Assembly District of New York County, wrote that so-called slum clearance was creating "a wandering society of transient tenancies with no chance for the children to take roots" (36). The construction of affordable housing developments caused widespread tenant dislocation and disruption in many communities throughout the city. A sense of rootless wandering, impermanence, and separation from the familiar and the historical, fills the correspondence Moses received during his time as Chairman of the City Slum Clearance Committee. Unhappy New Yorkers who had been forced to move, sometimes more than once, from their buildings, blocks, neighborhoods, and boroughs, provided frequent epistolary critique. Alice Saul, in 1957, signs off her letter of complaint with "I don't know how you can face yourself if you realise the harm you have done to the people of this city. [. . .] I wish you bad luck" (Saul 1957: n.p.). Robert Caro dedicates two chapters in *The Power Broker* to the story of East Tremont, one of the neighborhoods that the Cross-Bronx was to cut through (a mile away from the neighborhood in which Berman grew up). Caro speaks with several former Tremont inhabitants, who stress the familial intimacy of the old neighborhood: "In its bricks were generations" (1974: 853). The Cross-Bronx, argues Caro, had by 1965 completely decimated that shared history.

A sense of loss and absence is what is long remembered by those who grew up in the Bronx during the period in which many of its neighborhoods were excised from the landscape of the city's memory. In an article for *The New Yorker* published after *The Power Broker*, Caro (1998) writes: "I asked these couples—or widows or widowers—to compare their present lives with the lives they had had in East Tremont, and the general picture that emerged from their answers was a sense of profound, irremediable loss" (51). Berman (1984b) writes frequently of the material unity and architectural cohesion of the mid-twentieth-century Bronx neighborhoods with which he was most familiar, as though already fearful that this completeness would soon be broken: "A few smaller houses, probably occupied by their owners, were, as ever, shabby but intact" (1984b: 20). "When I was a girl," author Vivian Gornick, who grew up in the Bronx on 181st Street between Vyse and Bryant, told me in an interview, "the whole world was the same. It was a completely coherent neighbourhood" (2015: n.p.).

The effect on the Bronx was tangible. As Jill Jonnes (2002) writes in *South Bronx Rising*, the "sheer scale of these public endeavours was altering the physical appearance of the borough, scarring and obliterating whole neighborhoods" (117). Berman indicates that the urban rot which had begun in the late 1950s had set in not only along the route of the Expressway, but throughout the landscape of the entire Bronx.[12] This rot proliferated "at a spectacular pace, devouring house after house and block after block, displacing hundreds of thousands of people from their homes like some inexorable plague" (1984b: 18.). Here Berman uses similar rhetoric about sickness and surgery to Moses, but from a different point of view. Where Moses believes he is purging the wounds of the city, Berman sees the same wounds as festering; the sickness is taking hold. Caro echoes Berman's words when he writes of post-Cross-Bronx East Tremont that the buildings that remained were nothing more than "ravaged hulks," resembling "blitzkrieged London" (1974: 893). As though to exemplify Caro's point, Howard Kaminsky, a local historian who grew up just south of East Tremont and moved out in 1964, told me in an interview that the Expressway "eviscerated the Bronx" such that it "looked like London after the Blitz" (2015: n.p.). Similarly, Gilbert Tauber, who grew up in the borough on Gerard Avenue between 165th and McClellan, informed me that he would walk past the construction site of the Cross-Bronx Expressway on his way to his school at 176th St., a few blocks north of the Cross-Bronx, observing the construction from either Walton Avenue or the Grand Concourse, as it was built incrementally. He described how he would come across a "huge gash in the ground and it was really kind of scary [...] it reminded you of pictures of bombed out cities in Europe" (2015: n.p.).[13]

The idea of orientation as an essential component of the fabric of the postwar city was tackled in a 1974 address to the Back to the City Conference in New York by James Marston Fitch, Director of the Historic Preservation Program at Columbia University, in which he referred to the city as "a theater of memory," continuing that familiar urban spaces form a "sort of physical matrix for your own experiences" and citing an example provided during his visit to Warsaw after the Second World War: "The city was all under rubble, and you couldn't say 'meet me at the corner of Fourth and Main.' The question of orientation was not just a physical one, it was a psychological one as well" (7). In 1966 the United States Congress had reaffirmed the preservation of landmarks as a national policy, stating that "the historical and cultural foundations of the Nation should be preserved as a living part of our community life and development in order to give a sense of orientation to the American people" (Pyke, Jr 2).[14] Lawrence Levy, Executive Dean of the National Center for Suburban Studies at Hofstra University, described to me the way in which inhabitants of cities organize their spatial memory: "folks who grow up in and live in cities, the people are a blur and the buildings become the fixed reference points, the backdrop for memory, and sometimes the soundstage." In order to make sense of vast urban space from a distance we must look for landmarks that allow us to distinguish, divide, and quantify space. But often when we seek out "objects of memory" which we had anticipated would be eternally anchored to the landscape, we sometimes find gaps where these should be present (Vidler 1992: 64).

When, in *Civilization and its Discontents*, Freud ([1930] 1961) compares the life of the city to the "life of the psyche," which can only retain its sense of history if it has remained "intact and its fabric has not suffered from trauma," it is difficult not to think of the Bronx and the tearing of its spatial fabric (18). Norman M. Klein writes in *The History of Forgetting* that modernity is best symbolized by the appearance of a "suture" (2008: 313) which physically marks the spot where the trauma of "Haussmanization" (for which in the case of the Bronx we can read "Mosesization") has altered both the landscape and one's perception of it. What are the consequences for a borough like the Bronx, which has seen its own fabric stretched and torn, its stitches unpicked? In his 2007 Introduction to *New York Calling*, Berman reflects on the visceral experience of visiting its strangely unoccupied spaces: "In 1979, 1980, 1981, I spent many lonely afternoons wandering through the Bronx's ruins. I couldn't believe the enormity of these ruins! They went on and on, for block after block, mile after mile. Some blocks seemed almost intact; but look around the corner, and there was no corner. It was uncanny!" (2007a: 19). As Berman walks through the borough he is occasionally "lulled to sleep" ((1982) 2010: 344) by the sense of the ordinary and the vaguely familiar as he re-traces his old neighborhood steps. Should you walk around Southern Boulevard or Longwood, he advises, you will find blocks "that feel so much like blocks you left long ago, blocks you thought had vanished forever, that you will wonder if you are seeing ghosts—or if you yourself are a ghost haunting these solid streets with the phantoms of your inner city." But upon turning a corner, "the full nightmare of devastation" is revealed in the form of "a block of burnt-out hulks, a street of rubble and glass where no man goes," which rudely awakens him. "For Freud," Vidler (1992) explains, "'unhomeliness' was more than a simple sense of not belonging; it was the fundamental propensity of the familiar to turn on its owners, suddenly to become defamiliarized, derealized, as if in a dream" (7). It is the shock of difference, the confrontation with an unexpected *tabula rasa*, which awakens Berman from his dream of the past into present-day alienation. The final pages of *All That is Solid* find Berman seeking and meeting signs of the past in the street he loved and abandoned: "I thought to end up with the Bronx," he discloses, "with an encounter with some ghosts of my own" ([1982] 2010: 345).

James Donald (1999) contends that the uncanny represents "the internal limit of modernity" (72). It is not a glitch accidentally produced; it is endemic to life in the modern city, which inevitably generates many uncanny experiences. The uncanny is about the derealization of the familiar; effectively, a kind of psychosomatic disorientation (to refer back to the 1974 remarks of James Marston Fitch). It is characterized by, as we have seen in Raymond Chandler, a sense of ambivalence, often represented by a disintegrating border between one hermetically sealed entity and another. It can denote "intellectual uncertainty about the shifting and collapsing boundaries between otherwise distinct categories of the strange and familiar, the past and the present, the other and the self" (Rau 2009: 184). It represents the "thinning of the membrane" between one seemingly distinct thing and another (Bowen [1948] 1976: 195). Writing about the Bronx of the early 1980s in "Views from the Burning Bridge," Berman repeatedly refers to fragmented and fractured buildings, cratered sidewalks, open spaces, and vacant lots. These are descriptions which recall the abandoned oil fields of *The Big Sleep*, the dilapidated buildings which sit across the street from the Cattleman house waiting to be torn down in *The Nowhere City*, the white clay sifting through the ceiling of Cuadros' subterranean home in "My Aztlan: White Place," or the eerie "thief's emptiness" of the Washington Avenue sidewalks in *A Meaningful Life* (Davis [1971] 2009: 120). "Now many tenement and apartment houses are cracked, burnt, split apart, caved in," Berman observes, with many blocks entirely "vanished or disintegrated into wreckage and debris" (1999: 71). Some blocks are "wide open and empty as deserts," others exist amid the urban detritus that speaks to the "shards of thousands and thousands of lives." He finds signs of incoherence and disintegration; the streets are in "various stages of demolition or decomposition" (1984b: 18). In Tom Wolfe's novel *The Bonfire of the Vanities* (1987), antihero Sherman McCoy gets lost in the South Bronx in his Mercedes. Having been unceremoniously dumped out of the Bruckner Expressway and on to Bruckner Boulevard, he grows increasingly anxious that he may never escape. Wolfe's bleak description matches Berman's, who was conducting his own expedition around the same time:

> Utterly empty, a vast open terrain [...] entire blocks of the city without a building left standing [...] The eerie grid of a city was spread out before him, lit by the chemical yellow of the street lamps. Here and there were traces of rubble and slag [...] the hills and dales of the Bronx ... reduced to asphalt, concrete, and cinders (86).

This sense of collapsing boundaries is made manifest in the uncanny landscape through which Berman walks like a flaneur in mourning, surveying the flattened, open space without a distinguishable frontier, as did Philip Marlowe in the outer limits of Southern California's "non space" (Jameson 2016: 86).

In exploring the origins of this upheaval, I interviewed a number of local people who had lived in the neighborhood during this period. Throughout the time I spent with them, the Cross-Bronx remained constant, both literally in the landscape of the borough that I could see, and in the conversations we had, disappearing and reappearing periodically, seamlessly, in every location as we walked and drove around. Gilbert Tauber said to me that the Cross-Bronx Expressway in particular created this sense of what *was* (familiar) and what *is* (unfamiliar) by constructing "a psychological barrier—whereas *before* you would go and visit Aunt Minnie twice a week, *now* to visit Aunt Minnie you've got this scary, noisy place" (2015: n.p.). I spoke to Joe Rosen, born in the East Bronx close to Tremont Avenue in 1953 (where he remained until 1972), who recalled having to cross to the other side of the Cross-Bronx to get to his school: "I thought I was going to another place" is how he describes his journey, continuing that it was "almost like a foreign country [. . .] 'I better bring my passport'" was the attitude, "because I'm going to the other side of the Cross-Bronx" (2016: n.p.). The evolution from the Grand Concourse to the Cross-Bronx had created a powerfully symbolic before and after.

The Negative Path: After the Cross-Bronx

In 2003 Berman writes that the eventual urban catastrophe that befell the Bronx began when "Robert Moses drilled his Cross-Bronx Expressway right through its center, destroying some of the most crowded (but intact) neighborhoods in the city, displacing thousands of people from their homes. The CBE was (and still is) a wound in the Bronx's heart" ([2003] 2016: 126–7). In *All That is Solid* he vividly recalls "vowing remembrance and revenge" while watching the bulldozers at work in his neighborhood ([1982] 2010): 295). Howard Kaminsky places blame in the same place for the end of the neighborhood as he knew it: "I knew early on that [Moses] was responsible for the city taking over my grandmother's house, and the entire block, and we knew that eventually it was going to be torn down [. . .] I mean as far as I'm concerned it was stolen. And I blame Moses for it" (2015: n.p.). For Berman, it was not just buildings that were decimated, but his sense of a geographically locatable childhood: "Robert Moses came into my life just after my bar mitzvah, and helped bring my childhood to an end, when he rammed a highway through the heart of my neighborhood in the heart of the Bronx" (1973: n.p.). In an essay titled "Never at Home: Jewish Writers and the Sense of Place," Berman's friend, the academic and cultural historian Morris Dickstein (2004), remarks fittingly that novels that reach back into the significant locational histories of their authors are often "less about location than about dislocation" (5). Where before the Bronx of Berman's childhood looked out on the Grand Concourse, now it is defined by the Cross-Bronx. We watch the transformation unfold as he takes us within the space of a few sentences through his memory of the Cross-Bronx as it replaces his receding recollection of the Grand Concourse, which used to stand in its place: "The Grand Concourse, from whose heights I watched and thought, was our borough's closest thing to a Parisian boulevard.

Among its most striking features were rows of large, splendid 1930s apartment houses [. . .] I saw one of the loveliest buildings being wrecked for the road" ([1982] 2010: 295). What are the implications when one is unable to lay claim to one's personal history through the prosthetic of space?

The denial or removal of history, Anthony Vidler (1992) contends, creates its own ghosts and forms its own history: "the traces of erasure form a kind of negative path, a route of obliteration into a past that is [. . .] always a present" (180). In this way the city can become marked by "a haunting absence, not a haunting presence" (183). Memory is not physically anchored to space, but it is symbolically anchored to space *as we remember it*, and often there is a gap between the two. In Italo Calvino's *Invisible Cities* (1972), Marco Polo says of his elusive ideal city that it is: "discontinuous in space and time, now scattered, now more condensed," and yet "you must not believe the search for it can stop" (164). Polo's city becomes more myth than matter in its re-telling, but its reality or unreality is ultimately of no consequence. Like Berman's Bronx, Polo's city transcends itself when it becomes a symbol—it can only really "begin to exist" through the repeated "signs" of itself generated by memory (19). This is a notion that Vivian Gornick articulated when she told me that her memories of the Bronx are both "attached to the concrete," and simultaneously would endure whether the material entity it was attached to survived or not: "What would it matter to me if it's actually there now? I think that's an illusion" (2015: n.p.).

Commenting on the thesis of Freud's *Civilization and its Discontents*, Berman notes:

> If we are willing to follow Freud and see the mind as a city, it may be fruitful to follow him a little further than planned to lead and see the city as a mind, a mind with unconscious depths and contradictory currents, a mind that can not only be in two places at the same time, but can also embody two (or more) times in the same place (1984a: 2).

What we remember is not what is necessarily real. But the remembered and the real, Berman argues, can be in the same place at the same time. The consequence is that our remembrance of the city as we knew it before is now fixed on a point of loss.[15] The point of origin around which these differences converge becomes a place, a real, tangible place, which is somehow linked to, or houses, a localized, locatable memory. Upon returning to these material sites of memory, we feel suddenly a chasm between what we remember and what we see. We feel a sense of alienation and betrayal: these places have been reconfigured, rearranged in our absence. This is perfectly articulated by Berman's sense of bereavement at looking out across the once-familiar landscape which is now an alien wasteland; a construction site: "standing above the construction site from the Cross-Bronx Expressway, weeping for my neighbourhood" ([1982] 2010: 295). Berman describes with great pathos the scene of destruction as the bulldozers rolled in, reducing his home to ashes: "My friends and I would stand on the parapet of the Grand Concourse, where 174th Street had been, and survey the work's progress [. . .] and marvel to see our ordinary nice neighbourhood transformed into sublime, spectacular ruins" (292–3). For Moses and his crew were not simply blasting through concrete and steel, they were obliterating the physical locus of memory—effectively demolishing a landmark of history. This inspires that sense of the sublime expressed by Fredric Jameson (2016) as he considers Philip Marlowe's world beyond the urban; here, Moses is the one who flattens the world, making it formless and uncertain.[16]

For Berman and his friends, surveying the wreckage of their home, the annihilation of a city's memory that those in power did not care to preserve presents to them an acute and tangible moment that perfectly expresses the discrepancy between memory and history. "History," Halbwachs ([1952] 1980) explains in *The Collective Memory*, "is neither the whole nor even all that remains of the past" (64). There are "two sorts of memory," he continues, the first being "internal or inward memory" and the second, "external memory," or alternatively "'autobiographical memory' and 'historical memory'" (52). Historical, social, external memory "represent[s] the past only in a condensed and schematic way" and can be mapped spatially by "clearly etched demarcations" (52, 82). Meanwhile, our personal memories present "a richer portrait with greater continuity" (52). These are more collective in nature, and thus retain the parts of the past which are "capable of living in the consciousness of the groups keeping the memory alive" (80). Memory is not so easily mappable as history; it is marked instead "by irregular and uncertain boundaries" (82). When Berman describes his walks around the Bronx as visits to his "inner city," ([1982] 2010: 344) he is perfectly summarizing the concept of the "autobiographical memory" as found in the "mobile city" and the "soft city."[17] These cities can exist independent of time or place. They represent a psychic split tearing through the walls of the mind and of memory; something which is real and unreal, there and not there.

M. Christine Boyer ([1996] 2001) builds on the work of Halbwachs when she argues in *The City of Collective Memory* that while history (that which is made visible in the landscape, or Halbwachs' "historical memory" (52)) is "manipulable and re-presentable in a play of lost significance," memory is "plural, alive, and cannot be appropriated" (67). Boyer contends that history "fixes the past in a uniform manner [. . .] reorganizes and resuscitates collective memories and popular imagery, freezing them in stereotypical forms [. . .] sets up a fictional space manipulating time and place, and re-presenting facts and events" (66–7). Meanwhile, memory, defined separately and distinctly, "occurs behind our backs, where it can neither be appropriated nor controlled" (67). This definition of history, in the context of *All That is Solid*, is given physical form in the Cross-Bronx Expressway and in Moses' plans for the future of New York City. Memory, that which used to be visible in the landscape and now remains only in symbolic form, is represented by the ghostly presence of the Grand Concourse; a "negative path" running in parallel (Vidler 1992: 180).

Michel de Certeau suggests in similar terms that it is the "childhood experience that determines spatial practices," and that this experience "later develops its effects, proliferates, floods private and public spaces, undoes their readable surfaces, and creates within the planned city a 'metaphorical' or mobile city" ([1980] 1984: 110). In this way, we create two spatial realities: within this "planned city" is enclosed the "mobile" city—respectively, the city of the eye and the city of the mind's eye. In a 1977 *New York Magazine* article, Professor Stanley Milgram details his experience of returning to his childhood neighborhood in the Bronx in the 1960s. Like Berman, Milgram is met with the profound material change of a new expressway; in his case it was the Bruckner Boulevard Expressway. However, he is able to navigate his way around. "Mental maps are drawn from a city's buildings and avenues but they are not the same as the physical reality," he explains (Duncan 1977: 52). This chimes with Brooklyn-born author Lynne Sharon Schwartz's characterization of what it means to see the invisible city: "my husband and I met in the Phoenix Theatre at a play, Shaw's *Saint Joan*, it was on East 12th Street and Second Avenue, and whenever we'd pass by there, we'd say 'oh you know that's where the Phoenix was.' Of course it's not there [. . .] but we would kind of *know*" (2015: n.p.).[18] Milgram writes that, much like the idea of the mobile or metaphorical city, there is also the "soft city," the implications of which mean that "you can mold the city to your own needs and peculiarities. [. . .] It is not hard and unyielding but takes on the impress which each individual gives to it" (Duncan: 62). (This notion of the impress recalls Plato's description of memory as a "waxen tablet" upon which various impressions could be made depending on its firmness or permeability (Marshall and Fryer 1978: 5)).

Vivian Gornick, whose memoir *Fierce Attachments* pieces together her childhood in the Bronx during the 1940s, returned to her old neighborhood three decades later. She told me that she wished to better-represent 181st Street and its environs authentically for the purposes of autobiographical reproduction, but discovered that so much had changed that her attempt to revisit sites of the past was redundant. So instead she turned to her own memory to re-create her history, which she found had outlasted the neighborhood itself: "we went up there and it had all changed [. . .] I was so panicked about not being able to get it, I said 'now concentrate,' and I wrote the scene. So, there it was. Whether it was actually as I remembered it, what does it matter? But I didn't need to actually see it" (2015: n.p.).[19] The gap between *what was* and *what is* was also evident when Howard Kaminsky talked to me about the history of the borough, simultaneously describing what he saw around us in the present-day in the context of this history. Howard drove me around his old stomping grounds, narrating the landscape as we stopped and started, prompted into a parallel vision of what used to exist: the row houses, the concrete of the schoolyard where he used to play softball, large old apartment houses that were torn down, his father's candy store, formerly a grocery store that had been known for kosher pickles. His reminiscences peppered with references to absence and negation: "This is a high school that was never here. This is a public school that I went to that never looked like that" (2015: n.p.). The reminiscences of Bronx residents like Kaminsky and Gornick are full of discontinuities—my interviews with them were peppered with remarks concerning what they could see no longer existed in the built environment, these absences jarring them out of their recollections, creating bumps in smooth surfaces. In a 2001 article for the *New York Times*, Gornick recounts that upon her return to her childhood neighborhood almost two decades after she left, she felt a "sense of disconnect [. . .] Jack's Appetizing was now Rivera's Auto Parts, the shoe repair Bar-B-Que Chicken, the hardware store a pawnbroker" (Gornick 2001: n.p.). Shellie Sclan, Berman's wife, relayed to me that she has her own "lost worlds" (Berman [1982] 2010: 35), such as a particular Russian-Turkish bath she used to frequent ("I really physically emotionally miss it. It's been replaced by Spa Castle" [Sclan 2016: n.p.]), or the route along the subway line of the 6 train to Spring Street downtown, where she now feels "like Rip Van Winkle," waking up in a world far removed from her expectations, a world where she sees "everything double [. . .] I have this memory of what was there before." There are places in the city which are able to take her back, one just has to know where to look. Sometimes, she would really *know*, but would need to physically return to be sure, and what she was looking for "wasn't there, it was someplace else," requiring a shifting along the vacillating urban space/time continuum. Nothing is the same—every place Vivian Gornick could have pointed to as a child as a local landmark, or Shallie Sclan sought out as a long-time resident, has been, inevitably, replaced.

Fredric Jameson (1988) argues in "Cognitive Mapping" that our modern global reality cannot be represented accurately by us as individuals because it is defined by what is *absent* to us—what we can no longer see and perceive—rather than what is present, visible, and therefore representable (Jameson 1988: 350). He writes that the "mental unmappability" of certain cityscapes, which are unmappable because those who live in them have become alienated from their physical reality, has consequently led to a split between "the here and now of immediate perception" and the "imaginary sense of the city as an absent totality" (353). When we remember, we are attempting to recall something which is no longer there; to bring the absent into the present. Walter Benjamin ([1927–39] 2003), when writing about the Arcades of Paris early in the twentieth century, describes them as "*a past become space*" (923); a century later, Henri Lefebvre ([1992] 2004) writes that the center of the city "bears the imprint of what it hides, but it hides it" (34). The literal rubble of Berman's past is a manifestation of the way in which the past can "*become space*"—by reminding those who traverse it of what used to exist there. But what if, instead of rubble, we could manifest something intact and complete? What if the past could "*become*" a space that is both impressionable and mappable?

At the end of *All That is Solid*, such a space takes the imagined physical form of a Bronx Mural.[20] This Mural, Berman suggests, could run alongside eight miles of the Cross-Bronx, so that the driver's view would become "a trip into its buried depths" or a vision (or hallucinatory flashback) of "houses, even of rooms full of people just as they were before the Expressway cut through them all" ([1982] 2010: 341, 342). Here is the Cross-Bronx, again, smashing through Berman's symbolic history and the formerly intact buildings; it is the before and after of his life. In the absence of the familiar and the empirically real, Berman's borough becomes dominated by the symbolic. To this "forest of symbols [. . .] where axes and bulldozers are always at work," (289) why not add our own symbols, Berman seems to ask, in the form of what Vidler calls a "harbinger of the unseen" (167)? For Berman these harbingers should remain somehow visible, because "a world in which all ruins have been cleared away" or made invisible, "is a world that wants to forget" (1984b: 23).

His remedy is that the past (in the form of these houses, these "rooms full of people just as they were") should not be forgotten as the modern conception of progress in postwar urban space seems to demand, but should instead continue to exist and to run in parallel. Berman sees the "rich and strange experience" of the Mural, which conjures "fantasies" and "ghosts" ([1982] 2010: 343), as providing access to, or an outline of, the parts of the city which are felt (memory) but not seen (history). This is a project to anchor memory at the heart of history. Its actual construction would mean that the unseen and absent (memory) becomes the seen (history), or at least the memorialized.

Berman believes that dialogue is necessary. By this he means dialogue between history, that is, what is tangibly real and visible in the present (the Cross-Bronx) and memory, that is, the symbolic (the Grand Concourse), the conjunction of which would take the form of the Mural. Such an ongoing dialogue means that "modernists can never be done with the past: they must go on forever haunted by it, digging up its ghosts, recreating it" ([1982] 2010: 346). To be modern, Berman tells us, is to "experience personal and social life as a maelstrom, to find one's world and oneself in perpetual disintegration and renewal" (345). We must find a way to make a home in the maelstrom, he argues, but we must also accept that this home is haunted. After all, as de Certeau ([1980] 1984) pronounces, "Haunted places are the only ones people can live in" (108). In order to survive in the modern urban world, you must create a dialogue with the ghosts you are haunted by, even if one of those ghosts is yourself.

No Other Place

In a 1984 article for *The Village Voice*, Berman writes about having returned to his old neighborhood four years previously in terms that speak to the performance of a pilgrimage of sorts. This is similar to Vivian Gornick's 2001 essay "My Neighborhood: Its Fall and Rise," suggesting that there is a certain audience for nostalgic returns to the ruined place of one's birth. The timing of Gornick's article should also be noted; it was published less than three months before the attacks of September 11, 2001, after which, Gornick told me, the very concept of nostalgia in the city became obsolete: "it was so hard to think about the city as it ever was before that moment" (2015: n.p.).

Berman explains in his *Village Voice* article that he and his family had often spoken of their home on 1460 College Avenue ("we would talk about 'our house'" (1984b: 18)), the apartment building where they had lived for twenty years. None of them had been back. "No one had heard anything about the building since the fires, collapses, and abandonments had begun. Maybe no news was good news, but during the plague years none of us could bear to go back and take a look." In his short story "The Cost of Living" (1950), the author Bernard Malamud, writing about the Brooklyn of his childhood, articulates this same fear of looking directly at the haunted spaces of the past that now mean too much to glance at: "Afterwards when Sam went by the store, even in daylight he was afraid to look, and quickly walked past, as they had the haunted house when he was a boy" (Malamud [1950] 1985: 185). Just as Berman describes in *All That is Solid*, his words contain the sense that a return is somehow forbidden, or at least bad luck, as though the fleeing residents of the South Bronx were repeating the Biblical escape from Sodom (recalling Didion's words in *Where I Was From*: "Were not such abandonments the very heart and soul of the crossing story? [. . .] Never dwell on what got left behind, never look back at all?" ([2003] 2004: 198–9)). But Berman does return, setting out to rediscover what he felt he had lost. He explains, as though feeling he must justify his wanderings, that "Many modernisms of the past have found themselves by forgetting," continuing that the modernists who came later in the 1970s had to, conversely, "find themselves by remembering" ([1982] 2010: 332). Either way, he implies, we can only be "found" in our history, through our relationship with the past. Berman chooses to find himself through communing with the latter type of 1970s modernism, in order to "generate a dialogue with my own past, my own lost home, my own ghosts" (340). But Berman's home is haunted. "I want to go back to where this essay started, to my Bronx, vital and thriving only yesterday, ruins and ashen wildness today." Such a house can, if "condemned to history or the demolition site" as Anthony Vidler states, produce its own ghosts and become an "object of memory [. . .] an instrument, that is, of generalized nostalgia" (1992: 64).

In *All That is Solid*, Berman describes the act of walking through the South Bronx as an adult; as a child of the pre-Cross-Bronx Bronx, this is a process of recognition followed inescapably by mourning. Returning after a long absence he is reunited with neighborhood blocks that "feel so much like blocks you left long ago, blocks you thought had vanished forever, that you will wonder if you are seeing ghosts—or if you yourself are a ghost" ([1982] 2010: 344). As time went by Berman found it increasingly unbearable to walk in the shadow of the past; he felt that the "ruins" (he repeats the word frequently, pointedly) were overwhelming his sense of what had preceded them. So much of what he knew is gone, he writes, that "we know we will never feel so much at home anywhere again" (325). He confesses in the Afterword, written in 2010, that during the 1970s he had "walked through those ruins obsessively," seeking a "core of meaning" inside the skeleton of what used to be (352). He quotes Octavio Paz (1973), who laments the fact that because modernity cuts itself off at the root, willing itself forward, it is therefore "unable to return to its beginnings" (Paz 1973: 162). Berman expresses a desire to overcome this inability by continuously returning to the site of memory which now seems bereft, its insides carved out, leaving only holes and cracks in the landscape which speak to what used to exist. Anne Friedberg (1993) writes that the nostalgic pull which Berman articulates here is a form of compulsion—the compulsion "to repeat" which is "based in the desire to return" (189). Berman finds himself determined "to go back," his display of repetition compulsion setting him on an endless loop ([1982] 2010: 340). In his Introduction to *New York Calling*, Berman ponders this pull backward, writing of *All That is Solid* that he "came to feel I couldn't finish till I had gone back to where I'd started. So I went back [. . .] What was I looking for?" (2007a: 18–19).

What does Berman want to go back *to* exactly? So much of his Bronx, "our Bronx," has gone; he knows he will "never feel so much at home anywhere again. Why did it go? Did it have to go?" ([1982] 2010: 325). As Roberta Rubenstein (2001) writes in *Home Matters*, the very notion of home is not just "a physical structure of a geographical location but always an emotional space" (1). Berman explains, as though feeling he must justify his flaneur-like wanderings, that "the look towards home is a look 'back,' backward in time [. . .] back into our own childhood, back into society's historical past" ([1982] 2010: 333). All that seemed solid in his own life has fallen apart, and though he recognizes that the past is always "in a process of disintegration" he finds himself compelled to seek out signs of that disintegration ("When I talk about ruins, I'm an interested party" (1984b: 18)), just as he watched the fall of the Grand Concourse as a boy. Nostalgia, from the Greek *nostos* (a return) and *algos* (painful), describes a sense of longing for something, for a particular space or place from which one is "separated by distance and time" (Friedberg 1993: 188). It is, in short, homesickness. As Hugh Haughton puts it in his Introduction to "The Uncanny," this feeling "reminds us not only that there is no place like home, but that, in another sense, there is no other place" (Haughton 2003: xlix). There is no place like home; home is that "no-place." What to do when your point of origin, your center, could not hold? For Berman, there is a home somewhere, buried in the Bronx, that has been lost to him. Though he chose to leave, he can't help but look back; though the return is painful, he can't help but revisit. There is no other place, but that place is no-place. In his search for "something solid" he instead finds himself "embracing ghosts" ([1982] 2010: 333).

The overwhelming sense that something has been omitted from the physical text of his history permeates much of Berman's writing. In his work on the Bronx he writes in terms of mourning and bereavement. "As I saw one of the loveliest of these buildings being wrecked for the road," he tells us, "I felt a grief that, I can see now, is endemic to modern life" (295). In 1955 Berman and his family had moved into the Northwest Bronx, at his father's behest, settling at Claremont

Park. In a 2013 lecture, Berman waxes lyrical about these halcyon days and the verdant landscape of their new neighborhood: "It was very green, there were the remains of forests. My sister and I missed the old neighborhood, but our parents were happy in the new one. They had a room of their own [. . .] they would walk in the woods hand in hand" (2013: 3). In his program notes accompanying the play *The Day the Bronx Died*, Berman goes so far as to compare the South Bronx as was to Arcadia: "I started to write this essay with the phrase, 'I, too, grew up in the South Bronx.' Then I realized how much my words sounded like the classical elegiac motto, Et in Arcadia ego, 'I, too, was in Arcadia'" (1993: 208). Though he cannot help but note the ominous melancholy that accompanies such a vision, as he continues: "And I remembered [. . .] that even in Arcadia, death is there. It rings true, all right. People who grew up in the Bronx [. . .] can't seem to write about our sweetest, happiest childhood years without implanting deep shadows in the landscape." The effect of his father's sudden death only six months after the move is explicitly linked to Berman's fascination with urban ruin and renewal:

> We moved because of what my father said was coming to our neighborhood, and indeed what did come, not instantly, but soon enough: RUINS [. . .] The whole episode would be a perfectly ordinary "move to the suburbs," at a time when millions of people were making that move—except that, six months later, suddenly, my father died of a heart attack. Our family crashed and plummeted. Our life was shattered, in a place where we hardly had a life. People had a hard time getting to our new house, to mourn with us; mostly they didn't come. I became obsessed forever with the destruction of cities (2013: 3–4).

In *On the Town* (2006a), his investigation into Times Square and its chequered past, Berman writes about the connection he made between his father and downtown Manhattan. He consciously links the bereavement he felt at the loss of his father with his hesitance at returning to that part of the city for some time after his father's death. "I remember how I knew 'downtown' was there, just a subway ride away, and I knew I'd been there only yesterday, or maybe the day before, yet today, with my father dead, it sounded so hopelessly far away" (2006a: xxiv). This point is reiterated in a paper presented in 1997:

> It was my father who first took me to the Square. In the early 1950s, on Saturday afternoons, we would go to the Paramount and the Palace theatres and Lindy's and Tofinetti's restaurants and the lobby and café of the Astor Hotel. Afterward, we would hang around the streets and check out the people and the signs. [. . .] All those places and spaces were magical, as he was, like him (d. 1955), they were all torn down before their time. For a time I walked in empty spaces alone (1997: n.p.).

Here Berman gives us further examples of what Milgram deemed the "mental maps" (Duncan 1977: 52) of this "mobile city" (de Certeau [1980] 1984: 110), a city which has taken on Berman's "impress" (Duncan 1977: 62), rendering a series of seemingly insignificant city landmarks as deeply ingrained with meaning and history. In *Invisible Cities* (1972), Marco Polo reveals that each description of the many cities he has seen in the realm of Kublai Khan could be an echo of Venice, his hometown: "Every time I describe a city I am saying something about Venice" (Calvino [1972] 2013: 86). In much the same way, for Berman it is the Bronx, Tremont, 1460 College Avenue, which he sees refracted in splintered fragments throughout the larger urban tapestry of New York City. For Berman, memory is a place, or a series of places, the distance to and from which cannot necessarily be calculated; a distance which becomes, after his father's death, almost impossible to breach.

Grief underlies this city of collective memory, like the oil that sits beneath the earth in Chandler's *The Big Sleep* and the water that alternately bursts through and retreats into the land in Lurie's *The Nowhere City* and Waldie's *Holy Land*. Each of Berman's texts contains signs and traces of Berman's attempts to process his sense of loss—the loss of his neighborhood, his childhood, his sense of personal history, his father (each folded inside the other). As Halbwachs ([1952] 1980) notes, "Any inhabitant for whom these old walls, run-down homes, and obscure passageways create a little universe, who has many remembrances fastened to these images now obliterated forever, feels a whole part of himself dying with these things" (134). These feelings of loss have deep roots; often Berman asks himself what more he could have done to prevent these losses, finding himself wanting. Could he have stopped "the dread road from being built?" ([1982] 2010: 326). For though he lays the blame for the end of his childhood at the feet of Robert Moses, he is also unflinchingly honest about his own choices with regard to his separation as an adult from the site of his youth. He confesses that regardless of the path bulldozed through the Bronx, he would have ultimately, embodying the very spirit of modernity, left his childhood home of his own accord. "Men need to recover their roots," he writes in 1966, "not to sink into, but to grow out of" (1966: 1). This is something nearly everyone I spoke to who had grown up in the Bronx repeated. Howard told me that everyone in his neighborhood eventually moved: "the children, they wanted something better," (2015: n.p.) while Vivian confirmed that "We all wanted to get out. As children nobody dreamed of repeating this life" (2015: n.p.). Berman repeats this notion that abandonment was necessary in one of many notes he made while researching Robert Moses: "Our hearts break for these neighborhoods now that they're gone—but when we ourselves were growing up in them, didn't most of us basically want out?" (1974: n.p.).

In a 1975 paper for *Ramparts*, Berman anticipates what he will later conclude in *All That is Solid*—that we are culpable for our own desertion of the past, and that this is the tragedy of our modern lives: "a tragedy in which we ourselves turn out to be implicated, a lot more deeply than we think" (1975: 38). The Cross-Bronx, he muses elsewhere:

> gets you out of the Bronx in eight minutes flat. I think sadly of a time that life in the Bronx was so sweet that you wouldn't want to get out of it at all. (Was it really so sweet? Can real life ever be as sweet as your memory of your lost childhood?) When I do ride Moses' road, I feel at once elated, as if I'm in touch with the deepest springs of my life, and horrified, as if I'm trampling on loved ones' graves (1973: n.p.).

He recalls a conversation in 1967 with a fellow-Bronxite, anticipating that in a discussion about Moses and the Cross-Bronx, they would feel the same pain at the demise of their neighborhood. Instead, the man expresses a sense of satisfaction that the highway would destroy any trace of their childhood homes: "Fine, he said, the sooner the better" ([1982] 2010: 327). For this is the paradox of modern urban life: we are as desperate to grow up and leave ourselves behind as we are to preserve that which we abandon. Or as Berman puts it when describing the rush to get out and move on: "We fight back the tears and step on the gas" (291).

4

The Palimpsest

Paula Fox and L. J. Davis in Brooklyn

Betty Smith's *A Tree Grows in Brooklyn*, published in 1943, charts the formative years of Francie Nolan as she comes of age in Brooklyn, a neighborhood in flux even in 1912 when the novel begins. The novel opens:

> You took a walk on a Sunday afternoon and came to a nice neighbourhood, very refined. You saw a small one of these trees through the iron gate leading to someone's yard and you knew that soon that section of Brooklyn would get to be a tenement district. The tree knew. It came there first. Afterwards, poor foreigners seeped in and the quiet old brownstone houses were hacked up into flats ([1943] 1974: 1).

Almost sixty years after the period in which Betty Smith's novel is set, Sophie Bentwood, the protagonist of Paula Fox's *Desperate Characters* (1970), echoes Francie's musings when she expresses concern about the poor "foreign" people next door and wonders aloud about the fates of her neighbors whose homes are sold to the new, entrepreneurial arrivals to her neighborhood. Two recent buyers, we learn, are a "brave pioneer from Wall Street" and "a painter who got evicted from his loft on Lower Broadway," rather different new arrivals to Francie Nolan's neighbors ([1970] 2003: 5). Much like Paul and Katherine Cattleman in *The Nowhere City*, Sophie and her husband Otto are depicted in the novel's opening pages in a state of erosion that equals that of their neighborhood. "What happens to the people in them when the houses are bought? Where do they go?'" asks Sophie (5). This is a question bleakly answered by L. J. Davis' *A Meaningful Life* (1971), in which Lowell Lake, gifted with a full scholarship for a PhD program at the University of California, Berkeley, takes it upon himself instead to go East, to Brooklyn, to rehabilitate an old brownstone rooming house. This is a rather ironic reversal of the expected route for explorers, as repeatedly articulated by Joan Didion, and indeed an inversion of Paul Cattleman's impulse to "Go West, Young Man" (Lurie [1965] 1994: 11). Where Paul seeks the future in Los Angeles, Lake expects the past in New York.

This chapter takes *A Meaningful Life* and *Desperate Characters* as focal points in a wider discussion of the restoration and preservation of history by the brownstoner cause in Brooklyn during the 1960s and 1970s. I also draw on *Brown Girl, Brownstones* by Paule Marshall (1959), and *A Walker in the City* by Alfred Kazin (1951). In the pursuit of preservation, how is the past actually utilized and transformed in literature of this period? What does preservation signify to these characters? How does the relationship between external and internal spaces present itself? In order to answer these questions, I trace the emergence of both the brownstoner movement and gentrification in mid-twentieth-century Brooklyn.

Signs of Authenticity

Brooklyn, which had started its life as a pleasantly pastoral suburb, became after the Second World War a place from which its inhabitants were desperate to escape. Not so many decades later, they would be desperate to return. When I interviewed Richard Fine, who grew up in the Flatbush/Bensonhurst neighborhood of Brooklyn during the 1950s (his mother came to New York from Europe at the age of seven), he explained the irony of the borough's modern allure: "All of the people who killed themselves to get the hell out of here, now their grandchildren are paying a fortune to move back into the neighbourhoods" (2015: n.p.). Lynne Sharon Schwartz, who grew up in East Flatbush, speaks of the borough in similar terms when recounting the recreation of the neighborhood for her 1989 novel *Leaving Brooklyn*: "The book was published in '89 and I wrote about [Brooklyn] as a very dull provincial place, which is how I remembered it, everybody just wanted to get away and most of us did [...] But now it's transformed. Now it's a historical novel!" (2016: n.p.). The closure of the *Brooklyn Eagle* newspaper, the departure of the Brooklyn Dodgers (who infamously went West), the folding of the Brooklyn Navy Yard, the arrival of African Americans from the South, who were migrating to find work and escape horrific Jim Crow politics, the expansion of the suburbs, and the growth of the Interstate Highway System, have all been put forward as explanations for the postwar decline of the borough.[1]

Regardless, a strong sense of nostalgia permeates Brooklyn narratives both pre- and postwar, with inevitably unfavorable comparisons made.[2] In *A Walker in the City* (1951), Alfred Kazin writes of his childhood haunts in Brownsville, Brooklyn, as experienced in the late 1920s to early 1930s. As he passes by the various sites of transformation, Kazin notes the familiar spots which have become strangers to him: the lumber yard which is now a housing project; the wholesale dry-goods store where his mother bought his first shirts; the clapboard Protestant church on Blake Avenue, now torn out like a tree uprooted. The parents of one participant at the "Brooklyn Transitions" book discussion group that I attended in 2015 came to the Park Slope neighborhood in 1978, and they continue to live in the same house that they originally moved into between Seventh and Eighth Avenues. This man professed that his ability to point out what each store or house or bar used to be was his birth-right as a New Yorker. The melancholic awareness of the imminent erasure of the places that one loves is perhaps best exemplified by Colson Whitehead in his famous assertion that "You are a New Yorker when what was there before is more real and solid than what is here now" (2003: 4). Being in a position to know exactly what has changed, to *see* what you have lost and to quantify that loss, seems to come somewhere close to defining what it means to be a long-time citizen of this particular city.

Kazin quantifies his own loss as he notes the townhouses and lumberyards that have been replaced by housing projects, the brownstone mansions that have become boarding houses, the movie theatres now converted for a different use. For Kazin, buildings mark boundaries in space. Memories bind these buildings to the land, upon which invisible lines are drawn, made tangible by the tenements and stores in which the speaker's memories are housed. The new housing project he sees, for example, has created a new space "down the center of Brownsville, from Rockaway to Stone," and "clean diagonal forms" have been carved into the streets that look out onto the project, with everything but his childhood school excised from the newly streamlined area (1951: 12). Walking past these "indistinguishable red prisms of city houses," Kazin is forced into the remembrance of "what they had pulled down to make this *project*—and [. . .] I could not quite believe that what I saw before me was real" (13). The juxtaposition between the past and the present, the expected and the empirical, creates a surreal schism in his mind:

> There is something uncanny now about seeing the old vistas rear up at each end of that housing project. Despite those fresh diagonal walks [. . .] the streets beyond are so obviously just as they were when I grew up in them, that it is as if they had been ripped out of their original pattern and then pasted back again behind the unbelievable miniatures of the future (14).

In Kazin's uncanny vision quoted here, like the observations of Marshall Berman as he wanders the streets of the Bronx, we find an example of what Suleiman Osman (2011) defines as Brooklyn's "tectonic cityscape" (2011: 22). Despite the attempt to render the area virgin land, the very visibility of the old tenements that remain on either side of these "fresh diagonal walks," and the irrepressible nature of the streets themselves, demonstrates that the city's skeleton can still be found (Kazin 1951: 14). The past is available, but not in the form one might have expected, and perhaps it is not your past, but that of the city itself, which has internalized a million histories and layered them on top of each other.

Paule Marshall articulates a similar sense of the past as achieved through the visibility of difference. Her novel *Brown Girl, Brownstones* details the experience of one Bajan community living in Bedford-Stuyvesant in Brooklyn in the years just before and during the Second World War. Just as, thirty years before, Betty Smith's Francie Nolan had anticipated the arrival of the next wave of immigrants, Selina recounts the Brooklyn lives of generations of white "Dutch-English and Scotch-Irish" which unraveled "in a quiet skein of years behind the green shades" and ultimately made way for the West Indians who "slowly edged their way in" in 1939 (Marshall [1959] 1982): 4). At the beginning of Marshall's novel, her heroine Selina Boyce does not feel a sense of belonging within her house, which seems to her to be "the museum of all the lives that had ever lived here" rather than a home (5). At its conclusion, she gazes at the buildings beyond Fulton Park, watching the kinetic life of the streets that persists in the rubble of the neighborhood's former glory. The scorched earth that lies in wait for the project that will be constructed atop its urban burial ground provides a scattershot cemetery for bits and pieces of the past, now de-contextualized and deprived of function: a homeless stoop which "still imposed its massive grandeur" here, a "carved oak staircase" leading nowhere, there (310). She understands the impossibility of imprinting oneself on such a landscape, but, wishing to memorialize, she tosses a silver bangle over her shoulder. Marshall captures the futility of such an act: "The bangle rose behind her, a bit of silver against the moon, then curved swiftly downward and struck a stone. A frail sound in that utter silence." Already, whole blocks of brownstones have been "blasted to make way for a city project," the wind picking up that perennial Brooklyn scent of "crushed brick and plaster," moonlight catching "the heaped rubble in a fretwork of light and shadow," all of which waits to be replaced by "the new city houses" which have already been constructed (310).

At the end of *Brown Girl, Brownstones*, Selina Boyce describes the Bed-Stuy neighborhood of the 1940s around Fulton Park as "ruined" and belonging "to the winos who sat red-eyed and bickering all day, to the dope addicts huddled in their safe worlds and to the young bops clashing under the trees," where previously it had been home, on a similar spring evening, to "the mothers [who] would have been sitting there, their ample thighs spread easy under their housedresses, gossiping" (309). Just beyond the outskirts of the park, the "ravaged brownstones," once occupied and drawn inwards toward an internal life, sit dark and empty. David Gissen (2013) writes in *Manhattan Atmospheres* that during the postwar period of acute urban crisis (as outlined in Chapter 3), New York, like so many other American cities, "became degraded physically and financially [. . .] The site of this time period, which extends from the end of an industrial era to a postindustrial one, has been termed the 'crisis' or 'disaster' city" (1). Kenneth T. Jackson (2004) reports in *The Neighborhoods of Brooklyn* that throughout the same era, "Rioting became a constant threat, arson was on the rise, and poverty, labor strikes, and racial tensions seemed to be the only stories the outside press reported about Brooklyn," a trend that would continue through the 1950s and into the 1960s (xxix). Despite this, by 1969, eminent journalist, author, and Brooklyn émigré Pete Hamill had written that somehow nostalgia had "worked its sinister charms" (31). Compared to the empty experience of the suburbs, the "Old Neighborhood" didn't seem so bad: "A little at a time, people started to drift back."

This return was not a complete coincidence. In the second half of the twentieth century, New York provided a particularly acute example of the consequences of deindustrialization for cities wholly dependent upon specific industries to stay economically alive, as Samuel Stein (2019) explains in *Capital City*: "from the 1950s to the 1990s, the city lost 750,000 manufacturing jobs while its land values soared from $20 billion to $400 billion" (45). Real estate had plugged the enormous financial hole the city found itself in, ultimately transforming itself from "a secondary to a primary source of urban capital accumulation." However, as outlined in the previous chapter, projects and practices such as redlining, the Home Owners' Loan Corporation risk criteria, the expansion of the suburbs, and urban renewal, effectively shut out immigrants, the poor, and people of color from any financial avenues which would otherwise have enabled them to participate in the same housing market which, by the 1960s, had begun to flourish for other "young urbanites [. . .] artists and professionals" (47). Indeed, it was mostly their housing stock which the young urbanite brownstoners (the term stemming from the name of the stone from which many of the most desirable properties in Brooklyn are made) were moving into, thanks to the very practices that ensured the decline and abandonment of particular neighborhoods, thereby turning them into "low-cost properties" ripe for renovation. As noted in Chapters 1 and 2, when land is transformed into real estate, it becomes something more than a garden for cultivation; more even than territory alone. Space itself becomes marketized. In the present day, the air above the heads of New Yorkers has become a commodity through what is known as "upzoning," whereby "planners allow developers to own a new piece of the sky, turning everyone's airspace into someone's property" (62). Space is no longer space alone, rooted, inhabited, alive. Space is property, a resting place for capital; it is abstracted from human experience and dematerialized. How can memory be imprinted upon such a landscape, which has been zoned, redlined, renewed, purchased, turned into "privately owned public space" (Kayden 2000: vii)?

The neighborhood movement of which Lowell Lake becomes a part began to emerge during the 1950s, continuing in earnest and becoming more widespread throughout the later decades of the century. In a 2009 *New York Times* profile, L. J. Davis states that Lake's decision to move is an attempt to: "give meaning to his life by refurbishing the house and the slum it's in the middle of, and of course it just completely dominates his life." The author himself did "more or less the same thing" at the same time, having "undertaken the project on a large and decayed brownstone on Dean Street near Hoyt." It was, says, Davis, "one of the most dangerous, poorest neighborhoods in New York [...] of course the neighborhood got much more desirable over time." He said he sold the house, which he had purchased for $17,000, for $2 million" (Konigsberg 2009: n.p.). In *The Invention of Brownstone Brooklyn*, Suleiman Osman (2011) explains that the so-called brownstoner movement, now closely aligned with the concept of gentrification, was galvanized by the desire for an alternative to the "overmodernized skyscrapers, suburban tract homes, and the 'wild' ghetto" (14) which were on offer elsewhere in the city. The word "gentrification" (stemming from the word "gentry") was coined by sociologist Ruth Glass (1964) in her Introduction to the 1964 book on the subject of postwar London, titled *London: Aspects of Change*. She observed that working-class parts of the city were being increasingly accessed by the middle classes, who were buying up the "Shabby, modest mews and cottages" and transforming them into "elegant, expensive residences" (xviii). "Once this process of 'gentrification' starts in a district it goes on rapidly until all or most of the working-class occupiers are displaced, and the whole social character of the district is changed."[3] Stein (2019) writes that the process of gentrification comes in three waves: investment, disinvestment, reinvestment (49), and once this process is complete, entire cities are transformed "from places into products" (48). Thus, cities become products to experience, not places to inhabit.

Sharon Zukin ([2009] 2010) argues that the so-called "gentrifiers" sought to put down roots "in the old city identified with origins rather than with new beginnings" (5). The idea of origins, which are not singular but rather "built up of layers of historical migrations," like many accumulative roots, represent a moral right "to inhabit a space, not just to consume it" (5–6). It was the search "for an authentic urban experience," Zukin asserts, which led people back to Brooklyn during the period of acute urban crisis that began during the 1960s (5). During this same period the movement trickled down to the white and white-collar professionals who were unable to afford the rising rates of Manhattan, finding more affordable housing in the borough's surrounding areas. Brooklyn neighborhoods like Brooklyn Heights, Cobble Hill, and Carroll Gardens were viewed as "organic and authentic" spaces (Osman 2011: 14). Indeed, it was a desire to preserve "the 'authentic' city" which has been "the goal of historic preservationists" since the 1960s (Zukin [2009] 2010: xi).

Authenticity is a key term here. In *Sincerity and Authenticity*, Lionel Trilling ([1971] 1972) ties the idea of authenticity to something quasi-religious; humans have fallen from some primordial state of grace, and as a consequence seek out a return to an original authentic space. Comparing it to "sincerity," which is defined as "the absence of dissimulation or feigning or pretence," (13) Trilling suggests that authenticity is "a more strenuous moral experience [. . .] a more exigent conception of the self and of what being true to it consists in" (11). Richard Handler (1986) writes that the search for the authentic is the search for "the unspoiled, pristine, genuine, untouched and traditional" (2). Examining Trilling's thesis, Handler explains that the concept of authenticity and that of sincerity emerged with the birth of the modern world out of the medieval. In the pre-modern world, God was responsible for the "hierarchical whole in which humans and all other features of the natural world are subordinate parts," (3) whereas with modernity came a sense of the individual which allowed people "to locate ultimate reality within themselves," with society, not God, the entity that ordered and defined the world. Sincerity therefore became a question of "the congruence between one's outer position [. . .] and one's inner or true self." It was demanded "not for the sake of the self but for that of others, as a means of honest social relationships." Authenticity on the other hand is about "our individual existence, not as we might present it to others, but as it 'really is,' apart from any roles we play." It expresses an anxiety about "being, about 'reality,' or, more particularly, about our lack of reality, about our lives which seem [. . .] 'unreal.'" Authenticity is a concept filled with an acute consciousness of an essential spuriousness; a lack of inherent value within the individual experience that has become homogenous and repetitive.[4] This is what certain gentrifiers seek when they scour the city for its authentic spaces; for them the concept is "predicated on a sense of the *in*authenticity of their own identity and networks" (Brown-Saracino 2009: 176). In such a world, the search for authenticity "is related to the standardization and homogenization of the world marketplace [. . .] people have begun to seek out new ways of distinguishing themselves from the masses. They now collect experiences, especially ones that they associate with a sense of authenticity or realness" (Benz 2016: 463). Of course, the search for this "realness," as though it is a tangible substance, often throws up instead mere reproductions; "social construction[s] based on that individual's assumptions and preconceptions, which may or may not be accurate" (464). In this scenario, anything could be "the real thing," as long as it approximates what is viewed as such. Even "seediness," once considered undesirable by previous generations which "saw dirt and danger in the asphalt jungle," is now sought out as "a sign of authenticity" (Zukin 2008: 726–7).

In a new age of "globalisation and rapid change," Japonica Brown-Saracino posits, a previous desire among gentrifiers for "progress and transformation" may give way to new concerns, foremost among which is "a desire to preserve the authentic and fragile, whether a dilapidated Victorian home, [or] a two-hundred-year-old landscape" (2009: 265). Preservation is another key term—not just of buildings, returning them from dilapidation to uncannily mummified glory, but in terms of a desire to retain remnants of a collective urban identity, a throwback to the kind of small-scale community for which Jane Jacobs was an advocate.[5] For Brown-Saracino, social preservationists and homesteaders both place a high value on "cultural and aesthetic congruity [. . .] They seek unification of a place's social and physical traits" (169). Both groups are concerned with "preserving place characteristics, such as the built or natural environment" (250). "What are we preserving?" Michael Kimmelman, *New York Times* architecture critic, asked rhetorically at a 2015 symposium: "We're preserving a notion of the city" (2015). Randall Mason (2009) writes that preservation strategy was predicated on translating "historical consciousness into urban forms and spaces," or in other words, on "'spatializing' historical memory" (xxiv). The search for both authenticity and preservation is not only about place, but also about time. Both reflect a desire to find the ideal city incarnate in a singular time which does not change.

In a 1974 address to the Back to the City Conference at the Waldorf-Astoria in New York City, which was sponsored by the Brownstone Revival Committee of New York and attended by more than 200 representatives of community preservation organizations, National Trust for Historic Preservation President James Biddle states that these so-called "clock stoppers" are "part of today's efforts to reverse the deterioration of our man-made environment," thereby defining the brownstoners as an effective opposition against city planners like Robert Moses, who was deemed a prime impresario of urban demolition (Biddle 1974: 2). At the same conference, architect and preservationist James Marston Fitch states that "under the guise of urban renewal or urban redevelopment, the assumption was widespread [. . .] the only way to rebuild our cities was to bulldoze them, clear the ground, start over. In retrospect, the lunacy of this proposition should have been clear to all of us" (1974: 6). Moses wanted to rebuild the city, ignoring what was already present in the built environment. The brownstoner movement, and the gentrification that followed, wanted to restore the city in order to not just pay homage to, but actively *recreate*, which tangible components of the past could still be found and physically excavated. Mason contends that thanks to modernity, more traditional ties "of memory and community were strained or broken altogether," and thus "the preservation movement responded by trying to heal the rupture" (2009: xxv). But the work of the preservationists at this time led to the creation of "a spectacle" of the past rather than a genuine recreation (xxvi). Though arguably the movement, being led by those who resisted what Zukin characterizes as a "forced march to progress," ([2009] 2010: 222), was a result of and a response to the events reflected in my chapter on Berman and the Bronx, the consequences of both ideologies in action, unintended or otherwise, are not dissimilar. Both the city planning of the modernists, and the preservationist desire to save buildings deemed historically significant, privilege history over memory. For Moses, this was expressed in terms of favoring its onward momentum. For the brownstoners it was expressed in terms of their creation of restored architectural artifacts which appropriate and fix the past through the preservation of a visible outward shell.

In *A Meaningful Life*, when restoring his brownstone home, Lowell Lake attempts to strip what physical evidence of the past he finds, of its layers, to scrub it clean, in order to reach back to something primordial, to some kind of "real" and original past which seems to kill the very thing that gives it meaning. He brings to life instead some kind of undead replica; the uncanny in tectonic form. Lake personifies what Osman describes as the brownstoners' drive to "symbolically [strip] layers off the built environment to restore a seemingly authentic past" (2011: 23). In *Desperate Characters*, Otto and Sophie Bentwood struggle to contend with the many changes in the urban fabric of the external world. As Martha Conway writes in her review of the novel, it seems that "the world outside their renovated brownstone is turning over on its side" (1999: 173). The interior spaces they frequent, their Brooklyn brownstone included, prove increasingly inadequate shelters from the storm of historical progress found in the outside world. Fox delineates the slow erasure of the past as articulated by the incremental encroachment of history in the rarefied lives of the brownstoners. The Bentwoods spend much of the novel moving from one internal space to the next, rather than aligning themselves with the outside world. The world beyond the familiar walls of their various memory palaces is treated with censure and disapproval, its language an incomprehensible foreign tongue they do not wish to learn.

A Bomb Through the Window: *Desperate Characters*

In *Desperate Characters*, the outside world is often on the verge of encroaching on the interior spaces inhabited by the Bentwoods and their cohorts, and indeed on several occasions does manage to trespass. Territory is invaded, for example, in the form of the incessant ringing of the telephone, an aggressive knock at the door, a rock through a window, and an actual home invasion. Early in the novel, Otto expresses his belief in the dependable impenetrability of their home. To him this is "powerfully solid [. . .] the sense of that solidity was like a hand placed firmly in the small of his back" (Fox [1970] 2003: 4). But as Marshall Berman tells us, all that is solid inevitably melts into air, and through the course of the novel Otto's sense of imperviousness is called into question on several occasions. As James Peacock (2015) writes in *Brooklyn Fictions*, throughout *Desperate Characters*, Paula Fox provides visceral reminders that "the couple lives on a socioeconomic frontier," and that "each rude interruption of their lives [. . .] reminds them how porous the frontier is" (132–3). This frontier is not just one of socioeconomic difference, but one which demarcates history and memory. Their Brooklyn brownstone, their farmhouse, and the homes of their friends, are all bulwarks against history's devouring capacities.

Fox quickly establishes the nineteenth-century brownstone belonging to the Bentwoods as a porous space, symptomatic of the couple's own fragility: it is a space vulnerable to external pressures. Their home is defined first by its commitment to the past as emphasized by their choice of interior décor, such as the "oval willowware platter Sophie had found in a Brooklyn Heights antique shop," and the "Victorian secretary" (Fox [1970] 2003: 3). Her choice of furnishings is evidence of what Alan Radley refers to as "a difference in the maintenance of a particular conception of 'the Past' and the effort to be given over to remembering" (1990: 51). Sophie's decision to display signs of an antique disposition represents the "material codification" of a desire to "deliberately evoke a sense of continuity, deliberately invite remembering." The internal spaces of her home manifest "the fabrication of the past through a construction of the material world" (53). Sophie is trying to make the past—her past—tangible in the form of her choice of interior decorations (like Katherine Cattleman), but the use of the word "fabrication" is suggestive of an inherent artifice in her cultivation of a certain look (the dual meaning of the word "fabrication" recalls the vocabulary used by Joan Didion). Sophie constructs and fabricates the past, choosing to display self-consciously historical pieces.

The house is also described in terms of its lack of internal compartmentalization. Fox's descriptions of their home confer an openness to the point of near-translucent penetrability which is compounded by the heightened visibility both of their own lives cracked open and that of their neighborhood-at-large: "The old sliding doors that had once separated the two first-floor rooms had long since been removed, so that by turning slightly the Bentwoods could glance down the length of their living room" ([1970] 2003: 3). Throughout the novel, acts of aggression committed outside the home increasingly wend their way inside what should be an impenetrable space.

The first invasion comes in the form of a stray cat, which Sophie initially observes through the glass door that leads to the back yard. The cat is in possession of a shade of fur that is "the gray of tree fungus," suggesting an insidious creeping; it is deemed "unprincipled and grotesque," somehow exhibiting human qualities that mark it as destructive and sinister (3, 4). Sophie takes it upon herself to feed the stray and her hand is horribly mauled in thanks. The cat and the houses on what Otto deems the "slum street" opposite are aligned by Otto's view through which they coalesce: "Across the yard, past the cat's agitated movements, he saw the rear windows of the houses on the slum street. Some windows had rags tacked to them, others, sheets of transparent plastic [. . .] A fat elderly woman in a bathrobe shouldered her way out into the yard and emptied a large paper sack over the ground" (4–5). What emerges from this passage is not just the merging of cat with neighborhood—something possibly rabid, starved, ugly, unsanitary—but also the high level of visibility. Otto is able to see almost directly into the houses of those living close to him; the materials used to create a sense of separation and compartmentalization are gossamer-thin to the point of translucence, like substandard versions of the steel and glass used in his own home. Such materials speak to an essential insubstantiality or illusory quality. The flimsy plastic sheeting and crystalline glass create nothing more than a mirage of permanence; each blockade to sight and entry is easily transgressed. Proved equally as illusory is the security of Otto's fortress of white middle-class solitude. The difference between "the slum people" (12) and the families in possession of a "superior comprehension of what counted in this world" is marked by their respective uses of "rags" versus "cloth" to mask the lack of traditional white shutters behind the panes of glass at their windows. New residents are thus demarcated from old, with the latter paid little heed outside of censure, despite their precedence. As Lance Freeman (2006) points out, the use of words like "slum," which Otto applies to both people and streets adjacent to himself, has particular connotations and can be placed alongside similar terms such as the "ghetto, the inner city, the 'hood,'" which are frequently applied as "monikers for black neighbourhoods," conjuring up "places that are off-limits to outsiders, places to be avoided after sundown [. . .] isolated pockets of deviance and despair" (1). What happens, Freeman asks, when "commerce, the middle class, globalization, if you will, comes to these forlorn neighbourhoods?"

Signs of the urban blight that characterized particular Brooklyn neighborhoods during the 1960s can be found in the Bentwoods' walk to Henry Street. Fox describes street lamps having been smashed, driving one family out of the block, the deficit of visible police officers ("except in patrol cars on their way to the slum people" ([1970] 2003: 13)), and the ubiquity of detritus, both human and animal. Further en route, Otto recalls the memory of a policeman's declaration that their own neighborhood "is really pulling itself together, doesn't look like the same place it was two years ago" (15). Resistance to change, despite Otto's attempts to do so, is futile. Though he is snobbish about the neighborhood of Brooklyn Heights, the destination of the party thrown by their friends Flo (producer of musicals) and Myron (psychoanalyst to the stars) Holstein ("He wouldn't consider buying a house on the Heights. . .horribly inflated prices [. . .] house prices enunciated in refined accents, mortgages like progressive diseases, 'I live on the Heights'" [15]), he recognizes that the rapid price inflation of property there is just as insidious as the refuse found on their block: "Of course, the Bentwood's neighborhood was on the same ladder."

Despite some difficulties during the 1950s, Brooklyn Heights retained its aura of unimpeachable class (high, with prices to match) throughout the mid to late twentieth century. Even Lowell Lake's wife, intractably set against moving back to Brooklyn, makes an exception for this particular zip code: "Unless it's the Heights, I'm staying right here. Or maybe Albemarle Road. Is it the Heights?" (Davis [1971] 2009: 88). Unlike the Cross-Bronx Expressway in the South Bronx or the Santa Ana Freeway in East Los Angeles, Brooklyn Heights escaped its potential bisection. Historian Francis Morrone, while recounting the history of the borough to me in an interview, reveals that Gladys Underwood James, who was the heiress to the Underwood typewriter fortune and knew Robert Moses, personally intervened to prevent the Brooklyn Queens Expressway from being pushed along Hicks Street (i.e., through the center of Brooklyn Heights). Mrs. James requested that the Expressway be instead diverted along the river front. Not only did Moses agree to the diversion, but he also proposed the construction of a new Brooklyn Heights Promenade. Though Mrs. James' interventions are disputed, there is little doubt that the socioeconomic makeup of the neighborhood gave it the clout to refuse the mighty Moses.[6] The Promenade (sometimes called the Esplanade), was cantilevered over the Expressway, opening completely in 1951. The Expressway itself was rerouted instead through the Brooklyn neighborhood of Vinegar Hill (running another ten miles through the Navy Yard and Williamsburg) which was conveniently home not to heiresses but to Irish and later Lithuanian immigrants. According to the *Home-Buyer's Guide to New York City Brownstone Neighborhoods*, published in 1974, the sheer aesthetic pull of the Promenade, which runs along the north-western edge of the neighborhood, "began to brace the area against further decline" (*Home-Buyer's Guide* 1974: 10). Conversely, Vinegar Hill and its environs experienced "a cycle of decline that wasn't reversed until the 1990s" (Campanella 2019: n.p.).

By 1965, Brooklyn Heights had been designated a New York City Historic District (the first district to have been decreed so), and by the 1970s the Brooklyn Chamber of Commerce was advertising the Heights as reflecting "once more the luster of her Victorian heyday" ("The New Brooklyn" 1973: n.p.). The same neighborhood is distinguished in the 1974 *Home-Buyer's Guide to New York City Brownstone Neighborhoods*, as "the archetype of urban renaissance in New York" (*Home-Buyer's Guide* 1974: 10).

The discovery of a broken window in the Holsteins' bedroom, its glass smashed by a stone hurled from the street, seems both a continuation and a reflection of Sophie's earlier attack. An attack on a neighborhood like this, however seemingly minor as a stone through a window, is symbolic of its true vulnerability to the forces of historical progress outside its fortress of cozy nostalgia. As Fox states in a 2015 interview: "All the antagonisms through history are played out through that window" (Fox 2015: n.p.). The hole in the window makes a mockery of the attempt to insulate those on the inside from those on the outside.

As they approach their destination, Sophie's wounded hand, another manifestation of contamination, balloons to such a degree that it resembles "a tarantula" (Fox [1970] 2003: 20). Her presence in her host's bedroom, where he has taken her to study her swollen hand, thus becomes imbued with potential violence. Even the mantelpiece accoutrements seem to vibrate with a colonizing ill-intent, the faces of the "small pre-Columbian statues [. . .] looking, oddly enough, as though they were outside the room but about to enter and sack it" (21). Outside the house all seems calm; inside is a different matter. In *Delirious New York*, Rem Koolhaas ([1978] 1994) examines the relationship between the external and internal life of a multi-story building. The external is, in his estimation, split from the internal world of the building in order to spare the outside world "the agonies of the continuous changes raging inside it. It hides everyday life" (101). He argues that a building's exterior represents the logic of urban planning and development, its face turned to the world outside implacable, while the interior contains the swell and storm of the human emotion and chaos which threatens to overwhelm it. Here, an act of violence, committed on the outside, lies in evidence on the inside of what should be another "powerfully solid" (Fox [1970] 2003: 4) white middle class Brooklyn home. Just as Sophie attempts to ignore the results of the cat bite, so Mike Holstein breezes past another worrying incursion ("'Oh, well, it's nothing.' He smiled at her and patted her arm" [23]). Otto's former business partner Charlie Russel rather perfectly articulates this willful denial of change and its repercussions later in the novel when he says to Sophie that "when people change slowly and irrevocably and everything goes dead, the only way to cure them is a bomb through the window" (37). The hole in the window undermines the attempt to demarcate space; indeed it makes the external and internal worlds into one open space. Mike makes several attempts at calling doctors on Sophie's behalf, to no avail ("'There are only answering services,' Mike said, putting the phone down" (21)); the trilling of the phone without answering call, or the expected caller, on the other side, is repeated several times throughout the novel.

The sense of insidious infiltration follows the Bentwoods back to their home. They are greeted by an unexpected telephone call, the noise ringing aggressively, the speaker at the other end silent, and as though to further emphasize their vulnerability in the face of an increasingly invasive external world, the same gray cat sits, impervious, at their back door. The discovery that it is Charlie Russel—who recommends the use of explosives to awaken the dormant middle class from their complacent slumber—who calls and does not speak is further evidence that the world outside threatens annihilation. Otto, characteristically, does not wish to pick up the phone, because "I never hear anything on it that I want to hear anymore" (27). Alexandra Schwartz (2017) affirms that what lies outside their home is what the Bentwoods "have spent so much time and money fending off—the poverty and resentment that lies just beyond their well-painted front door, which they sense could combust into violence against them at any moment" (2017: n.p.).

Later that night Charlie knocks at the door ostensibly wishing to see Otto, but expends much energy instead warning Sophie that the old ways are passing; that she and her kind will soon be obsolete. He is determined for Otto, a man who repeatedly refutes any notion of change in his world, to acknowledge that "something important has happened" (Fox [1970] 2003: 37); that neither of them will "survive" (39) this new world. In turn, Sophie tells Charlie that her family will end with her, compounding the inevitable cease and desist of such old ways of life. Having suffered two miscarriages, she and Otto have no children, and her only other surviving relatives are distant cousins in Oakland. Her parentage, interestingly, is split between the Old World (her father was half-French) and the New World (her mother is Californian, and Sophie's parents were, of course, in California real estate). By the time Sophie is once again safely ensconced inside her enclosed world, its domestic interiors have taken on a "shadowy, totemic menace" (47) that speaks to these fears that the life they knew no longer exists, and indeed has been replaced, surreptitiously, with something strange.

The once-familiar household objects begin to take on an uncanny strangeness. The notion that seemingly inanimate objects are capable of being cognizant, and that the home itself is, somehow, capable of watchfulness, recurs throughout the novel. Leaving for the Holsteins' party, Otto expresses a desire to catch the furtive house unawares ("He yearned to throw open the door he had only just locked, to catch the house empty" (12)), and later expresses concern that particular rooms feel "faintly hostile" (94). The prevalence of that which Freud would deem an uncanny stillness about their home is increasingly articulated, as though the material world within it possesses a kind of kinetic energy that is halted whenever she enters a previously empty space: "Chairs, tables, and lamps seemed to have only just assumed their accustomed positions. There was an echo in the air, a peculiar pulsation as of interrupted motion" (47). Sophie's world is changing, and all of her previous notions of being exempt from such changes have proven futile. She is not safe from the vicissitudes of the world outside because they have made their way inside her own home; she, in fact, has let them in.

In *Home Matters*, Roberta Rubenstein (2001) describes a particular kind of grief, a "cultural mourning," which is experienced spatially and caused by the loss of "something with collective or communal associations" (5). This kind of grief is expressed by the Bentwoods throughout *Desperate Characters* in different ways. Although Otto frequently articulates a certain rancor regarding the present in comparison with the past, for Sophie it is her sense of dislocation and imminent exile from a familiar space which causes her most consternation. Otto is a man who is burdened by the past but does not wish to be part of the future. "I *want* to be left out," he declares. Sophie tells him, with some resentment, that he is "barely in the right century" (Fox [1970] 2003: 10–11). She reaches for memory where history fails her, retreating into spaces which should provide an unbroken continuity with the past. Mickey Pearlman (1989) details the connections made between enclosed spaces and "the often negative power of memory" (138). Pearlman argues that one's experience of memory can be a spatial one; how we decide to fold our past into our present "determines our perception of emotional and actual space" (140). Leaving first the anxiety-riddled interiors of the easily penetrated Brooklyn home, and later in the novel a ransacked, violated second home, Sophie detaches from every aspect of the material life that previously defined her, descending instead, like Carmen Sternwood and Maria Wyeth, into a halcyon land of controlled memory within which she can insulate herself from the external world that seems so threatening. She dreams of her old love Francis Early, her memories contained in rooms untouched by anything else in her life, as though they are cordoned-off crime scenes. Her encounters with him all occur within internal spaces: at his office on East Sixty-first Street, at the Morgan Library, in the back seat of taxis, in a bar where they meet in clandestine fashion. Next, she drifts into a reverie about her childhood home, replete with small, visceral details: "the skimpy parlor of her childhood, her father and a friend speaking late into the evening while she lay drowsily on the Victorian sofa" (Fox [1970] 2003: 117). These still, tranquil visions of internal life contrast with her apocalyptic fears of the potential horror which had previously been limited to the outside world, but had now infiltrated her various inner sanctums.

Tamara K. Hareven and Randolph Langenbach (1981) write that particular components of the built environment can provide a continuity that the rest of the cityscape lacks. When one's way of life has been swept away, buildings for example are one of the few tangible remnants which "survive as silent witnesses" (114). The desire for such buildings to remain standing is not, they argue, synonymous with a wish "to return to the old days." Rather, it represents a wish that the memory of a life once known "should not be unhinged from reality through the destruction of the principal elements of its setting." Where Sophie's sentimentality about buildings, objects, and locations is more akin to the localized homesickness described by Marshall Berman, Otto's nostalgia is for a period of time that now lies behind him.

Further infiltrations of the outside into the inside world occur in the second half of the novel. The first comes in the form of a Black man wishing to enter the house and use their telephone. The doorbell rings and the Bentwoods are frozen, expecting only bad things to come from the outside world desiring entry. "How apprehensive they both were," thinks Sophie, "like people waiting for bad news" (Fox [1970] 2003: 98) (a response which neatly summarizes their behavior throughout the course of the novel). Upon opening the door, they are greeted by a barrage of noise which extends its reach inside the house before the speaker himself crosses its threshold. "A man's voice rose and fell in accents of hysteria. Otto backed into view, followed by a young Negro man waving his hands." Otto allows the stranger inside. The emotional immediacy of this first encounter exceeds that of any other thus far in the novel bar the stray cat; for the first time the Bentwoods engage with a human being who dwells in the world just outside their back door. In *October Cities*, Carlo Rotella (1998) points out that a large component of the rhetoric of fear around urban decline was centered around race. "Although the list of contributing factors tends to be long and various," he explains, "the widely recognized urban crisis of the 1960s [...] was and is constructed as fundamentally a matter of violent racial conflict" (215). The postwar transformation of cities was configured around "a parallel set of physical reconfigurations and ethnic successions," with the convergence of many conflicts occurring alongside the ethnographic transformation galvanized by "the absolute and relative growth of black, Hispanic, and (later) Asian populations to remake the city's social landscape" (218). As Robert Beauregard (1993) notes, during the postwar years of urban decline through to the early 1970s, there emerged "a single theme that unified its various fragments" (169). That theme was race, and the response was "one of fear and eventually panic." The encounter here between the Bentwoods and the stranger is harmless, despite the emphasis on his "hysteria" and the kinetic energy expressed by his wildly waving hands. The outsider departs, leaving nothing but knee-jerk expectations in his wake: "Robbery and murder appeared before her in two short scenes" (Fox [1970] 2003: 98). The narratives around urban decline, Rotella argues, frequently coalesced around the issue of race, in order to "reduce the complexity of urban transformation to sharply representable and narratable form" (1998: 215). This took the form of "racially coded violence," such as, for example, the "figure of 'the mugger'" which since the 1960s has been "implicitly assumed to be black or Hispanic" (215).

The second intrusion is the nightmare of invasion fully realized. Upon visiting their country home in Queens, they find objects broken, strewn about and disturbed, and personal items mishandled and out of context: "lamps broken, the Paisley fabric of the couch cover torn into strips, cushions gutted, and over every painting or photograph a giant X had been drawn with barn paint" (Fox [1970] 2003: 130). Otto takes this act of vandalism, and the muted reaction of the caretaker and his family, as a directive that he himself is unwanted and unnecessary: "'it all said one thing to me. It said, *die*'" (140). Despite her declaration to Otto that it was "*just furniture*," (139) Sophie mourns the loss of her things, defining herself as a collector: "She went into the living room and looked around the bare walls. All the sweet, pretty things were gone, things she had found in junk shops or picked off the ground, or bought in antique stores" (140). For Sophie, such objects create a sense of permanence, a connection to the past even if this is someone else's past, acquired at a second-hand remove. Strangers having infiltrated her home are a rather ironic extension of that ethos—there is no explicit, innate sense of territory or ownership that defines it as specifically theirs outside of the power of money to buy components of their surrounding landscape. Note Otto's purchase of the barn beyond their purview in order to further control and own his environment, and his construction around the farmhouse of "a low picket fence, not because they had close neighbors, but because he had been compelled by his sense of order to distinguish between what belonged immediately to the house and what belonged to the open fields" (128). Similarly, there are no objects within the house that did not originate through purchase by other peoples' hands. Thus its occupation by outsiders is not so much a frightening sign of inexplicable modern times, but a continuation of this cycle of colonization and displacement. This time it is the Bentwoods who have been displaced, with talk of the occupation of other spaces in Flynders by other unfamiliar parties compounding the sense of its inevitability: "One couple—you wouldn't believe it—they lived in someone's old barn for two months before we spotted them" (137). Much like Didion, who writes in "Slouching Towards Bethlehem" of spaces inhabited by peripatetic youths in the San Francisco of the late 1960s, Fox here is articulating the encroachment by "outsiders" upon spaces both urban (back in the downtown Brooklyn of the Bentwood's primary abode) and pre-urban (the amorphous Flynders farmland). The Bentwoods see themselves as victims of a kind of misalignment—unwanted elements are invading their territory on both fronts in insidious and explicit ways, making them strangers in their own homes—but do not consider that they themselves, as active participants in this cycle of ownership and exile, are also invaders (some would call them "pioneers" - a loaded word which I unpack later in this chapter).

The outside world has infiltrated this rarefied inner sanctum through the *perception* of threat, its potential not yet realized, but felt as intensely as an imminent act: "'I had some morbid image,' she said. 'I thought they might have been here, too.' 'Not yet,' he said" (143). Her neighbors seem to move closer and closer toward her own space, until a mere look from across the street feels like a violation. Everything has become a fatalistic portent of future doom ("Was it the phone call she was afraid of? Or was it that she knew she would refuse those inoculations?" (151)), to the point where she too is a signifier, a carrier in fact, of this same decline. Sophie herself has become subsumed inside the external maelstrom; the ultimate manifestation of the collision between internal and external worlds. "*God, if I am rabid*" she thinks, "*I am equal to what is outside*." She sees, suddenly, that the world around her is under siege; that all of her efforts, and those of other neighborhood preservationists, have been a mere cosmetic enhancement, having no permanence whatsoever. All that is solid does indeed melt into air in Sophie's estimation; her world is transient, and bordered by lines increasingly translucent and unstable.

The Walls Weren't Really Solid: *A Meaningful Life*

In *A Meaningful Life*, Lowell Lake also experiences a domestic crisis, though his is far more literal than the existential devastation wrought upon the Bentwoods. When he first arrives in New York, he settles for a time in Manhattan, and does so as though having sunk placidly into a state of unconsciousness: "He couldn't remember anything but highways and tunnels. He felt like a man emerging from some kind of coma" (Davis [1971] 2009: 54). During this period, Lake's already vacuous persona further diminishes. His memory becomes increasingly faulty to the point where he cannot remember growing the mustache that protrudes from his face: "I think you grew it in 1967," his wife Betty offers, "'Sometime around there'" (70). His wife, "Betty from Flatbush," is originally from Brooklyn and so for her this is a return home (13). Visiting his in-laws in Flatbush, Lake is given a somewhat compacted history lesson about the flow and flux of other Brooklyn residents: "our people moved out of that neighbourhood 20 years ago," says his wife's mother, as though accusing him of going backward in time when others had worked to leave such places behind (as Betty Smith illustrates) (158). A decrepit next-door neighbor bemoans the state of the neighborhood compared to its former glory, longing for the way things used to be "40 years ago" (171). Significantly, Lake appears to have lost one of the few attributes he had as a child: "He did well in school, largely because he had an excellent memory" (8). The failure of Lake's memory and the absence of identity are of a piece with his sudden desire to grapple with "real life and the significant issues of our time" by moving to Brooklyn (87). The absence in Lake of what David Lowenthal (1985) describes as "Self-continuity" is caused by his lack of recall (1985: 197). In place of this it seems a sense of historical authenticity is best conferred by his proximity to the "stage set of historic buildings" that Brooklyn becomes for him (Zukin [2009] 2010: 6). His lack of personal history could perhaps be rectified by gaining possession of a greater sense of place, with the historical significance of that place made obvious by the buildings in the neighborhood he moves to.

Lake's nostalgia and sense of the past is more a vicarious experience of the "cultural mourning" (as also experienced by the Bentwoods) than an authentic one (Rubenstein 2001: 5). He yearns for a period of time he never experienced himself, choosing to replicate and re-live this experience through the piecing back together of *signs* of the past in the form of his dilapidated brownstone and the semblance of antiquity therein. In *Dwelling in the Text*, Marilyn R. Chandler (1991) outlines the prominence of domestic space in many American novels: "In a country whose history has been focused for so long on the business of resettlement and 'development,' the issue of how to stake out territory, clear it, cultivate it, and build on it has been of major economic, political, and psychological consequence" (1). This aligns with what Richard Slotkin (1973) describes as the American "'myth of the frontier'—the conception of America as a wide-open land of unlimited opportunity for the strong, ambitious, self-reliant individual to thrust his way to the top" (5). The building and maintenance of a home on such a landscape is therefore both a "kind of autobiographical enterprise—a visible and concrete means of defining and articulating the self" (Chandler 1991: 3), and a continuation of a national narrative (or "mythogenesis" as Slotkin would define it (1973: 4)). Like Sophie Bentwood, Lake seeks to define himself through his property and the relics within. However, in his case, the property says nothing of autobiography, only biography—that of another man, not Lake himself, who remains a cipher. Having decided to buy the building he had originally sworn off, Lake becomes fixated with its original owner, Darius Collingwood, "foremost corporation lawyer in the Northeastern United States" (Davis [1971] 2009: 101). It is his (invented) history of which Lake is so enamored ("'Bankrupt at nineteen. A colonel at twenty-three. A part of history'" (130)) and the sense that, through his ownership of Collingwood's house, Lake can access and become part of that historical significance.

Late in the novel, Lake meets Mr. Warsaw, a man who is just as obsessed as our protagonist with identifying himself as a kind of facsimile of a history beyond and before his own life. Warsaw perfectly encapsulates the myopia and obsession that form the archetypal qualities of a brownstone acolyte. The narration of his domestic accoutrements speaks to the notion of their bearing witness to a history that somehow transfers to *him*, making him more significant and impressive by association: "'No one else had bought in the neighbourhood when we arrived. We were the first. Our house was built in 1873. The Pouch family owned it. Some of the original furniture was still in the basement.' 'That's interesting,' said Lowell. 'Our place was built by Darius Collingwood'" (180). The so-called "clock stoppers" (Biddle 1974: 2) like Lake and Warsaw are searching for a "timeless city that never changes" (Zukin [2009] 2010: 29).

In thrall to the urges of gentrification, upon first arriving in Brooklyn, Lake sees himself as one of the original adventurers into unknown territory, part of a new group of "Creative young people [...] buying houses in the Brooklyn slums, integrating all-Negro blocks" (Davis [1971] 2009: 87). Lake finds himself caught between approximating a history that is long gone and denying his own part in the defacement of the more-recent past. He frets that he has not met the right sort of people that would corroborate his vision of the neighborhood. Instead he has met "a substantial number of Negroes and Puerto Ricans" but they, of course, cannot possibly represent a "reasonable cross-section of this or any other neighborhood" and so do not count (178). The name of this neighborhood is Fort Greene , "a largely African American and actively industrial area near Downtown Brooklyn" (Stein 2019: 128). In *There Goes the Hood*, Lance Freeman explains that this neighborhood is known as alternately Fort Greene and Clinton Hill, with the two names often used interchangeably: "In the past, the area known as Clinton Hill was considered part of a larger neighbourhood known as Fort Greene. Indeed, to this day many residents still consider the neighborhood to be part of Fort Greene" (2006: 34). Neighborhood boundaries shift and vacillate through time; particularly when it comes to their real estate desirability or lack therefore (much like the South Bronx, as detailed in Chapter 3). People of color had been present in Fort Greene since its inception, and by 1860 "approximately half of Brooklyn's black population lived in the Fort Greene area" (38). By the middle of the twentieth century, this neighborhood had become "a predominantly black community," albeit because Black people who had joined the great migration from the South (and from the Caribbean) to Northern cities "were typically relegated by housing discrimination to marginal and declining neighbourhoods" (38). During the mid-twentieth century, Brooklyn became second only to Harlem in terms of desirable neighborhoods in which Black people wished to settle in New York, living "mostly along the axis at Fulton Street and Atlantic Avenue stretching from the downtown and Fort Greene areas through Bedford and Stuyvesant and into Brownsville and East New York" (38).

Instead of living in this reality, Lake dreams instead of Darius Collingwood (who, it transpires, only lived in the Lake abode for six months), thumbing through his antique memoirs until its pages crumble into "a pile of brittle brown flakes that got smaller and smaller the more you handled them" (Davis [1971] 2009: 167) (recalling the "flakes of paint fallen on to his desk [. . .] broken, meaningless messages" that Paul Cattleman's historical research becomes (Lurie [1965] 1994: 156)). What little is left of these autobiographical boastings is kept in a safe-deposit box alongside Lake's birth certificate (or the replica thereof), as though the two are as interchangeable a part of his identity as the other items in the box: "his lease, his deed, and five canceled bankbooks" (Davis [1971] 2009: 167–8). He longs to have as much meaning and longevity as this place gives him by association: "'I bought the old Collingwood place out in Brooklyn,' he told people when they asked him what he was doing with himself these days," a phrase which is paraphrased and repeated throughout the novel in a tone that modulates from pride to desperation (164).

In first laying claim to this territory, Lake is aiming to forge some kind of integrated persona for himself amid the fragments. He will now be a hero of the venerable city, rather than a pathetic interloper in a foreign land with which he has no history: "In his mind's eye he saw himself striding down the littered streets [. . .] exciting the envy of his colleagues in Manhattan because of all the rooms he owned" (87). Because, of course, the space he has purchased is already inhabited, the question of how real or lasting his occupation and his new-found identity can be, remains. With no prior relationship with the place, he has as little connection to Brooklyn as he had to Manhattan. He sees himself as a kind of frontiersman, and in many ways he is—expressly because he is following in the footsteps of other so-called American "pioneers" of old (like the "brave pioneer from Wall Street" who becomes the Bentwoods' neighbor (Fox ([1970] 2003: 5)) by attempting to colonize a land that is already occupied. Arguably the Californian pioneers about whom Joan Didion writes are the antecedents of the Brooklyn gentrifiers portrayed by Davis and Fox. The word "pioneer" is frequently deployed to describe various members of the new brownstone generation, making the movement another iteration of the early settlers' crossing story and their decision to "Go West" (Lurie [1964] 1994: 11). In his 1982 article for *Dissent*, "Gentrification: Towards a New Apartheid?" Jim Sleeper describes a block association meeting in which the hostess calls one of the young professionals who has lived on the block in question for ten years "'one of the pioneers!' —in front of some older Italians who've been raising their kids on these stoops since the 1930s" (1982: 1). Jim Stratton (1977) notes the parallels between the frontiersmen and 1970s gentrifiers: "From the moment the earliest settlers learned they could profit by evicting the present tenants and replacing the old housing stock with log cabins the New World was locked on a course of Out with the Old, Up with the New" (7). Samuel Stein (2019) explicitly traces the brutal history of "manifest destiny" to its most recent incarnation within the exploitative real-estate market, which only spreads wealth in one direction by removing it from people of color (36). Lake casts himself in the mold of those who, as Richard Slotkin describes, defined national character and aspiration "in terms of so many bears destroyed, so much land pre-empted, so many trees hacked down, so many Indians and Mexicans dead in the dust" (1973: 5).[7] For Lake this is not so much a question of taking advantage of market forces as it is about the myopic search for *authenticity*.

Lake possesses only an imaginary history with this new space: "Actually, the thing about the street was that there was nothing strange about it at all: with its tall trees and old houses of brick and clapboard, it was the kind of street he'd grown up expecting he would live on" (Davis [1971] 2009: 94). In *The City in Literature*, Richard Lehan (1967) contends that we encounter the city in our imagination, thanks mostly to the reproductions of art and literature, long before we encounter it in person. Thus, an alternative reality is constructed in our minds before we physically stand before it. This is a narrative created in anticipation, as opposed to in retrospect, and this personal, subjective realm of the imagination can be a form of escape, allowing us to shut out "the urban, commercial, and industrial world that ha[s] become hostile. Under such pressure the city as a physical place [gives] way to the city as a state of mind" (76). In similar terms, Davis writes that Lake is seeing the street in terms of "ambience instead of objects, interspersed with brief, vivid glances of things he really wanted to see, like bark and brickwork and turrets with sharp conical roofs" ([1971] 2009: 94–5). Lake wants to see the past he expects, and so he looks past everything that does not conform to this expectation.

The schism between the imagined and the real that Lehan describes, and which Lake articulates, encourages artificiality. The "reality" of the neighborhood is contrived through the distortions of Lake's desires, rather than discovered and exactly reproduced. This act, according to Lehan, changes one's understanding of the city from a place experienced from the *outside in*, to one experienced from the *inside out*—from the objective (based on collective history) to the subjective (based on individual memory). Lehan writes that the favoring of inner reality in narrative form means that the outer reality of the world beyond this perspective becomes opaque, and that how one chooses to exert one's power of perspective—from the outside in or the inside out—can be defined as a "parallax view. When we focus on the foreground, the background become vague; when we focus on the background, the foreground blurs" (1967: 80). In the same way, subjective memory (internal) is ignored when objective history (external) is focused upon and vice versa. In Lake's case, a certain nostalgia for an imagined history clouds his vision.

Lake allows for palatable signs of the past as he walks along Clinton Avenue to Lafayette; streets which are, he observes, "lined with tall old trees, real country trees" with roots which "had tumbled the sidewalks and cracked the curbing," and bordered by brick structures "dating from the last century" (Davis [1971] 2009: 93, 91). But the presence of people of color, also entrenched in the neighborhood alongside its bucolic aspects, is conversely something to turn a blind eye to, or actively avoid. His wife sees their existence as a sign of the undesirability of the neighborhood ("In Brooklyn there's only one place where colored people are, and when you see a lot of them standing around, you know that's where you are too. Let's go" (92)), while Lake attempts to ignore them in favor of a whitewashed nostalgic perspective, through the fog of which he only vaguely discerns both his wife and neighbors as diversions from his parallax view: "It was the same way, distracted by his wife and Negroes, that he was seeing things now" (94). Lake does not wish to acknowledge any kind of historical Black presence, despite the empirical reality of the Fort Greene neighborhood, seeing only his own hermetically sealed (and invented) homogenous history projected outwards: "the kind of street everyone lived on when he was a kid" (94).

The first building that the Lakes examine in the neighborhood is the real-estate office, which, characteristically for a novel about deconstruction, is part of a larger structure itself "in the process of being either torn down or repaired" (95). The office is missing half its cornice, all of its upper windows are broken, and many of the other rooms in the building are "filled with bags of garbage and broken television sets." Every aspect of the building in which the real-estate office is housed is in the process of falling apart and overflowing with the remains of former lives like some Baudelairean vision of a rag-picker's paradise. Like the street on which the Bentwoods live, the vicinity of the real-estate office in *A Meaningful Life* is surrounded by the spoils of uncollected trash, with "several burst bags of garbage stacked up in the lee of the stoop, along with the remains of a pair of tubular kitchen chairs and a V-8 engine block" (95). Despite signs of life in the form of its remains and refuse, the simultaneous barrenness of the sidewalks leads them to assume a sinister character. Much like the destroyed environs of Berman's Bronx haunts and the eerie sense of lack in Waldie's childhood home, here an anxiousness abounds: "it was the kind of emptiness that suggested if someone else was moving in it too, he probably didn't mean you well," to which the shattered glass, busted storefronts, and scorched buildings are testament (120). It is a "thief's emptiness," suggesting something that was once present has been forcibly absented, unnaturally stripped of life; uncanny, even. Like the pre-urban, somewhat wild, landscape of the world beyond the border provided by the freeways of Los Angeles, as portrayed by Chandler, Lurie, and Didion, external, public spaces in Brooklyn are "low and all spread out and unconfined" (121). Space here is uncontained and uncontrollable, making Lake (like Marlowe when placed in the great outdoors) feel indistinct, "small and infinitely fragile" within its boundless territory.

The Lakes proceed along Washington Avenue, the real-estate man regaling them with the history of the neighborhood. He tells them that it "slummed up after the war [. . .] Before that it was by far the most fashionable part of Brooklyn, and only millionaires could afford to live in it" (99). According to *Brooklyn By Name* (2006), the neighborhood of Fort Greene through which they now pass was nicknamed Brooklyn's Gold Coast; thanks to its "large villas and leafy boulevards, the area was once populated by a number of Brooklyn's prominent captains of industry" (2006: 76). By the middle of the nineteenth century, Fort Greene had grown rapidly, thanks in part to the development of the Brooklyn Navy Yard at the beginning of the century. Early on, the neighborhood was "an electric mix of stately mansions and broad streets interspersed with pockets of run-down housing, immigrants, and a sprinkling of blacks," but as the nineteenth century bled into the twentieth, it's attraction for New York's elite wore thin, and by the 1930s "there was strong evidence of Fort Greene's decline" (36, 37) which only deepened during the 1960s and early 1970s.

Here, again, we find Robert Moses implicated. In 1954, during the first decade of the postwar urban renewal project, a five-block area of Fort Greene/Clinton Hill was declared "suitable for clearance and renewal" by the Slum Clearance Committee (Davis 1970: 39). L. J. Davis, wearing his reporter's hat, interviews Ralph Steinhauer, who had managed an art supply store in the area since 1946: "'It was ridiculous to call this place a slum before they showed up,' [. . .] 'But they did their damnedest to turn it into one.'" Between 1954 and 1963, when five large income cooperatives were finally erected on the site, the neighborhood slid into a desperate decline; some houses were demolished, some stood empty, and some were converted into rooming houses. In a 1958 *New York Times* article titled "Brooklyn Slums Shock Officials," journalist Ira Henry Freeman outlines this decline: "Fifty years ago this row at 123 to 129 Lafayette Avenue had been proper, private one-family homes with the high stoops and English basements of the period. Today the mortar is crumbling from the outside walls and the plaster on the interior is in large part destroyed. Nearly every window is broken, the frames being boarded over with scrap wood or cardboard" (31). The area had been successfully "slummed up" (Davis [1971] 2009: 99), setting the scene for Lowell Lake's entry onto a sparsely populated stage.

In the early years of the 1970s, this part of Brooklyn became "the site of some of the earliest gentrifying activity" (Freeman 2006: 40). Lance Freeman writes that by 1973, Fort Greene/Clinton Hill was being described as "a 'revival neighbourhood,' a place where 'brownstoners' and renovators sought out homes to be rehabilitated." In 1974, the *Home-Buyer's Guide to New York City Brownstone Neighborhoods* writes that in this neighborhood: "New families have bought rooming houses and converted them without the scary experience of the pioneers in some other neighborhoods" (*Home-Buyer's Guide* 1974: 17). However, its gentrification "did not occur in a continuous and steady fashion. The same article that described Clinton Hill as a revival neighborhood also pointed out there were no 'especially good streets,' rather the 'brownstoners were scattered throughout the neighborhood'" (Freeman 2006: 41). The random vacillations of neighborhood real estate are not kind to Lake. He is informed toward the end of the novel by the (still nameless) real-estate man that he happened to buy on a block that is "going down" as though literally descending into a subterranean hell ([1971] 2009: 193).

When at last the Lakes come to it, the Collingwood edifice (soon to become Lake's home) is a charismatic place, replete with "wrought-iron railing," "ornamental brickwork," "wide brownstone steps," and "thick brownstone columns that supported a kind of porch or miniature fortress" (101). Lake is, of course, immediately struck by a "powerful subconscious craving that defied analysis" because he is using the house as a means of defining and aligning himself with history (100). The agent exhorts them not to look upon the wreckage of the street, but to instead imagine the possibility of the houses which demand only a modicum of repair to restore them to their former glory. Here we find again the juxtaposition of seeing and imagining, of ignoring the present and superimposing an image of the past. The townhouse of Lake's particular dream was built between 1800 and 1885 and made of various materials including the all-important brownstone, placing him definitively in the brownstoner camp.

The inside of the townhouse beloved by Lake tells a different story to its handsome exterior. The 1974 *Home-Buyer's Guide to New York City Brownstone Neighborhoods* airily reports that in Fort Greene/Clinton Hill, "a rooming-house population has been displaced," but only in a "mild and gradual way" of course (*Home-Buyer's Guide* 1974: 17). These are terms which *A Meaningful Life* belies. The first sign that the Lakes are unwanted interlopers (or neo-pioneers) comes in the form of Henry Gruen, part-curmudgeonly-caretaker, part-unwilling-gatekeeper, who refuses at first to let them cross the threshold. The interiors of the house, once they are able to view them, demonstrate that this is a space in a state of total disrepair. Not only is the entire Collingwood building already occupied (fulfilling, in fact, its original purpose as a rooming house), but the walls and floor are filthy, the stench of water damage fills the air, and every surface bristles with "a gray fur of dust and soot" (Davis [1971] 2009: 104). The house itself seems uncannily sentient; populated by others who are mostly perceived but not seen, and with doors opening and closing of their own accord: "It was sort of like being in a haunted house, except that the house wasn't haunted, it was inhabited" (138).

Inside, Puerto Rican and Black tenants dwell in every room, all living in cramped, often unsanitary conditions within spaces that have been compartmentalized and subdivided to within an inch of their lives: "'Probably there was a door in that wall,' said the real-estate man, 'connecting this room with the one we were just in. Actually, this place hasn't been cut up as badly as some'" (109). This description recalls both Betty Smith's account of brownstone houses being "hacked up into flats" ([1943] 1974: 1) back in 1912, and Rem Koolhaas' dissection of juxtaposed external versus internal realities in *Delirious New York*, in which he contends that the internal world of buildings "hides everyday life," asserting that while architectural interiors contain the individual and the irrational, this is masked by the façade of the exterior, which turns its implacable face to the world outside ([1978] 1994: 101). Each room in Lake's brownstone acts as the set of a whole microcosmic world; a series of rooms within rooms revealed like Russian dolls and echoing the subdivision of internal spaces in Raymond Chandler's novels. There are twenty-one (and counting) rooms: a "sewing room," a "master bedroom," a "ten foot tall" turret room the size of a barrel, a series of "little rooms incredibly close together, clustered around a central foyer" that formerly acted as "servants' quarters," and the subterranean space that houses the furnace is also home to one Mrs. Blouse and several small children (Davis [1971] 2009: 108, 111, 112, 113). The interiors (like those of Waldie's Lakewood home) are flimsy and near-decomposed, so insubstantial as to melt into one another. Lake is under the impression that "the walls weren't really solid but composed of some substance that would yield and engulf anyone unwary enough to lean on them" (115). Space here is both segmented *and* somehow infinitely *open*. Tenants are happened upon as though by accident within their own homes, sometimes barely discernible in such indistinct spaces: "At the table was sitting a small brown man. For some reason [. . .] Lowell had failed to notice him before. [. . .] Next door was another sewing room. It was darker than Henry's place, smelled powerfully of cigars, and was occupied by a crone who remained in the shadows, her presence barely visible but powerfully felt" (106–12).

Such visits expose the tenants in various states of being, like a collection of still life portraits that are literally still: "Upstairs in the largest room a family of Puerto Ricans was eating supper at a big, plastic-looking table; they became utterly motionless the moment the real-estate man and his little party trooped in" (112). Accumulated objects represent the stuff of lives, interrupted. Henry Gruen's dwelling is full of wreckage, as though demonstrating its existence as a petrified ruin in need of excavation. Scores of newspaper cuttings line the room, coalescing with other similar items such as "rags," "scraps of old bed sheets," "squares of Woolworth oilcloth," and "cheap lace curtains" (109) akin to the rags, sheets of plastic and blankets that hang from the windows of the houses opposite the Bentwoods' home ("Across the yard, past the cat's agitated movements, he saw the rear windows of the houses on the slum street. Some windows had rags tacked to them, others, sheets of transparent plastic" (Fox [1970] 2003: 4)). The sense of multiple histories pervades the entire Collingwood estate and Henry's room specifically; the story of each covered window is "separate and distinct," the layers of each covering "never completely overlapping" (Davis [1971] 2009: 109). Other histories are present here, just about visible, though faded, dispersed, ragged, palimpsestic.

Lake and his wife spend their days removing the layers of the past with which the house is thickly lined: "Lowell couldn't guess how many more layers there were, each one cleaner than the last; they seemed to go down for inches more" (129). With much gleeful abandon he starts "demolishing," "ripping" and "obliterating" all remnants of "his impoverished predecessors," (133) continuing in the same vein by ridding the building of its preexisting tenants, completely ignorant and unsympathetic to the reasons for their refusal to leave. Writing about *Desperate Characters*, Alexandra Schwartz asserts that

Brooklyn's wealthy residents, like the Bentwoods and the Holsteins "think of their improved homes as an outward sign of inward virtue," a criticism that can be extended here to Lake. "They don't bother to notice the resigned dread of the poor they are busy displacing" (2017: n.p.). Lake's life at last has meaning, but it is bestowed upon him through the destruction of the lives of others both past and present.

Gradually, as the tenants move out, Lake is left with the "vacated apartment" to take apart room by room as though engaged in "smashing someone else's dishes for no good reason," an analogy which reinforces the sense of wrongfully acquired ownership (Davis [1971] 2009: 140). "The people had to go just the same as the partitions before Lowell could start putting things back the way they belonged, and that was that," he declares, before painstakingly dismantling every artifact that might testify to a history that he does not wish to acknowledge: "'My bed,' said the old man [. . .] 'My cabnit. My chester draws.' 'They're all downstairs,' repeated Lowell in a loud, firm voice. 'They're downstairs by the garbage cans. Help yourself'" (136). But the former occupants of the former boarding house cannot all be "as it were, plastered over" (Peacock 2015: 135). Signs of the past persist despite Lake's best efforts: "the person who had occupied this room, alone of all the dozens of people who had occupied this house, had kept his window clean both inside and out" (Davis [1971] 2009: 164). Lake is constantly reminded of those who had called the now-skeletal remains of the building home in previous years.

The return of the repressed past occurs one small uncanny instance at a time, associated here with the inherent danger of open spaces. The folly of an unlocked door or window, also expressed in Chandler's novels and in *Desperate Characters*, recurs. In the latter, there is an almost ritualistic closing and locking of doors, particularly at the very beginning and the very end of the novel. When Sophie is bitten by the cat, it is a result of her failure to seclude herself safely inside her home. Fox writes this scene with a sense of inevitability, as though this was a long-anticipated event: "I can't unlock the door again, she said to herself. 'It's done,' Otto said. He sighed. 'Done, at last'" (Fox [1970] 2003: 8). This is reversed and repeated toward the end of the novel when the cat is caught and Otto curses the rigmarole of unlocking the door: "the elaborate sequence of steps needed to unlock the door—hook, key, insert, reach, turn again" (94). In *A Meaningful Life*, first, this danger is applicable to others ("'The door was open,' he remarked gruffly, assuming an expression that he hoped would intimidate the old man" (Davis [1971] 2009: 135)) and later, to himself ("'Leave the door open,' said his visitor with obvious exasperation and contempt. 'I wouldn't leave the door open'" (178)), until the open door of his own home provides access to real horror: "The front door was standing wide open [...] Minutes passed. Then, with a stumble and a wheeze, a shadow of a man appeared in the doorway" (199).

Approaching the novel's conclusion, the landscape of Lake's neighborhood sinks further into the glut of decline. The surrounding streets show frequent signs of human life outside (albeit not the kind of human life that Lake wishes to see, being mostly Black and poor), but are peppered with blasted buildings, the interiors of which are home to broken windows, unhinged doors, and unfurnished living rooms. Lake's house, now emptied out of all internal domestic paraphernalia, appears to him as a huge, formless mass that incubates the same sense of potential threat inside as the open expanse of Brooklyn streets outside: "the house took on the devastated look of the streets, as if it had been attacked, not recently but months ago, by a squad of compulsively tidy commando assassins" (190). Its vacuity is disturbing, and the signs of its former life that persist speak to yet another past having been rubbed not-quite-clean off the walls. Lake notes the "jagged outlines," "heads of pipes," "holes [...] scattered here and there" that are all that remain of his inept attempts at restoration. The house now stands vulnerable and open to the outside world.

"The house," writes Marilyn Chandler, "is frequently treated as a schematic reiteration of the character of the central figure in a story" (1991: 10). The Brooklyn house, acting as Lake's double or mirror, must also be cleaned of any signs of an unwanted narrative. By the end of *A Meaningful Life*, Lake's brownstone looks "ready to be demolished" along with the rest of the disintegrating block (Davis [1971] 2009: 190). In the dying days of his residence in Brooklyn, Lake sees hideous visions of carnage in the buildings around him. In a series of strange (and, later, murderous) events, heralded by the sudden disappearance of the old ladies next door, Lake experiences an existential crisis of material and immaterial selfhood. Upon returning to his West Side apartment block, the place looks at first glance to have been looted and robbed, but it turns out that the only thing missing is him; he has been erased: "Not a single one of his belongings was anywhere to be seen [...] not a single one of the discards, nor the tiniest scrap of debris, bore the unique and recognizable stamp of his personality" (209). Much like the recollections of Maria Wyeth, the Sternwoods and D. J. Waldie, who piece together a narrative by redacting certain aspects, Lake's story has become increasingly porous and subject to excision. The apartment has been excised of any mark of his existence, just as the brownstone albatross has been emptied out. His very identity seems subject to the same decline as the Brooklyn house, so complete is his psychological alignment with its well-being. Ultimately Lake turns into a kind of Potemkin human, nothing more than a smooth external façade that provides a screen for absence.

As though complicit in his wish for eradication, this house has also rid itself of all signs of the fatal struggle between Lake and an unknown assailant (the mysterious man who appears in the doorway). Lake is removed from his murderous actions, his conscious knowledge of exactly what he is doing depicted as a murky, unknowable prospect: "Meanwhile his body continued down the stairs in his shoes, and every time he woke up, he found himself on a lower step" (199). Like Carmen Sternwood, he sinks into a state of amnesia when performing such sordid tasks that would ordinarily prove impossible, unthinkable. When disposing of the body, he finds himself "in the middle of a thought that he couldn't remember having" (200), he makes use of tools to do so which then disappear ("he was in the backyard, pouring water over himself from a bucket [. . .] There was no sign of the bucket"), and he goes through the motions of the entire ordeal as though in a dream replete with irrational time-lapses. In a moment reminiscent of Philip Marlowe recounting his story to the police in *The Big Sleep*, Lake verbalizes his sense of dislocation: "Lowell perceived the events of the next hour in an odd way, sort of like a movie from which big hunks had been edited, totally at random." The garbage pan into which Lake deposits the dead body is gone, plaster has replaced blood spatter, and holes have replaced gore until "all trace of the deed had vanished" (214).[8] It has been purged in an orgy of destruction seemingly without purpose or end, the entire place gutted until even items of genuine historical significance are removed: "Mr. Busterboy and his men also broke a number of windows and accidentally dismantled, smashed up, and threw out one of the irreplaceable parlor fireplaces" (212). In an article titled "You Can Have Your Brownstone . . . And Rent It, Too" published in 1974 in *The Brownstoner*, the author remarks that the "creation of apartments and public halls can cost a lot in lost brownstone charm. But you can save the charm. It's just that there's a lot of work involved, a lot of supervision—as in any renovation" ("You Can Have" 1974: 6). A similar article listing tips for brownstone hunters exhorts readers not to "be too hasty with that crowbar" ("Special Report" n.d.: 5). Setting such advice against the increasing hysteria of Lake's renovations seems to make the sagacity of *The Brownstoner* likewise delusional; saving "the charm" of this brownstone seems entirely beside the point by the time we reach the novel's bitter end.

Freud writes in "The Uncanny" of houses which are no longer comforting vestibules for family life, enclosing the domestic sphere within a warm brick grasp, but have instead become places from which one feels estranged and inside which one feels anxious. The term represents what had been secret, private, coming at last "into the open" ([1919] 2003: 132). Freud articulates a series of closed, impenetrable private spaces having been perforated and opened out, rendered transparent and exposed to public view (outlined previously with regard to Marshall Berman's descriptions of the uncanny nature of open spaces). Likewise, in Lake's Collingwood home, borders and partitions are eliminated completely, the house now so internally nebulous that it gapes with a dangerously infinite space: "They made enormous holes in the walls and ceiling, and you had to be extremely careful where you walked to avoid falling suddenly into the room directly below" (Davis [1971] 2009: 212). Stripped of its layers it is now characterized by a sense of pristine novelty, full of "fresh plaster and newly sawed wood," but bereft of meaning (213). It does not belong to Lake, does not bear the "mark of his hand"; so thorough was the job of Mr. Busterboy and his men that even *he* has been scrubbed from existence, just as he has attempted to scrub the existence of his domestic antecedents from the brownstone walls.[9] History (or what the city chooses to put on display with regard to its past) replaces with relentless efficiency that which does not fit within its remit.

In her examination of the living history museum, Colonial Williamsburg, Virginia, and its uncanny replication of a former reality, Ada Louise Huxtable (1997) describes the process of restoration as "a difficult and unclear procedure at best; unreality is built into the process" (16). The same can be argued of the restoration committed by Lake, for whom a borrowed, regurgitated past is just as good as a real one. But this is of course problematic. Huxtable continues that to restore something back to some primordial form of itself means "re-creating a place as someone thinks it was" (recalling Richard Lehan's words regarding encountering the city first in one's imagination), a process which is likely to move or destroy anything that does not fit that expectation. The elimination of signs of the passing of time that filled the period between the point of origin and the present also represents the destruction of "exactly the stuff of which real history and art are made." In this way "the intrinsic qualities of the real are transformed and falsified by an experience that is itself the ultimate unreality" (17). In short, historical reproduction should not be equated with the genuine artifact of memory.

Judith N. DeSena and Timothy Shortell ([2012] 2014), in their study of gentrification in Greenpoint, Brooklyn, ascribe a similar ideology to gentrifiers as Huxtable does to preservationists, arguing that the former are more interested "in the aesthetic quality of the built environment and support the idea of historic preservation through restoration to original façade [. . .] there is more social status and economic value in places designated 'historic'" (80–1). In a 2018 article for the *New York Times Magazine*, Willy Staley looks at urban theorist Philip L. Clay's 1979 book, *Neighborhood Renewal*, in which the author outlines the four key stages of gentrification. Clay explains that first of all, "pioneers" arrive in a seemingly derelict neighborhood in search of cheaper rent; they are followed by the middle class, after which comes the displacement of "the original population" and after that arrives the wholesale ownership of the neighborhood by private interests such as banks, developers, and the very wealthy. Ironically, the original "pioneers" are at this stage also priced out, with many beginning the whole process again elsewhere (Staley 2018: n.p.).

Staley suggests that in its present-day incarnation, the most significant issue gentrification has produced is that of "cultural ownership," and the greatest harm it has caused was "something psychic, a theft of pride." It is the "perceived appropriation" of culture that is the most integral aspect of gentrification. He argues that the "flow of global capital," represented at its peak in a neighborhood by the final phase of Clay's four stages, results in an ironing out of its every crease. Similar to the "cartographic lie" (Waldie 2010b: n.p.) of the Los Angeles map now showing the "corrected" version of its streets downtown without the discordance of the original grid, this smoothing out of history so that it aligns with current expectations continues, asserts Staley, until the neighborhood in question is as "featureless as a river rock" (Staley 2018: n.p.). *A Meaningful Life* presents a world in which the restoration of history is privileged over the preservation of memory, as illustrated by Lowell Lake's obsessive pursuit of various external façades that speak to an *idea* of the past at the expense of the more chaotic, private, and insular spaces which typify the more nonconformist aspects of personal memory.

As previously recounted in Chapter 3, M. Christine Boyer contends that history commandeers the past, disrupting it so it appears in the present as "historical theatre" which "acts out" rather than lives "the past [. . .] slowly turning former events into an imaginary and fictional museum" ([1996] 2001: 67). Likewise, in *What Time Is This Place?* Kevin Lynch (1972) reasons that when a historical object is reconstructed, often it is the "ancient form" which is given precedence over the "old materials" (32). The external life of such an object, the obvious outlines of its *form* and structure, is considered of great import in terms of historical value and authenticity. Lionel Trilling suggests that we come to understand and quantify authenticity in the same way as curators seek to assign value to antiquities in a museum, "where persons expert in such matters test whether objects of art are what they appear to be or are claimed to be, and therefore worth the price that is asked for them" ([1971] 1972: 93). It can be extrapolated that according to the doctrine expressed by Lynch, "*only* the external historical shell need be preserved or reconstructed" (1972: 32 emphasis added), whereas its hidden internal life does not warrant such attention. Indeed, "internal physical modifications" are in fact "allowable." When he writes that "'Outsides' are public, historic, and regulated, while 'insides' are private, fluid, and free," Lynch is suggesting much the same thing as Boyer and Koolhaas. History—what is worth preserving—is presentable, visible, external. Memory—housed within the shell of that which is publicly preserved—is unregulated, obscure, internal.

By the end of *A Meaningful Life*, Lake is left to contemplate an existence as "blank and seamless" as the interiors of the house, a space now devoid of signs that time has passed through it. His future looks "much like his past," passing quickly and without much of significance to demarcate one year from the next (Davis [1971] 2009: 214). Shut up in his house, he pays little attention to the world outside. But beyond the blank walls, the street itself shows signs of continuing life: "From the street outside came the sound of laughter and shouting, bottles breaking, voices droning in the warm air, and children playing far past their bedtime." As in *Brown Girl, Brownstones*, instead of being contained in houses, life is here on the outside, on the street itself: "the roomers' tangled lives spilled out the open windows, and the staccato beat of Spanish voices, the frenzied sensuous music joined the warm canorous Negro sounds to glut the air" (Marshall [1959] 1982: 309). Having previously been a site of uncanny emptiness, the street is now a place of renewal. Lake may have failed to purchase himself a meaningful slice of history, but the street, representing the world beyond the walls of the brownstone, is able to internalize it.

Other Layers from Below

Early in *Brown Girl, Brownstones*, Selina surveys one "interminable Brooklyn street," and though she does not feel a sense of personal history, notes the presence of antiquity in material form: the touches of "Gothic, Romanesque, baroque or Greek" which "triumphed amid the Victorian clutter," an "Ionic column" here, a scowling gargoyle there, and cornices hung alternately with "carved foliage" and "Gorgon heads" scattered along the way (Marshall ([1959] 1982): 3–4). With its visible ties both to a colonial past and to the birth of the grid system, Brooklyn exhibits many "architectural and social imprints" in its built environment (Osman 2011: 22). Remnants "of past and present" lie on top of one another, "the sediment from each historic cityscape seeping into the others" (22–3). Likewise, Boyer contends that in what she calls *The City of Collective Memory*, we will find "different layers of historical time superimposed on each other" which will "culminate in an experience of diversity" ([1996] 2001: 19). In order to "read across and through different layers and strata of the city" city-dwellers must "establish a constant play between surface and deep structured forms, between purely visible and intuitive or evocative allusions" (21). Berman posits a literal translation of this advice when he suggests the construction of a Bronx Mural, but perhaps there are other ways to both see and read these different layers of the city's history. The experience of "diversity" which is generated from the spectacle of these myriad layers made visible in the cityscape, and indeed from the very perception of difference felt but not always seen, necessitates the interplay between that which is empirically visible, and that which is beneath the city's surface but is understood to exist through intuition and allusion—through memory.

For Francie Nolan, Brooklyn is "a magic city and it isn't real [...] It's mysterious here in Brooklyn. It's like—yes—-like a dream. The houses and streets don't seem real. Neither do the people" (Smith [1943] 1974: 306). The inference is that Brooklyn is a distant phantasmagoric vision; an intangible memory on the cusp of obscurity. In her 1985 Brooklyn-set novel *Mainland*, Susan Fromberg Schaeffer writes that "In the past, nothing ever changes. In Brooklyn, nothing does either. It's not so much a place as a vale of time" ([1985] 1986: 19). It is this ambivalent quality that has made Brooklyn sufficiently obscurely defined enough (see also its ambiguous neighborhood boundaries) to be, as Martha Nadell (2010) puts it, "both an old and a new country, and for some, a transitional place in between" (114).

Lynne Sharon Schwartz described New York in an interview with me as a *pentimento*, because, she said, "when you paint a picture, if you start scraping off the top layer, other layers from below start showing up" (2016: n.p.). Some layers are scoured so violently they are almost wholly erased, yet endure in a more ghostly form, haunting the canvas. The National Gallery defines the term *pentimento* as a change made by the artist in question during the course of painting: "These changes are usually hidden beneath a subsequent paint layer. In some instances, they become visible because the paint layer above has become *transparent with time*" ("Pentimento" n.d.: n.p. emphasis added). In the collection of oral histories from mid-twentieth-century Brooklyn residents, *It Happened in Brooklyn*, Karl Bernstein (who was the assistant principal at Meyer Levin Junior

High School, situated between East Flatbush and Kazin's Brownsville) expresses a clear alignment with this way of thinking about his city, and specifically here about Brooklyn: "I search the borough for my past. I drive past an abandoned building on Atlantic Avenue in East New York. Once it was the Borden Dairy Plant; now, all that remains are two beautiful mosaics of Heidi and the cows on a yellow-brick wall" (Frommer and Frommer 1993: 238). Here the palimpsest of endlessly overwritten texts becomes the pentimento, a more forgiving way of seeing the Brooklyn cityscape, allowing for the reemergence of the past over time, rather than its erasure. The past, in "tectonic" and material form, endures, though it may not map precisely and recognizably on top of memory (Osman 2011: 22). Houses and their occupants may change, but these changes signify something that is consistent in Brooklyn; some historical traces, slowly repeating and revealing themselves, do remain.

As Betty Smith suggests, if you do not wish to bear witness to the inevitability of change in a place which is fixed in memory if not in time, perhaps you should close your eyes to it: "If in the years to be she were to come back, her new eyes might make everything seem different from the way she saw it now. The way it was now was the way she wanted to remember it. No, she'd never come back to the old neighbourhood" ([1943] 1974: 363). The alternative is, perhaps, to wait for the past to become visible; to become transparent with time.

Conclusion

It was not long after I moved out of the house I had lived in with my family for more than twenty years that I visited the childhood home of my oldest friend. She had grown up there, remained until she went to university, and it was only after her mother had died that she went home less and less, finding it too difficult to spend time in a space so filled with now painful memories. I too had spent most of my time there after school (and at my grandmother's, in the same neighborhood) until I was twelve years old, as her mother would pick us both up while my parents worked. Her father finally sold the house when my friend was in her late twenties. He knew the couple who had bought and renovated it, and years later invited my friend and I to go and take a look. It proved to be a disquieting experience. My friend saw the swing-set which we had used as a launching pad to pull out all the flowers from the rhododendron bush opposite with our feet, and the kitchen table where her mum had sat us both down to explain why this had been a very bad idea, and where on other occasions we had sat and failed to do our homework together because we were giggling too much (her mum told us off all the time for that too). She saw the bedroom upstairs with the mirrored cupboards we had always thought were so glamorous, and the long velvety curtains in the living room downstairs that we used to hide behind, and the bathroom where we had acted out sketches in front of each other and where we always, always burned our hands on the too-hot towel rail. She saw the bedroom door that she had slammed so many times during arguments with her mum.

But the house itself did not show us these things. The swing-set had been removed and there was a greenhouse in place of the old shed which housed the giant mythical spider I was terrified of but never saw. The velvet curtains and the mirrored cupboards were no more; the kitchen table had been replaced; the bedroom door now closed on a study. Even the shape of the house was different, having been expanded and extended so it no longer resembled even in dimension what she saw when she looked at it in her mind's eye. The rhododendrons had not flowered. I decided I could never go back to my own childhood house. My friend felt one of the last physical connections to her mother grow fainter.

What does all this have to do with memory and the built environment in twentieth-century American literature? Well, it has something to do with memory and history. Thinking about this experience made me consider the ways in which the two might be distinct. Memory—what we saw when we looked around the house we knew so well. History—what the house itself showed us. We experienced a kind of double vision. This is a very small example of what those who live in cities experience on a much larger scale. History as experienced in the city is something all of its citizens share. It is both private and public; intimately connected to our sense of personal memoir, and explicitly an expression of a collective past. It is built by both our own self-narrative, and the very public, material evolution of urban space.

Modernity in the city is made manifest by a cycle of destruction, renewal, and preservation. This cycle, characterized by conflict and collision, frequently causes physical fractures in urban space which in turn cause psychic, figurative ruptures in the internal "metaphorical city" that we carry within us (Certeau [1980] 1984: 110). Space is interrupted, and history begins to feel likewise discontinuous. Here and throughout this book I have used the term "space" to signal both physical space and subjective or psychic space.

Instead of carefully unpicking the stitches that had held neighborhoods together for generations, such processes as urban renewal slice through the tapestry. What had come together naturally over time is ripped up, replaced, patched together. This leads to the separation of memory from history. The past which was previously discernible in a material sense (in the form, for example, of a childhood house, a boulevard, or a string of stores with a long local history) is no longer visible, and so a distinctly *absent* past develops that runs parallel to the past which has retained its visibility. The double vision of history (the urban space of the physical landscape) versus memory (the spaces of the psychic landscape) comes into existence. In other words, the emotional experience of space is synonymous with memory and the physical experience of space is synonymous with the processes of history.

So, one begins with the idea that the sense of conflict in urban space is a result of the disorienting and destabilizing cycle of modern urban renewal and destruction. After this, the hermetically sealed urban landscape, which should surely externalize both memory and history as one, is now open and porous, liminal and discontinuous. It is in the city's in-between spaces where individual memory reveals itself, where collisions between alternative perspectives of time and space and between rival conceptions of history and memory play out in the built environment. Such spaces are defined by their inherent liminality, in that they are open and borderless; in-between spaces are transitional spaces where one supposedly self-contained thing threatens to spill over into or merge with another. As outlined in Chapters 1 and 3 in particular, Freud would deem such spaces uncanny because they are defined by the collapse of integrity and the perception of difference. The double vision in which we are able to see both history and memory but at the same time perceive the difference between them, represents the liminal edges of our spatial experience of the city. It is important to emphasize that the revelation of memory as a distinct prospect to history is dependent upon making discontinuity visible in the built environment. The psychic or emotional experience of space occurs most frequently in the physical spaces that are characterized by this conflict, by discontinuity, because here it is obvious that there has been a rupture of some kind and we can thus clearly perceive the difference between the image we have in our minds of what this space should look like (according to our own personal recollections) and the reality in front of us in the landscape.

Sometimes as a result of this perception of difference we feel the urge to recreate the city we see before us in the image of how it appears to us in memory, which feels more complete. This is a form of nostalgia, and it finds physical expression in the remaking of material space via methods like gentrification. Nostalgia is, in short, the space between where we are now and the places of the past. David Lowenthal (1985) tells us that in its original seventeenth-century form, nostalgia was diagnosed by a Swiss physician as a physical complaint experienced by those whose brains clung to "traces of ideas of the Fatherland" (46). It is also defined by Anne Friedberg (1993) as "an algia, a painful return" (189). It represents a longing for a place that can only cause pain should you succeed in going back to it. Nevertheless, the desire to return home persists.

Rather than something which prevents the reconciliation between history and memory, discontinuity is a necessary (and unavoidable) component of life in the modern city. Discontinuity makes visible the messy contortions of history. Discontinuity has a greater power to reveal the past than nostalgia, because where the former points out the city's wounds, the latter pretends they never existed.

My Introduction refers to Lewis Mumford's maxim that "In the city, time becomes visible" (Mumford 1940: 4). The focus of each of the writers I have discussed has been how this maxim has manifested itself. I chose each writer because of the particular ways that they each consider how the built environment is able to make time visible and, indeed, to cultivate what we remember of the time that has passed through these spaces. In the context of this book, the "time" that Mumford writes of is translated as history. In other words, urban spaces are able to make *history* visible.

At the center of this book has been an examination of both the distinction and the relationship between history and memory, and how this is experienced spatially and articulated by each author. Integral to this exploration is the modern and modernity, in terms of how they manifest themselves in the urban spaces of New York, Los Angeles, and, in particular instances, in California more widely. Boyer ([1996] 2001) writes that the modern view of the city reflected a desire to "master and dominate" it and to experience it in "a coherent and integrated manner" (3). Yet conversely, modernity in the city achieves the opposite, making urban spaces feel incoherent, dispersive, and uncanny. One aim of modernity in this context, as per my discussion of Marshall Berman, was to question and distance "the relationship between history and the city," instead of "holding onto an Enlightenment or nineteenth-century view where even architectural styles, it was argued, followed a progressive and linear development." Yet despite the machinations of modernity, "our desire for authentic memories and city experiences reveals an empathy for lost totalities" (4). What happens to memory when what we expect to see in physical monuments to our past is not in fact visible? Does memory die too, or become more powerful in its invisibility? The double vision through which we continue to see both what is intimate, personal, lost, and what is collective, tangible, and evident, endures.

How to retain a connection to a personal sense of history in such places? If we follow the advice of Frances Yates ([1966] 1978), the solution is to be found in the memory palace. It is necessary, she tells us, to find a "loci" that is familiar and filled with items to aid recollection, such as an unfrequented building inside which we may wander and repeat her mnemonic technique (18). But not all memory palaces provide a sanctuary for authentic memory. Some are more like Norman M. Klein's imago: false friends rather than safe harbors. For Chandler, the memory palace is Philip Marlowe's apartment, a place where the detective can make himself a whole person again. But the Sternwood mansion, on the other hand, has very little in it on which to focus anyone's mnemonic technique. For Cuadros and Gamboa in East Los Angeles, there is nothing to return to, only to drive past. Berman's palace is 1460 College Avenue, a place to which he cannot bring himself to return and which thus becomes swathed in myth. In fact, for Berman, the whole borough of the Bronx (and by extension much of the city of New York) is his memory palace, yet it is so full of holes that memory seeps out, dissipating in the wide-open spaces of the modern city. Maria Wyeth, whose childhood home was blasted into oblivion, has internalized this insular blankness and purposefully avoids settling in anything resembling a home that could remind her of a painful history. The Mar Vista property of Mr. and Mrs. Cattleman, devoid of any personal effects, is under constant threat of obliteration by bulldozer or perhaps even flooding. The many ancestral houses referred to by Didion in her personal essays are similar to Yates' memory palace in that they are filled with significant objects to be memorialized. But does she see herself in the objects she examines, or just remnants of other peoples' history? Perhaps it is California's Holy Land which is her true memory palace. Waldie lives in his palace rather ambivalently, Lake has purloined a palace full of the memories of others, and the Bentwoods find the sanctity of theirs cannot outlast the changes brought by history to their doorstep. Every house, or equally meaningful space, in this book is in one way or another a "visible and concrete means of defining and articulating the self," even if that home, and indeed that sense of a self with any kind of hinterland, is absent (Chandler 1991: 3).

Home is where we embed our autobiography, becoming a text in which we ourselves are inscribed and can be read. This familiar physical locus may be what is needed, but what we are left with instead in cities like Los Angeles and New York is, as Klein (2008) explains, "an empty lot where a building once stood" (4). The search for, or the rejection of, a stable home, one which is often associated with childhood, recurs throughout each chapter. But such a place is hard to come by in cities like these. Each chapter in this book is filled with examples of absences and empty spaces in every text, which signify that something has been silenced or removed. All speak to a degree of grief, loss, and homesickness (itself a form of nostalgia) for this very absence that sits at the heart of everything. The act of remembering is complicated by the proliferation of these empty lots and what Kevin Lynch (1972) refers to as "external historical shell[s]" bereft of any internal meaning in the urban spaces of both New York and Los Angeles, cities which for many lack familiar architecture and topography (32).

Waldie and Berman both articulate an anxiety about empty spaces. "Now, for the first time, your room is empty, not merely unoccupied" writes the former about the chasm created by his father's passing, after which his house is "largely a void" (Waldie 1996: 3, 42). For Berman it is in the space outside his old home, which he describes as "open and empty as the desert," where this same sense of absence is discovered (1984b: 20). In *Play It As It Lays* the porousness of internal spaces, like the apartment on Fountain Avenue, threatens to overwhelm that space with the repressed content of unwanted human waste, bubbling subterraneously like the oil beneath the surface of the earth in *The Big Sleep*. Every physical structure in *All That is Solid* has already collapsed when we find Berman wandering the Bronx, while in both *A Meaningful Life* and *Holy Land* the houses which are central to each narrative are insubstantial spaces that threaten to fall apart. At the end of *A Meaningful Life* Lowell Lake's brownstone rooming house is characterized by a disturbing vacuity, with "holes [. . .] scattered here and there," (190) and in the home of the Bentwoods: "The old sliding doors that had once separated the two first-floor rooms had long since been removed, so that by turning slightly [they] could glance down the length of their living room" (Fox [1970] 2003: 3). These houses seem borderless, so completely exposed to the world outside that they threaten to dissolve into their external surroundings. Lake comments as his brownstone is being refurbished that the walls "weren't really solid" and would "yield and engulf anyone unwary enough to lean on them," ultimately discovering that while on the property you had to be "extremely careful where you walked to avoid falling into the room directly below" (Davis [1971] 2009: 115, 212).

The grids and altered topographies represented in these texts make the machinations of the modern highly legible in New York, Los Angeles, and Lakewood (if not obviously rational, as in the case of California's ad hoc growth). The concrete troughs that run through Los Angeles in order to control and redirect the river find an echo in the concrete highway that runs through the Bronx. The extension of the freeway is important in *The Nowhere City* too, as it drives through previously intact neighborhoods that topple easily in its wake, as the Cross-Bronx Expressway did when it was first constructed. The Cross-Bronx created a barrier to accessing the past in space, wending its way directly through the center of formerly tightly woven neighborhoods and creating a new space with no past, no meaning beyond its own capacity to run people out of their own history. In Los Angeles, the freeway system (representing the modern) rather ironically follows the bed of the river (representing the city's pre-urban natural history), duplicating the path that it paved over and creating a parallel version of what came before.

In a similar fashion, as Waldie has written, Los Angeles' crooked heart represents the superimposition of a new grid over the original, new paths over ancient paths, making its new history just off-center, imperfect facsimiles. As Alfred Kazin (1951) observes, certain buildings in Brownsville, Brooklyn, have been "ripped out of their original pattern" (735). Likewise, in *Farewell, My Lovely*, Marlowe's disorienting visit to the canyons outside the city leave him with the feeling that he has "an amputated leg" (Chandler [1940] 2000: 210), an echo of Henry James' ([1907] 1994) comment upon his return to New York in *The American Scene* that its unfamiliarity is akin to having been "amputated of half my history" (46). Such "traces of erasure," as Anthony Vidler (1992) puts it, form a "negative path" (180). These erasures and substitutions take place physically on top of a now-suppressed landscape, be it the Native American trails, lost gardens, and paved rivers of California's agricultural past or the communal streetscapes of New York. The desire to blot out and extirpate the past creates uncanny pockets of space where evidence that it once existed there in a different, now invisible, form, endures, as in for example the Sternwood mansion, the streets of the Bronx, disturbing Los Angeles hotel rooms, empty Lakewood bedrooms, confused San Francisco houses, and dilapidated brownstone buildings.

Every iteration of the modern city in the various forms displayed throughout this book, be it gentrification and preservation or clearance and renewal, paves over the past and creates a duplicate that runs parallel. This is how memory is dislocated, to paraphrase Vidler (1992: 181). It is displaced and relocated in this parallel world, creating the double vision through which we see both the mobile city and the planned; Plato's imprinted wax tablet and the rigid historical grid; the autobiographical cartography of a mental map and the material reality of the streetscape.

Berman, unable to reconcile the physical ruins with what he remembers, becomes a ghost haunting the streets of his "inner city" ([1982] 2010: 344). He can still retrace old steps and orient himself, but his interior cartography is frequently blocked by external reality. Likewise, for Didion when she goes home to Sacramento; each time she is greeted by a "presentiment of loss" ([1966a] 2005: 108). The California of her childhood disappears—as Berman articulates, grief seems endemic to modern life. Her view of the past is fixed on a point of loss just as the whole crossing story is predicated on the same idea. Loss is in fact built into the landscape of her childhood and is part of her history and heritage. Leaving home is part of this too—she contributes to her own loss. "Hurry along as fast as you can," as Virginia Reed advises ([2003] 2004: 75), words Maria Wyeth submits to and Didion herself seems unable to ignore, as though they are both the embodiment of the California land itself, reaching out toward the ever-retreating horizon. There is constant anxiety that Didion will one day entirely lose her sense of the place; that it will be totally unrecognizable. Home is always "somewhere else" because it can never settle on a landscape that is itself never permanently settled. (Didion repeats this particular phrase in *Play It As It Lays*

([1970] 2001: 87), "Notes from a Native Daughter" ([1965] 2005: 137), "Some Dreamers of the Golden Dream" ([1966b] 2005: 18) and "Goodbye to All That" ([1967a] 2005: 178.) The previous cohesion of the landscape, which authors like Berman and Didion imagine used to exist, has been violently ruptured.

This sense of spatial disruption is also found in the fragmentation of Chandler's architectural interiors; the continual disruption of construction in *The Nowhere City* and its de-centered exteriors; and the displacement not only of citizens' conceptions of their environment (*Where I Was From*), but more literally of the citizens themselves *from* that environment (*All That is Solid*). In New York, the sense of a lack of permanence in urban spaces is created not through the danger posed by nature, but by modern city planning and its creation of rootlessness. In Los Angeles this same impermanence is a consequence of the whole garden having been turned into a machine. The synthetic environment of both cities as a result of these disruptions has been exposed as flimsy and liable to collapse, as exhibited in every text in various forms: in houses on the edge of cliffs; flooded living rooms; bulldozed neighborhoods; bodies dragged out of the ocean; feet crashing through an attic ceiling; broken windows; and invaded, vandalized country houses.

The spatial transformations in Los Angeles in particular seem to have had an effect on the experience of time in the city. Here, the space lost is equal to the time that cannot be accounted for. "I rang the bell," Marlowe reports toward the end of *The Big Sleep*, "It was five days since I had rung it for the first time. It felt like a year" (Chandler [1939] 2000: 148). The passing of time affects the logic found in dreams by speeding up and slowing down when necessary. The "dreamtime" of Los Angeles (Didion [2003] 2004: 17) makes the place feel "as if it weren't real" (Lurie [1965] 1994: 200). This is not unlike the way time functions in Brooklyn, which often seems "like a dream" as Betty Smith puts it ([1943] 1974: 306), or indeed a "vale of time" (Schaeffer 1985: 19). According to Lurie, Los Angeles is the "nowhen city" where time seems to be of no consequence ("Alison Lurie: The Nowhen City," n.p.). Indeed, the city is time-*less*. What if, instead of becoming visible, time in some cities becomes unseen? Los Angeles is spatially formless, indistinct, and so it seems inevitable that time within this space should pass in an equally structureless fashion. "Everything runs together," says Katherine in *The Nowhere City*; it is "so easy to lose track of time," remarks her husband ([1965] 1994: 144, 208); "time passes and I lose the thread," reports Didion, halfway between a dream and a nightmare ([1967d] 2005: 80).

The texts which represent both cities express an equal fixation with things being, or not being, intact and cohesive. The "broken, meaningless messages" that Paul tries to assemble for his history of the Nutting Institute (Lurie [1965] 1994: 156) are like Marlowe's description of trying to piece a disjointed, broken narrative together, creating something solid out of something "looser and vaguer" than he might wish it to be (Chandler [1939] 2000: 151). Seemingly arbitrary details are incrementally collated until they form a montage of sorts, which expresses in its way the whole case, the sum of its intricate parts. Both Paul's messages and Marlowe's broken narrative are like Maria's attempt to establish a pattern in the images she sees of her friend BZ's death: "I played and replayed these scenes and others like them, composed them as if for the camera, trying to find some order, a pattern. I found none" (Didion [1970] 2011: 14). The "scenes" of her past are disjointed and it seems impossible to render a cohesive narrative. Paul is unsuccessful because his client has no real interest in creating a historical narrative, just like Marlowe's clients never have a desire to know the truth beneath the story with the smoother finish, and like Maria who does not wish to relive the true sequence of events that led to her friend's death. Waldie also resists piecing together his own past, as does Lake, for whom the exaggerated tale of Darius Collingwood's history, the book telling the story of which crumbling into "a pile of brittle brown flakes that got smaller and smaller the more you handled them," is taken for a more impressive fact than the events of his own life, which by the end of the novel is synonymous with a house which could disintegrate at any moment: "Lowell had the uncomfortable feeling that at any moment the place could come popping apart like a cardboard cutout" (Davis [1971] 2009: 167, 169). In each case, fragmentation is the rule and not the exception.

Over and over again we learn that all that is solid eventually falls apart. The urban fabric splits, is worn down, becomes threadbare. The modern city is inevitably uncanny because of this; because it internalizes both the invisible memory of the individual and the visible history that replaces it at street-level. It contains multitudes, and sometimes these push at the seams that attempt to hold together the city's before and after. Artist Naima Rauam, whose studio around Water and Pearl Streets looks out over the former location of the Fulton Fish Market (now replaced by a very upmarket version of the South Street Seaport), explained to me in an interview that in New York it is "the old smashing up against the new, and the incongruity of everything" that makes it such a rich urban space to examine, as well as a deeply challenging city in which to live (2015: n.p.). "If you want to live in that environment," she continued, you "rise to the occasion. And if you can't, then you leave." Nostalgia in this city, I discovered to my surprise, is not sustainable. "It's not embedded in nostalgia," Vivian

Gornick acknowledges, continuing that "no city that's alive" would allow itself to be (2015: n.p.). As Howard Kaminsky explained to me: "If you don't like it, if you're uncomfortable with change, if you're going to fight it, then don't live in the city, and certainly don't live in New York" (2015: n.p.).

At the end of *A Tree Grows in Brooklyn*, Francie Nolan decides that, like Berman, she would rather retain the still image of her old home as she remembered it and therefore is loath to return to note the difference: "No she'd never come back to the old neighbourhood" (Smith [1943] 1974: 363). But this kind of nostalgia is in fact the enemy of memory. Acts of preservation, gentrification, renewal, clearance, and so on, are all much the same as acts of nostalgia in that they are mechanisms for restoring an idea, or an ideal, of past places. They each represent the same process of "re-creating a place as someone thinks it was" (Huxtable 1997: 16) in the search for "organic and authentic" spaces (Osman 2011: 14). The more I read about it, the more I felt that, rather paradoxically, gentrification can be a similarly disruptive process as that which was prescribed by Robert Moses as the means for forging a modern city. Gentrification affects the pretense that the processes of modernity have not passed through this space, trying to smooth over the cracks, plug the holes in the walls, and restore the original features in order to pursue this façade. In *A Meaningful Life*, we watch as Lake's neighborhood goes through the same cycle of modernity that Berman decries in *All That is Solid*, with buildings being chosen for clearance and destruction and the lives of Lake's "impoverished predecessors" not much cause for concern ([1971] 2009: 133). In both instances the theory seems to be that the only way to rebuild the city is to simultaneously start over and pretend that nothing has changed.

As I completed this book I began to wonder if not just the recognition but the pursuit of discontinuity could actually be helpful in its ability to jolt memory that may have been buried, dormant, beneath the smoothing out of history. Nostalgia, expressed at various moments by each of my authors, smooths everything out; it "hide[s] the discontinuities" (Friedberg 1993: 188).

It begins as a refusal to accept change, which manifests itself in the built environment as a concealment of any bumps, cracks, or fissures. When Gay Talese ([1964] 2003) writes about the construction of the Verrazano-Narrows Bridge that "all was flattened and smoothed by concrete," this is a description equally befitting the effects of gentrification (122). Like the glass world that Hisaye Yamamoto's Esther Kuroiwa passes through, finding it almost impossible to either see or leave traces of herself, Moses' highways likewise sought to prevent attachment, to iron out a journey so one is taken seamlessly from one impersonal space to another. Didion's own personal nostalgia tries to smooth over inconvenient truths through fabrication and mythology which provide a false sense of cohesion. Willy Staley (2018) uses the same vocabulary to describe the contemporary effects of gentrification when he writes in the *New York Times* that it represents the "wearing down [of] every bump and cranny" until the neighborhood is as "featureless as a river rock" (n.p.). As we see from the eventual erasure of the past in tangible form inside Lake's house, one consequence of his nostalgia is his glossing over of all displays that anything resembling a history before his own had ever existed there. Likewise, when Berman writes that "even the rubble was gone" after his family's departure from the Bronx, this represents the recognition that any sign of a forcible change had been removed (1973: n.p.). A city built on nostalgia is one that has had its layers of memory stripped back; it would be, as Vidler warns, a city that allows us a too-smooth journey across and through it, in which "we cross nothing to go nowhere" (1992: 185).

In Georg Simmel's 1903 essay "The Metropolis and Mental Life," he argues that the human mind is stimulated by difference, particularly the difference between "past impressions and those which have preceded" ([1903] 2002: 11). Boyer writes in similar terms that the spectacle of the myriad "layers of historical time" made visible can trigger the "experience of diversity" ([1996] 2001: 19). We can draw a line from these layers to Freud's "different contents" of time preserved in space ([1930] 1961: 18), which also galvanize the perception of "diversity" in the form of discontinuity (Boyer [1996] 2001: 19). As Freud suggests when he describes these "different contents" of the past, the layers of a city's history are buried but not dead. They all exist simultaneously in palimpsestic form. The remembered and the visibly real can coexist, but in the overlap between them there is a sense of difference.

For example, Selina Boyce and Alfred Kazin both perceive the past through signs of difference in the street, of discontinuity with their expectations, and are both forced into remembrance as a consequence. In Waldie's *Holy Land* memories are found in the silences and in the intentional gaps in the narrative, existing behind the Douglas fir walls and in the in-between spaces that the grid tramples over. In *A Meaningful Life*, Lake attempts to strip, both symbolically and literally, the "layers off the built environment" to get closer to the past that he feels can only be discerned in the original layer of this architectural pentimento (Osman 2011: 23). But destroying the historical layers destroys his capacity to see the discontinuities in-between each, which would have galvanized the perception of memory. In the end Lake turns what should be a space imbued with history into a space that is characterized by novelty—think of the "newly sawed wood and fresh plaster"—and ultimately it becomes "blank and seamless" (Davis [1971] 2009: 213, 214). The seam, or the "suture" as Klein puts it—a tangible sign that is necessary in order to perceive difference and therefore memory—is not in evidence (2008: 313). A city of nostalgia is seamless.

This seam, or suture, is similar to James Donald's "split within" modernity, or a sign that modernity has overextended itself, with the uncanny representing that which it has repressed pushing back against its limits (1999: 72). If we can see this split then we can see memory. With no sign of a split or suture—the seam in urban space that makes visible the places where history has covered over memory—there is no way to see that anything else used to exist. Both Los Angeles and New York are full of sown up wounds that would speak to the processes of history and what it has erased, if only they were *more* visible, not less.

Other splits, seams, or sutures come in the form of liminal spaces characterized by a tangible ambivalence or in-between-ness. One recurring example comes in the form of the many doors which populate each text. Maria Wyeth is unable to "go back" to her memories of the past when she is under hypnosis, because, as her therapist explains, she is unable to "open enough doors to get back" (Didion [1970] 2001: 143). Naima Rauam relayed that the elevated highway of the FDR Drive opposite her studio acts as "a curtain," behind which is the historic district of the South Street Seaport, and that to walk beneath the first to access the second is "like going through a door" (2015: n.p.). Waldie finally allows himself to recollect his father's death "behind a well-made, wooden bathroom door" (1996: 24) and it is on the other side of the Bentwoods' glass back door and imposing front door that stray cats, strange men, and former business partners stand, threatening intrusion into their insular world. Similarly, elsewhere in *Desperate Characters* the Holsteins' broken window represents an opening to the transformed world outside they try to ignore. In "Wilshire Bus," Esther stares out of the bus window "with eyes that did not see," until she suddenly finds herself caught in an unsettling memory magnified by glass (Yamamoto [1950] 1998: 37). The door (and on some occasions, the window) makes space ambivalent because it is both open and closed, an exit and an entrance, a hinge within space that makes it both one thing and its opposite. Doors interrupt the smooth surfaces of space, making them discontinuous. Boyer writes of the "liminally conjoined spaces" which are formed when a link between what is visible and what is intuitive is established ([1996] 2001: 21). In such a space it is possible to perceive, to come to a more authentic understanding of, the history that is both present in the surface of the city and hidden somewhere within it. Doors, when opened, provide a physical representation of these spaces, and as such can expose one to discomfort, danger, and heartache, which is why the prospect of opening them causes such anxiety. But opening them is also, symbolically, the key to the reconciliation of history and memory.

Another liminal space is the street. As Michael Kimmelman observed at the Museum of the City of New York's 2015 "Redefining Preservation" Symposium, buildings "don't exist in a vacuum, they belong to streets, neighborhoods, communities, which need to be nurtured holistically. And it is very often the spaces between these buildings which need to be safeguarded," continuing that Robert Moses, for example, may have built many housing units in New York, "but he didn't build neighbourhoods" (n.p.). The subtext here of course is that it is the "spaces between" buildings that require nurturing and a degree of preservation because it is in these spaces that a sense of shared history, of memory, is forged. As Maurice Halbwachs ([1952] 1980) writes about personal memories, as distinct from historical memory, these are characterized by their ability to live "in the consciousness of the groups" that keep it alive, and by their "irregular and uncertain boundaries" (80, 82). Nowhere in New York is it more possible to feel this sense of group consciousness and ambivalent borders than on the street.[1]

In his *Arcades* project, Walter Benjamin ([1927–39] 2003), ponders if it is possible to locate the past of the city (in his case, Paris during the early twentieth century) somewhere within its material environment. He discovers that it is in the street, "in *the space between* the building fronts," that one is able to walk "into a vanished time [. . .] into a past that can be all the more spellbinding because it is not his own, not private" (828, 416 emphasis added). When I was first in New York conducting archival research, I spent a lot of time trying to find ways of feeling at home and creating a space where I could feel a degree of familiarity. I wanted to somehow plug myself into the city's history and try vicariously to feel connected to it. During one of my conversations with Shellie Sclan (2016), she mentioned that when she first moved to the city in the late 1970s she would force herself out of bed on a Saturday morning, frustrated that she didn't know what she was doing with her life, and would go out and "just start walking. And things would happen" (n.p.). In this way she managed to piece together a certain coherence in her urban experience. She mentioned that she had loved being on jury duty for similar reasons: it meant that she would be required to walk uptown, thereby enabling her to get to know the city by getting lost in it. I took it upon myself to follow her advice, spending so much time walking to fend off a deep sense of loneliness (which felt a lot like homesickness) that, like Waldie, my mind was taken up by the grid; by numbers and corners and avenues and coordinates. Some days I would retrace the quotidian steps of Berman when he lived on the Upper West Side, taking in his beloved Upper Broadway, Book Culture on West 112th Street, Metro Diner at 2641 Broadway. It took time and concerted effort to make places more contained by frequenting them and rendering them local. I created an intimacy with the city any way I could. Despite the grid and the very defined areas—Upper West Side, Upper East Side, Lower East Side, Downtown, Tribeca, the West Village, Soho, and so on—everything seemed to flow inconspicuously, casually, from one space to the next. There is really no stopping there. You are caught in a flow all the time, despite traffic and density and distraction, it goes on and on. It is bigger than you. I felt part of something on the street itself, together with other walkers, moving in the same direction, navigating correctly and so acceptably enfolded into the city. You move with the gridded streets, and with the subway lines, and New York is with you, pushing you forward. One evening after a particularly long wander it started to rain. I ambled about the surrounding streets getting progressively more wet hoping it would stop before giving up and getting on the subway. While down there waiting there was a man playing the flute, and his sweet sound could be heard in between that metallic jolt and rumble of the train carriages going past. I thought—this is New York. The clash that is actually comforting, rather than a deafening collision.

At the end of both *A Meaningful Life* and *Brown Girl, Brownstones* the authors make it clear that real life, that which is able to endure in these Brooklyn neighborhoods beyond the experiences of their respective protagonists, is not inside landmarked or preserved buildings, but outside on the cacophonous street. The street *is* the city, not just a series of separate passageways that connect and organize it, but a cumulative dissemination of what it means to be a city. In one of the more famous passages from *The Death and Life of Great American Cities*, Jane Jacobs ([1961] 1965) describes New York street life downtown as an "intricate sidewalk ballet," following the flow of the people that inhabit and enliven Hudson Street in the midst of what seems to be rampant disorder (61). This flow is composed of "movement and change, and although it is life, not art, we may fancifully call it the art form of the city and liken it to the dance [. . .] to an intricate ballet in which the individual dancers and ensembles all have distinctive parts which miraculously reinforce each other and compose an orderly whole" (60). William H. Whyte, urbanist and author of, for example, *The Organization Man* (1956) and *The Social Life of Small Urban Spaces* (1980), was also a mentor to Jacobs and details, as she does, the vast scope of people who comprise the city's crowd and unwittingly organize its space. There are the regulars who populate the streets, entertain or harass those moving past them, dictate the trajectory of the crowd, create pockets of people stood still momentarily to observe or partake, draw scrutiny, and occupy sections of the street. Positioning himself at various points of urban density, Whyte observes the movements, chosen or forced, of the people on the street, writing that "Bad or good, the variety of street people is astonishingly wide. To appreciate this, stand still" ([1988] 2000: 270).

Echoing Walter Benjamin, who wrote in *Arcades* that the street is "the dwelling place of the collective" and the "familiar interior of the masses" ([1927–39] 2003: 423), Paul Goldberger comments in the Foreword to *The Essential William H. Whyte* that Whyte had a deep understanding of the fact that "as the architect Louis Kahn once said, 'a street is a room by agreement'" ([1999] 2000: viii). Just as Selina Boyce and Lowell Lake notice at their end of their respective Brooklyn narratives, in the city the street becomes a more intimate living space than one's living room. People live on the outside. Berman likewise extols the virtues of life outside on the streets, professing that in New York "if you look up to the top of the buildings, it is brand new, but at the level of the street, it is a couple of hundred years old" (2007a: 35). For Benjamin, Jacobs, Whyte, Berman et al., the street is really where a sense of home, community, history, *and* memory can be found, and this is particularly true of New York.

In the Holy Land of California, external space is always bordered at some point by the "red and yellow flags," the "white posts" (Sinclair [1927] 2008: 21, 23), the "white barrier" (Chandler [1940] 2000: 207), or the "red rags" (Lurie [1965] 1994: 162) that mark the point where the garden ends and development begins. In *The Nowhere City*, Paul and his mistress Ceci drive along Mulholland, "a narrow road along the crest of the mountains, badly paved, twisting and turning around heaps of earth and rock, skirting sheer cliffs of mud" (Lurie [1965] 1994: 161). At first it seems they will be able to drive out far enough to track down the arcadian fantasy that Paul is seeking: "Together, they started uphill along the dirt road, now only a track. After all, this landscape had its own kind of beauty, Paul thought. The smoky green and indigo of the hill behind the construction site, the intense blue sky, were exotic and interesting." But the devouring capacities of the external world in Los Angeles are curtailed by modern encroachments. There is always a limit imposed, often in the form of a literal machine in the garden where the trail of nature comes to an abrupt end: "But round the next bend, with the trucks and bulldozers still in sight, the road ended in a trash pile: a heap of smashed bottled, cans, and dead sticks and leaves" (162). Similarly, in *The Big Sleep*, when Marlowe accompanies Carmen Sternwood down to the oil fields, following, as Paul does, a "narrow dirt road" which is "fringed with tall eucalyptus trees" that takes them to the abandoned wells, they find nothing but decay and detritus: "rusted pipe, a loading platform that sagged at one end, half a dozen empty oil drums lying in a ragged pile" (Chandler [1939] 2000: 154–5).

The accumulation of trash as a symbol of the accretions of historical progress is reminiscent of Benjamin's "Angel of History," who sees history as a "single catastrophe, which unceasingly piles rubble on top of rubble and hurls it before his feet" ([1940] 2003: 392). The Angel would like to "piece together what has been smashed" but is prevented from doing so by the storm of progress which "drives him irresistibly into the future." The pile of rubble is left to grow. Here one thinks of Berman and his quest to sift through the rubble left behind by Moses' storm of progress in the Bronx. But the Angel's struggle is also mirrored by Paul Cattleman in his search for some prelapsarian past found piecemeal in the midst of the wider Los Angeles construction site and his discovery of the dilapidated hidden history of Venice Beach. It is echoed by Didion in "Slouching Towards Bethlehem" as she picks through the debris of the atomized lives of the children in San Francisco as they are blown into an uncertain future; by her survey of the California landscape and its exploitation, mile after mile of sales and subdivisions piling up in her rear-view mirror; and by Maria Wyeth's fears of being overwhelmed by the human waste that threatens to flood every flimsy interior in which she takes brief refuge, her narrative collapsing behind her as she hurls herself toward the horizon. It resounds in Marlowe's repeated discovery of the very fine line that delineates the wild from the cultivated in Los Angeles, a line which is both disclosed and covered by the refuse of the city, and in his long list of bodies discovered out in the wilderness of the Greater Los Angeles area, seeming to pile up from one Chandler novel to the next like the Angel's "rubble-heap" that grows "sky-high" (Benjamin [1940] 2003: 392). It is mirrored by Waldie, trying to ignore remnants of difficult recollections in the structurally unsound buildings of Lakewood, built where the frame houses of encroaching urbanization meet the frayed edges of the garden, and by Cuadros (1994), who imagines the wreckage of his home buried "under dirt and asphalt, dust and neglect" (55). The City of Angels seems a fitting home for the Angel of History. In California, at the edge of the garden, in the slight gap between the built environment and its pre-urban shadow, there is a thin line of detritus that makes the transition from one to the other visible—another liminal space.

What is needed in order to perceive memory are the same discontinuities that processes like preservation and gentrification are designed to hide. The in-between, liminal spaces in cities are where the distance between history and memory comes alive. In New York, this is found in the dynamism of the street; in Los Angeles, in the margin or verge of the garden.

In my Introduction I wrote about Boyer's notion that walking through the city would make it more understandable and would allow its citizens to see both its urban spaces and its narrative history as cohesive rather than continuously disrupted. In fact, there is more discontinuity in evidence in the urban spaces of New York and Los Angeles than integrity or congruence. I also referred to Benjamin's "A Berlin Chronicle" ([1932] 1986) in which he tries to understand and read his own past through the selection of the various significant buildings which have been important to him throughout his life; buildings which become "a system of signs" on his own personal map (5). Benjamin explains that his perspective on autobiography is that it is about sequence, but not necessarily about one unbroken chronological sequence: "autobiography has to do with time, with sequence and what makes up the continuous flow of life. I am talking of a space, of moments and *discontinuities*" (28 emphasis added). Discontinuity is a necessary component of life in the modern city due to its capacity to unveil the presence of a buried or evicted history. Attempts to reconstruct the past and impose a cohesive narrative on a discontinuous form can actually rob it of its authenticity. The "fragmentary meanings" we discover on our walk through our own inner cities, as they alternately meet and part from the material city, should be left as they are (Boyer [1996] 2001: 25).

So, we must accept that a house built by nostalgia can never be a real home. But the question remains. How to make a home in a world in ruins? In the process of writing this book, I came to the realization that a common theme among these authors is a strong sense of grief. 'Where is my home?' they seem to be asking the reader, or themselves, over and over. Even the authors and characters who are still able to access their childhood homes (or to live in them, as Waldie does), and even, conversely, those who run from home, seem to be in mourning for it. They long for the restorative feeling of home, but often this longing is for a world that no longer exists. The space that they walk through is not topographical, but internal. It is another country, one that they can no longer inhabit. Perhaps their memories, which cannot be located spatially, represent an attempt to create an ideal and intact home that cannot be confronted by reality. After visiting my friend's old house I wrote in my diary that it didn't seem to belong to us anymore. I told her, and myself, that the new people didn't live in what I saw as "our house": "They live in their house. Ours is somewhere else." Each of the texts in my book present a similar vision of the city that lives on in the imagined spaces of memory, continuing to exist even after the city itself has melted into air.

Notes

Introduction

1. Soja argues in *Thirdspace* (1996) that space, when interacted with by humans, can be understood in three ways: it is perceived (it can be mapped), conceived (it can be imagined, represented), and lived. The latter is the titular thirdspace. Soja later writes that this space is "knowable and unknowable, real and imagined, at the edge and at the center," (1999: 276) connecting thirdspace to Derrida's linguistic trace; both are receptacles for what is simultaneously present and absent.

Chapter 1

1. See Kevin Starr's *Inventing the Dream* (1985) for more on what became known as the Booster Era (1885–1925).
2. "I should point out that I'm not able to drive. I walk to work, about a half hour's walk to my office, and the walk back is another half an hour. In that hour altogether, I would rehearse pieces in progress, try out new ones, and allow the rhythm of my walking to suggest alternative phrasings" (Waldie and Campbell 2011: 229).
3. In her 1962 song "Little Boxes," Malvina Reynolds sings of these suburban tract houses: "they're all made out of ticky-tacky/And they all look just the same." *Ear to the Ground*. Folkways, 2000 (album).
4. See Estrada (2005).
5. Starr (2005: 13).
6. Jenny Price (2006) writes in "Thirteen Ways of Seeing Nature in L.A." that because Los Angeles County, through its demonstrable environmental ignorance, designed the river's storm drains to empty *into* the channel, the river was "promptly turned [. . .] into L.A.'s Grand Sewer" (n.p.).

Chapter 2

1. Credit to Lawrence Ferlinghetti's *A Coney Island of the Mind* (1958) for the inspiration here.

2 For further reading about the environmental evolution of Sacramento, I refer the reader to *River City and Valley Life: An Environmental History of the Sacramento Region* (2013), edited by Christopher I. Castaneda and Lee M. A. Simpson. For a more comprehensive history related to environmental and topographical changes in California as a whole, see *California: A History* (2005), by Kevin Starr.
3 In *Capital City* (2019), Samuel Stein, a trained planner, argues that we now live in a world of the *"real estate state"* in which "the price of land [has become] a central economic determinant and a dominant political issue" (5, 4).
4 See *The Machine in the Garden* (1964) by Leo Marx.
5 For more information about the Donner-Reed party and their California crossing story, Michael Wallis' *The Best Land Under Heaven* (2017) makes for compelling reading.
6 This section was inspired by Karen Jackson Ford's reading of *The Scarlet Letter* by Nathaniel Hawthorne in *Gender and the Poetics of Excess* (1997).
7 Nabokov writes in *Ada, or Ardor: A Family Chronicle* (1969): "Maybe the only thing that hints at a sense of Time is rhythm; not the recurrent beats of the rhythm but the gap between two such beats, the grey gap between black beats: the Tender Interval. The regular throb itself merely brings back the miserable idea of measurement, but in between, something like true Time lurks" (538).
8 This is paraphrased from the opening line to Didion's "The White Album": "we tell ourselves stories in order to live" (Didion [1968–1978] 2005: 195).
9 See Rodney Steiner's (1981), *Los Angeles, the Centrifugal City*, Dubuque, Iowa: Kendall/Hunt Publishing Company.
10 For more on roadside architecture, see the discussion between Robert Venturi and Denise Scott Brown on "ducks" vs "decorated sheds" in *Learning from Las Vegas* (1972), written with Steven Izenour.
11 For further reading on architectural anachronism see also *Learning from Las Vegas* (1972) by Robert Venturi, Denise Scott Brown, and Steven Izenour, and Dolores Hayden *The Power of Place: Urban Landscapes as Public History* (1995).
12 Lurie herself lived in Mar Vista in the late 1950s, disclosing that this was due to its affordability because "a freeway was about to be built over it. While we lived on the block, other people began moving away to avoid the dropping trees" (Lurie "Alison Lurie: The Nowhen City": n.p.).

Chapter 3

1 A recommended counterweight to Berman here is Perry Anderson's 1984 paper "Modernity and Revolution," which provides a critique of Berman's take on modernism.

2. Moses was an admirer of Haussmann, writing in 1942 that "he grasped the problem of step-by-step large-scale city modernization" (Moses 1942: 65).
3. As Roger Starr put it, "Mr Moses sliced up the rich and powerful with his tongue, knocked down the poor and weak with his bulldozer" (Starr 1979: n.p.).
4. For further information on these plans, see Anthony Paletta's 2016 essay for *The Guardian*, "Story of cities #32: Jane Jacobs v Robert Moses, battle of New York's urban titans."
5. Architectural critic Paul Goldberger also provides an alternative reading of Moses' work and Caro's analysis of that work in a 2007 article for *The New Yorker* titled "Eminent Dominion."
6. In 2007, after over thirty years of Robert Caro's portrait of Moses having defined the man, a new (some would argue revisionist) vision of Moses was put forward via Kenneth T. Jackson and Hilary Ballon's *Robert Moses and the Modern City*, and three simultaneous exhibitions at the Museum of the City of New York, the Queens Museum of Art, and the Miriam and Ira D. Wallach Art Gallery at Columbia University. A similarly reinterpretative guide to Moses and his works took the form of a collection of papers presented at a 1988 Hofstra University conference, published in 1989 under the title *Robert Moses: Single-Minded Genius*, edited by Joann P. Krieg.
7. For more on the fiscal crisis and its impact on US cities during this period, see Jonathan Mahler's *Ladies and Gentleman, the Bronx is Burning* (2005) and *Fear City* by Kim Phillips-Fein (2017).
8. I can't help but think of Moses when I come across the Book of Job's assertion that Kings and rulers of the earth "built for themselves places now lying in ruins" (*New International Bible*, Job 3.14).
9. In May 2018 however, a *CNBC* article claimed that the South Bronx was "in the midst of a revival" and is known in some real-estate circles as "SoBro" (Bukszpan and David 2018: n.p.).
10. Howard Kaminsky calls it "the world's longest parking lot" (2015: n.p.).
11. Where did everyone who left the Bronx go? Many went to the newly constructed Co-op City, a housing project built under the auspices of the Mitchell-Lama program, which Moses was responsible for developing. It was built on top of what had been a huge amusement complex called Freedomland, itself constructed over marshland. A year after its opening in 1970, it had "sucked out what remained of the South Bronx's middle class, leaving those who remained in a virtual ghost town" (Worth 1999: 3).
12. For an alternative reading of Moses' impact on the Bronx, see Ray Bromley's 1998 paper "Not So Simple! Caro, Moses, and the Impact of the Cross-Bronx Expressway," published in *The Bronx County Historical Society Journal*.
13. Berman explains this fixation with comparisons between London during the early 1940s and New York after the Second World War in "Roots, Ruins and Renewals":

"For many of the people who grew up in World War II, the vision of the ruins of that war, which reduced so many cities to ruins, became an ineradicable obsession long after the last of the rubble had been carted away" (1984b: 23). See also Sharon Zukin's *Naked City* ([2009] 2010).

14 As a related aside, Geri Solomon, Assistant Dean of Special Collections and Hofstra University Archivist, told me in an interview that in New York there have always been particular landmarks that one would use for the purposes of orientation. Post-9/11, navigating the city was a much more disorientating experience. There are certain buildings that one always looks for, she explained, and the Towers had formed one such orienting mark on the city's cartography. After their loss, the landscape was etched with an enormous scar, as though a botched operation had been performed, which disfigured New York's built environment.

15 Before our excursions in the spring of 2015, the last time Howard Kaminsky had been in his old neighborhood was the late 1960s with a cousin who had also grown up there and had relocated to Florida. How did his cousin feel when he came back? "He cried [. . .] It was so different from what we knew, what we had grown up with" (2015: n.p.).

16 This marvelling at the destruction of the urban environment, and its description as "sublime" (Berman [1982] 2010: 293), also arguably anticipates the debates concerning so-called "ruin porn," of which Detroit in particular provides many examples. See: https://www.john-adams.nl/detroit-ruin-porn-architecture/

17 "Soft city" was a term first coined by Jonathan Raban in his 1974 book of the same name.

18 Here I am reminded of Joseph Mitchell, journalist and author who reported for *The New Yorker* for over twenty years, painting indelible portraits of the people he met at (among other places) the Fulton Fish Market and South Street Seaport. In August 1992 he was interviewed for *New York Newsday*, the journalist commenting that "Sometimes when Mitchell looks at a building, he won't see the present-day fast-food joint but the speakeasy it replaced. 'The past is obliterated,' he says, 'but somehow it's still there'" (Streitfeld 1992: n.p.).

19 Lynne Sharon Schwartz said much the same to me when I asked her about reproducing her childhood neighborhood for her novel *Leaving Brooklyn* (1989): "I use it a lot, I can remember everything, I can tell you the blocks going from East New York Avenue up to Eastern Parkway one after the other and I've written a lot about that. [. . .] When I want to write something about the past I just remember it" (2015: n.p.).

20 Berman acknowledges his debt here to Chicana artists like Judith Baca, who grew up outside Los Angeles on the edges of the San Fernando Valley. During the 1970s she created the half-mile-long *Great Wall of Los Angeles*, "a linear series of vignettes of the history of Los Angeles and California, emphasising the perspectives of

marginal social groups" (Avila 2014: 77). Murals as an art form date back to the pre-Columbian civilizations of the Americas and represented "a Mexican tradition of cultural expression [. . .] Chicano and Chicana muralists self-consciously invoked Mexican and indigenous traditions in their work, painting murals in the public spaces of barrios across southwestern cities" (168).

Chapter 4

1 See for example Suleiman Osman's *The Invention of Brownstone Brooklyn: Gentrification and the Search for Authenticity in Postwar New York* (2011) and Pete Hamill's 1969 article for *New York Magazine*, "Brooklyn: The Sane Alternative."
2 Brooklyn-born journalist and author Jim Sleeper recounts that he has "dreams, mournful dreams" about his childhood borough: "A sociologist calls this grieving for a lost home. I am convinced that countless people who left Brooklyn have felt that. The borough is haunted by ghosts for me [. . .] My greatest dream is to be able to get into a time machine and make it 1952 and just roam free across the borough" (Frommer and Frommer 1993: 237).
3 Gentrification is also defined by Judith N. DeSena and Timothy Shortell ([2012] 2014) as the "displacement of lower status communities by higher status" (1) and by Sharon Zukin (1987) as "the conversion of socially marginal and working class areas of the central city to middle-class [. . .] residential use" (1987: 129).
4 To quote the poet Edward Young: "'Born Originals [. . .] how comes it to pass that we die Copies?'" (qtd in Trilling [1971] 1972: 93).
5 There is of course a vast selection of literature available on the subject of the gentrification of New York City, which I touch on here but do not delve into in granular detail. This includes related issues pertaining to institutional racism inherent in particular housing practices, much of which goes beyond the remit of this book but is hugely important to a holistic understanding of the issue. For further reading, some recommended texts are as follows: *Naked City: The Death and Life of Authentic Urban Places* (2009), by Sharon Zukin; *How to Kill a City: Gentrification, Inequality, and the Fight for the Neighborhood* (2017), by Peter Moskowitz; *Gentrifier* (2017), by John Joe Schlichtman, Jason Patch and Marc Lamont Hill; *There Goes the 'Hood: Views of Gentrification from the Ground Up* (2006), by Lance Freeman; and *The World in Brooklyn* ([2012] 2014), edited by Judith DeSena and Timothy Shortell.
6 One example of a source which disputes this story is *New York Magazine*'s "The Brooklyn Heights Promenade Was a Robert Moses Head Fake," by Thomas J. Campanella (2019).
7 It must be noted that scholars such as Japonica Brown-Saracino (2009) have argued that there has been a failure to document "the multiple attitudes and practices

that characterize gentrification," which cannot all be simply categorized under the "frontier and salvation mentality" (8). She creates a more nuanced version of the gentrifier, articulating two distinct categories beyond that of the urban pioneers—"Social Preservationists and Social Homesteaders" (7).

8 At the Park Slope branch of the Brooklyn Public Library, I joined the "Brooklyn Transitions" book discussion group, which, on April 29, 2015, was discussing *A Meaningful Life*. During the discussion, an older gentleman, who had lived in Brooklyn his whole life, was so impressed with the novel's realism that he didn't even agree with me when I argued that it was a black comedy; a grotesque satire. *This is exactly Brooklyn in the early 1970s,* he told us he had thought to himself as he read the book. Francis Morrone agreed when I spoke to him about this; he argued that Davis is "not making any of that up. Almost everything that he describes, even the murder of the man is absurd but believable [. . .] You've got to realize it's not fantasy. L. J. Davis actually was writing from experience" (2016: n.p.).

9 For Neil Smith (1996) this is also a matter of class, contending that "urban pioneers" like Lake, "seek to scrub the city clean of its working-class geography and history" (25).

Conclusion

1 As Waldie emphasizes, history may wish for us to forget things that "the streets themselves remember" (Waldie 2010b: n.p.).

Bibliography

Abu-Lughod, Janet. (1999), *New York, Chicago, Los Angeles: America's Global Cities*, Minneapolis: University of Minnesota Press.

Affordable New York. (September 2015–February 2016), Museum of the City of New York, New York.

Agee, James. (2005), *Brooklyn Is. Southeast of the Island: Travel Notes*, New York: Fordham University Press.

Allen, David Bruce. (2017), Personal interview, May 5.

Alworth, David J. (2016), *Site Reading: Fiction, Art, Social Form*, Princeton and Oxford: Princeton University Press.

Anderson, Chris. (1987), *Style as Argument: Contemporary American Nonfiction*, Carbondale and Edwardsville: Southern Illinois University Press.

Anderson, Chris. (1989), *Literary Nonfiction: Theory, Criticism, Pedagogy*, Carbondale and Edwardsville: Southern Illinois University Press.

Anderson, Linda, ed. (1990), *Plotting Change: Contemporary Women's Fiction*, London, Melbourne, and Auckland: Hodder & Stoughton/Edward Arnold.

Anderson, Perry. (1984), "Modernity and Revolution," *New Left Review*, 144 (March–April 1984): 6–113.

Armstrong, Isobel. (2008), *Victorian Glassworlds: Glass Culture and the Imagination 1830–1880*, Oxford: Oxford University Press.

Auden, W. H. (1948), "The Guilty Vicarage," *Harper's Magazine*, May 1948: 406–12.

Austen, Jane. ([1811] 2004), *Sense and Sensibility*, ed. James Kinsley, Oxford: Oxford University Press.

Avella, Steven M. (2013), "The Indomitable City and Its Environmental Context," in Christopher I. Castaneda and Lee M. A. Simpson (eds.), *River City and Valley Life: An Environmental History of the Sacramento Region*, 1–10, Pittsburgh: University of Pittsburgh Press.

Avila, Eric. (2004), *Popular Culture in the Age of White Flight: Fear and Fantasy in Suburban Los Angeles*, Berkeley, Los Angeles, and London: University of California Press.

Avila, Eric. (2014), *The Folklore of the Freeway: Race and Revolt in the Modernist City*, Minneapolis: University of Minnesota Press.

Babener, Liahna K. (1984), "Raymond Chandler's City of Lies," in David Fine (ed.), *Los Angeles in Fiction: A Collection of Original Essays*, 109–33, Albuquerque: University of New Mexico Press.

Bachelard, Gaston. (1969), *The Poetics of Space*, trans. Maria Jolas, Boston: Beacon Press.

Ballon, Hilary and Kenneth T. Jackson, eds. (2007), *Robert Moses and the Modern City: The Transformation of New York*, New York and London: W. W. Norton.

Banham, Reyner. (2000), *Los Angeles: The Architecture of Four Ecologies*, Berkeley, Los Angeles, and London: University of California Press.

Barthes, Roland. ([1970] 1977), "The Third Meaning," in *Image, Music, Text*, trans. Stephen Heath, 52–68, New York: Hill.

Barthes, Roland. ([1979] 1997), *The Eiffel Tower and Other Mythologies*, trans. Richard Howard, Berkeley, Los Angeles, and London: University of California Press.

Baudelaire, Charles. ([1863] 1995), *The Painter of Modern Life and Other Essays*, trans. and ed. Jonathan Mayne, London: Phaidon.

Baudrillard, Jean. ([1986] 2010), *America*, London and New York: Verso.

Beauregard, Robert A. (1993), *Voices of Decline: The Postwar Fate of US Cities*, Cambridge: Blackwell.

Beauvoir, Simone de. ([1972] 1996), *The Coming of Age*, trans. Patrick O'Brian, New York and London: W.W. Norton & Company.

Beers, Henry A. (1894), *A Suburban Pastoral and Other Tales*, New York: Henry Holt and Company.

Benardo, Leonard and Jennifer Weiss. (2006), *Brooklyn by Name: How the Neighborhoods, Streets, Parks, Bridges, and More Got Their Names*, New York and London: New York University Press.

Benjamin, Walter. ([1927–39] 2003), *The Arcades Project*, trans. Howard Eiland and Kevin McLaughlin, Cambridge, MA: Harvard University Press.

Benjamin, Walter. ([1932] 1986), "A Berlin Chronicle", in *Reflections: Essays, Aphorisms, Autobiographical Writings*, trans. Edmund Jephcott, 3–60, New York: Schocken Books.

Benjamin, Walter. ([1933] 1999), "Experience and Poverty", in Michael W. Jennings, Howard Eiland, and Gary Smith (eds.), *Walter Benjamin: Selected Writings, volume 2, part 2, 1931–1934*, trans. Rodney Livingstone and Others, 731–6, Cambridge, MA and London: The Belknap Press of Harvard University Press.

Benjamin, Walter. ([1940] 2003), "On the Concept of History", in Howard Eiland and Michael W. Jennings (eds.), *Walter Benjamin: Selected Writings, volume 4, 1938–1940*, trans. Edmund Jephcott and Others, 389–400, Cambridge, MA and London: The Belknapp Press of Harvard University Press.

Bennett, Robert. (2011), "Tract Homes on the Range: The Suburbanization of the American West," *Western American Literature*, 46 (3): 281–301.

Benz, Terressa A. (2016), "Urban Mascots and Poverty Fetishism: Authenticity in the Postindustrial City," *Sociological Perspectives*, 59 (2), Summer: 460–78.

Berman, Marshall. (1966), *The Lower East Side: Portal to American Life, 1870–1924*, The Jewish Museum, New York, September–November 1966, Morris Dickstein Papers, Box 11, Folder 11: Professional Files – Berman, Marshall, Manuscripts and Archives Division, The New York Public Library, New York, New York, accessed April 30, 2015.

Berman, Marshall. (1973), "Expressway and Me: Personal Side," Draft for *Ramparts* article, 1973, Marshall Berman Papers, Box 12, Folder 37: Robert Moses: On Caro, *The Power Broker*, etc., Rare Book and Manuscript Library, Columbia University Libraries, New York, New York, accessed March 28, 2016.

Berman, Marshall. (1974), Handwritten notes, numbered 1–11, no title, no date. Marshall Berman Papers, Box 12, Folder 37: Robert Moses: On Caro, *The Power Broker*, etc., Rare Book and Manuscript Library, Columbia University Libraries, New York, New York, accessed March 28, 2016.

Berman, Marshall. (1975), "Buildings Are Judgement," *Ramparts*, 13 (6): 33–9.

Berman, Marshall. ([1982] 2010), *All That Is Solid Melts into Air: The Experience of Modernity*, London: Verso.

Berman, Marshall. (1984a), Application to the CUNY Graduate Center for National Endowment for the Humanities funding, 27 February 1984, Marshall Berman Papers, Box 37, Folder 8, Rare Book and Manuscript Library, Columbia University Libraries, New York, New York, accessed May 2, 2016.

Berman, Marshall. (1984b), "Roots, Ruins, Renewals: City Life after Urbicide," *The Village Voice*, September 4.

Berman, Marshall. (1993), "Life and Death in the Bronx," *Offstage Perspective*, 1993, Marshall Berman Papers, Box 13, Folder 24: "Life and Death in the Bronx," Rare Book and Manuscript Library, Columbia University Libraries, New York, New York, accessed March 28, 2016.

Berman, Marshall. (1997), "Too Much Is Not Enough: Metamorphoses of Times Square," Reworking of a paper given in Sydney, July 1997, Marshall Berman Papers, Box 37, Folder 9, Rare Book and Manuscript Library, Columbia University Libraries, New York, New York, accessed May 2, 2016.

Berman, Marshall. (1999), "Views from the Burning Bridge," in Lydia Yee and Betti-Sue Hertz (eds.), *Urban Mythologies: The Bronx Represented Since the 1960s*, 70–83, New York: Bronx Museum of the Arts.

Berman, Marshall. ([2003] 2016), "New York: Seeing through the Ruins", in Rebecca Solnit and Joshua Jelly-Schapiro (eds.), *Nonstop Metropolis: A New York City Atlas*, 119–28, Oakland: University of California Press.

Berman, Marshall. (2006a), *On the Town: One Hundred Years of Spectacle in Times Square*, New York: Random House.

Berman, Marshall. (2006b), "Review of *Moment of Grace: The American City in the 1950s* by Michael Johns," *Harvard Design Magazine*, 24 (Spring/Summer): 117–18, Marshall Berman Papers, Box: 16, Folder 9: American City in the 1950s: Harvard Design Review, 2005/2006, Rare Book and Manuscript Library, Columbia University Libraries, New York, New York, accessed March 28, 2016.

Berman, Marshall. (2007a), "Introduction," in Marshall Berman and Brian Berger (eds.), *New York Calling: From Blackout to Bloomberg*, 9–38, London: Reaktion Books.

Berman, Marshall. (2007b), Message to Brian Berger, April 1, 2007, Marshall Berman Papers, Box 9, Folder 3, Rare Book and Manuscript Library, Columbia University Libraries, New York, New York, accessed March 28, 2016.

Berman, Marshall. (2013), Lewis Mumford Lecture: "Emerging from the Ruins" (fourth draft), 2013, Marshall Berman Papers, Box 7, Folder 2, Rare Book and Manuscript Library, Columbia University Libraries, New York, New York, accessed May 2, 2016.

Berman, Marshall. (2017), *Modernism in the Streets: A Life and Times in Essays*, eds. David Marcus and Shellie Sclan, London and New York: Verso.

Berman, Marshall. (n.d.), "Why I Want to Write This Book", Marshall Berman Papers, Box 10: On The Town Drafts and related material on Times Square, Folder: no name/number, Rare Book and Manuscript Library, Columbia University Libraries, New York, New York, accessed December 12, 2015.

Biddle, James. (1974), "Press Release from the National Trust for Historic Preservation: National Trust President James Biddle Says 'Urban Pioneers' Are Modern-Day Preservationists", September 15, 1974, Back to the City collection, 1991.036, Box 1, Folder: Back to the City Conference – New York City, 1974, Brooklyn Historical Society, accessed September 25, 2015.

"Birth of the Boulevard." (n.d.), "Los Angeles Conservancy." Available online: https://www.laconservancy.org/birth-boulevard (accessed June 20, 2020).

Bowen, Elizabeth. ([1948] 1976), *The Heat of the Day*, Harmondsworth: Penguin.

Boyer, M. Christine. ([1996] 2001), *The City of Collective Memory: Its Historical Imagery and Architectural Entertainments*, 5th edn, Cambridge, MA: MIT Press.

Brady, Jennifer. (1984), "Points West, Then and Now: The Fiction of Joan Didion," in Ellen G. Friedman (ed.), *Joan Didion: Essays & Conversations*, 43–59, Princeton: Ontario Review Press.

Brodsky, D. (1981), *LA Freeway: An Appreciative Essay*, Berkeley, Los Angeles, and London: University of California Press.

Brogan, Hugh. ([1985] 2001), *The Penguin History of the USA*, London: Penguin.

Bromley, Ray. (1998), "Not So Simple! Caro, Moses, and the Impact of the Cross-Bronx Expressway," *The Bronx County Historical Society Journal*, XXXV (1): 5–29.

Brook, Vincent. (2013), *Land of Smoke and Mirrors: A Cultural History of Los Angeles*, New Jersey and London: Rutgers University Press.

"Brooklyn Heights Historic District, Borough of Brooklyn." Landmarks Preservation Commission document, November 23, 1965, Calendar No. 9, LP-0099, Brooklyn Heights Folder 1, Brooklyn Collection, Brooklyn Public Library, Central Library at Grand Army Plaza, Brooklyn, New York, accessed April 1, 2016.

Brown, Claude. ([1965] 2012), *Manchild in the Promised Land*, New York: Touchstone.

Brown-Saracino, Japonica. (2009), *A Neighborhood That Never Changes: Gentrification, Social Preservation, and the Search for Authenticity*, Chicago and London: Chicago University Press.

Bryson, J. Scott. (2010), "Surf, Sagebrush, and Cement Rivers: Reimagining Nature in Los Angeles," in Kevin R. McNamara (ed.), *Cambridge Companion to the Literature of Los Angeles*, 167–75, Cambridge: Cambridge University Press.

Buchanan, Ian. (2005), "Space in the Age of Non-Place," in Ian Buchanan and Gregg Lambert (eds.), *Deleuze and Space*, 16–35, Edinburgh: Edinburgh University Press.

Buhler, Stephen M. (2000), "The Burning of Los Angeles by Samuel Maio; *Holy Land: A Suburban Memoir* by D. J. Waldie," *Prairie Schooner*, 74 (2): 200–3.

Bukszpan, Daniel and Javier E. David. (2018), "The Bronx Sheds Image of Urban Blight, becomes Latest Target of New York City's Relentless Gentrification," *CNBC*, May 12. Available online: https://www.cnbc.com/2018/05/11/bronx-becomes-latest-target-of-nycs-relentless-gentrification.html (accessed May 16, 2018).

Burrows, Edwin and Mike Wallace. (1999), *Gotham: A History of New York*. New York: Oxford University Press.

Calhoun, Charles W., ed. (1996), *The Gilded Age: Essays on the Origins of Modern America*, Wilmington: Scholarly Resources.

Calvino, Italo. ([1972] 2013), *Invisible Cities*, trans. William Weaver, Boston: Houghton Mifflin Harcourt.

Campanella, Thomas J. (2019), "The Brooklyn Heights Promenade Was a Robert Moses Head Fake," *New York Magazine*, July 23. Available online: https://nymag.com/intelligencer/2019/07/the-secret-story-of-the-brooklyn-heights-promenade.html (accessed July 19, 2020).

Caparn, Harold A. (1906), "Parallelogram Park – Suburban Life by the Square Mile," *Craftsmen*, 10 (September): 767–74.

Caro, Robert. (1974), *The Power Broker: Robert Moses and the Fall of New York*, New York: Random House.

Caro, Robert. (1998), "The City-Shaper," *The New Yorker*, January 5: 38–55.

Casey, Edward S. (1987), *Remembering: A Phenomenological Study*, Bloomington: Indiana University Press.

Castaneda, Christopher I. and Lee M. A. Simpson. (2013), *River City and Valley Life: An Environmental History of the Sacramento Region*, Pittsburgh: University of Pittsburgh Press.

Caves, Roger W., ed. (2005), *Encyclopedia of the City*, Oxford and New York: Routledge.

Certeau, Michel de. ([1980] 1984), *The Practice of Everyday Life*, trans. Steven Rendall, Berkeley: University of California Press.

Cervantes, Lorna Dee. ([1981] 1982), "Freeway 180," in *Emplumada*, 20–1, Pittsburgh: University of Pittsburgh Press.

Chandler, Marilyn R. (1991), *Dwelling in the Text: Houses in American Fiction*, Berkeley, Los Angeles, and Oxford: University of California Press.

Chandler, Raymond. ([1939] 2000), "The Big Sleep," in *The Big Sleep and Other Novels*, 1–164, London: Penguin.

Chandler, Raymond. ([1940] 2000), "Farewell, My Lovely," in *The Big Sleep and Other Novels*, 165–367, London: Penguin.

Chandler, Raymond. ([1942] 1983), "The High Window," in *The Chandler Collection: Volume 2*, 7–196, London: Pan Books.

Chandler, Raymond. ([1955] 2000), "Letter to Roger Machell: 7 Feb. 1955," in Tom Hiney and Frank MacShane (eds.), *The Raymond Chandler Papers: Selected Letters and Non-Fiction, 1909–1959*, 206, London: Hamish Hamilton.

Chang, Jeff. (2006), *Can't Stop, Won't Stop: A History of the Hip-Hop Generation*, New York: Picador.

Clark, David L. (1983), "Los Angeles: Improbable Los Angeles," in Richard M. Bernard and Bradley R. Rice (eds.), *Sunbelt Cities: Politics and Growth Since World War II*, 268–308, Austin: University of Texas Press.

Cohen, Josh. (1998), *Spectacular Allegories: Postmodern American Writing and the Politics of Seeing*, London and Sterling: Pluto Press.

Connerton, Paul. (2009), *How Modernity Forgets*. Cambridge: Cambridge University Press.

Conway, Martha. (1999), "The Hand That Feeds You: Review of *Desperate Characters*, by Paula Fox," *The Iowa Review*, 29 (3): 173–5.

Costa, Richard Hauer. (1992), *Alison Lurie*, New York: Twayne Publishers.

Cuadros, Gil. (1994), "My Aztlán: White Place," in *City of God*, 53–8, San Francisco: City Lights Books.

Cunningham, Laura. ([1989] 2005), *Sleeping Arrangements*, London: Bloomsbury.

Davis, Colin. (2005), "Hauntology, Spectres and Phantoms," *French Studies*, 59 (3): 373–9.

Davis, Lawrence James (1970), "The Happy Reawakening of Clinton Hill," *New York Magazine*, 3 (26): 38–41.

Davis, L. J. ([1971] 2009), *A Meaningful Life*, New York: New York Review of Books.

Davis, Mike. ([1990] 1992), *City of Quartz: Excavating the Future in Los Angeles*, London and New York: Verso.

Davis, Mike. ([1998] 2000), *The Ecology of Fear: Los Angeles and the Imagination of Disaster*, London: Picador.

Dear, Michael. (1998), "In the City, Time Becomes Visible: Intentionality and Urbanism in Los Angeles, 1781–1991," in Allen J. Scott and Edward Soja (eds.), *The City: Los Angeles and Urban Theory at the End of the Twentieth Century*, 76–105, Berkeley, Los Angeles, and London: University of California Press.

Derrida, Jacques. ([1967] 1978), "Structure, Sign, and Play in the Discourse of the Human Sciences," in *Writing and Difference*, trans. Alan Bass, 278–94, London: Routledge.

Derrida, Jacques. ([1967] 1997), *Of Grammatology*, trans. Gayatri Chakravorty Spivak, Baltimore: John Hopkins University Press.

Derrida, Jacques. ([1993] 1994), *Specters of Marx: The State of the Debt, the Work of Mourning, and the New International*, trans. Peggy Kamuf, New York and London: Routledge.

DeSena, Judith N. and Timothy Shortell. ([2012] 2014), *The World in Brooklyn: Gentrification, Immigration, and Ethnic Politics in a Global City*, Lanham: Lexington Books.

Dickstein, Morris. (2004), "Never at Home: Jewish Writers and the Sense of Place," *Jewish Literary Supplement*, National Foundation for Jewish Culture, Fall 2004, Morris Dickstein Papers, Box 35, Folder 2, Manuscripts and Archives Division, The New York Public Library, New York, New York, accessed April 30, 2015.

Didion, Joan. (1956), "Sunset," *The Occident*, Spring 1956: 21–8.

Didion, Joan. ([1965] 2005), "Notes from a Native Daughter," in *Live and Learn*, 137–47, London: Harper Perennial.

Didion, Joan. ([1965–67] 2005), "Los Angeles Notebook," in *Live and Learn*, 170–5, London: Harper Perennial.

Didion, Joan. ([1966a] 2005), "On Keeping a Notebook," in *Live and Learn*, 107–19, London: Harper Perennial.

Didion, Joan. ([1966b] 2005), "Some Dreamers of the Golden Dream," in *Live and Learn*, 15–32, London: Harper Perennial.

Didion, Joan. (1967), Letter to Henry Robbins, 2 October 1967, Farrar, Straus & Giroux, Inc., Series I: Author Files, 1899–1998, Box 86, Folder: Didion, Joan. Slouching Towards Bethlehem. General. 1967–72, Manuscripts and Archives Division, The New York Public Library, New York, New York, accessed October 19, 2016.

Didion, Joan. ([1967a] 2005), "Goodbye to All That," in *Live and Learn*, 176–85, London: Harper Perennial.

Didion, Joan. ([1967b] 2005), "Marrying Absurd," in *Live and Learn*, 68–71, London: Harper Perennial.

Didion, Joan. ([1967c] 2005), "On Going Home," in *Live and Learn*, 131–3, London: Harper Perennial.

Didion, Joan. ([1967d] 2005), "Slouching Towards Bethlehem," in *Live and Learn*, 72–103, London: Harper Perennial.

Didion, Joan. (1968 [1969]), *Slouching Towards Bethlehem*, London: André Deutsch.

Didion, Joan. ([1968–78] 2005), "The White Album," in *Live and Learn*, 195–223, London: Harper Perennial.

Didion, Joan. ([1970] 2011), *Play It As It Lays*, London: Fourth Estate.

Didion, Joan. ([1976] 2005), "Bureaucrats," *Live and Learn*, 249–53, London: Harper Perennial.

Didion, Joan. ([1984] 1995), *Democracy*, London: Vintage Books.

Didion, Joan. (1984a), "Joan Didion: Staking out California," Interview by Michiko Kakutani, in Ellen G. Friedman (ed.), *Joan Didion: Essays & Conversations*, 29–40, Princeton: Ontario Review Press.

Didion, Joan. (1984b), "Why I Write," in Ellen G. Friedman (ed.), *Joan Didion: Essays & Conversations*, 5–10, Princeton: Ontario Review Press.

Didion, Joan. (2001), Interview by Christopher Bollen, *Christopherbollen.com*. n.d. Available online: www.christopherbollen.com/archive/joan_didion.pdf (accessed July 5, 2014).

Didion, Joan. ([2003] 2004), *Where I Was From*, London: Harper Perennial.

Didion, Joan. (2005a), "A Preface," in *Live and Learn*, 9–11, London: Harper Perennial.

Didion, Joan. (2005b), "Legends of the Fall," Interview by Susanna Rustin, *The Guardian Review*, May 21, 2005: 20–3.

Didion, Joan. (2006), "Joan Didion, The Art of Nonfiction No. 1," Interview by Hilton Als, *The Paris Review*, 176 (Spring 2006). Available online: https://www.theparisreview.org/interviews/5601/joan-didion-the-art-of-nonfiction-no-1-joan-didion (accessed June 2, 2014).

Didion, Joan. (2012), "Joan Didion: 'I think of myself as attached to California,'" Interview by Jonah Raskin, Sonoma State University. Available online: Sonoma.edu/users/r/raskin/interview:Didion.htm (accessed July 5, 2014).

Didion, Joan. (2017), *South and West: From a Notebook*, New York: Alfred A. Knopf.

Dillon, Sarah. (2005), "Reinscribing De Quincey's Palimpsest: The Significance of the Palimpsest in Contemporary Literary and Cultural Studies," *Textual Practice*, 19 (3): 244–5.

Dillon, Sarah. (2007a), "Palimpsesting: Reading and Writing Lives in H. D.'s 'Murex: War and Postwar London (circa A.D. 1916–1926),'" *Critical Survey*, 19 (1): 29–39.

Dillon, Sarah. (2007b), *The Palimpsest: Literature, Criticism, Theory*, London: Continuum.

Dines, Martin. (2015), "Metaburbia: The Evolving Suburb in Contemporary Fiction," in John Archer, Paul J. P. Sandul, and Katherine Solomonson (eds.), *Making Suburbia: New Histories of Everyday America*, 81–90, Minneapolis: University of Minnesota Press.

Donald, James. (1999), *Imagining the Modern City*, London: The Athlone Press.

Duncan, Susana. (1977), "Mental Maps of New York," *New York Magazine*, 19 December: 51–62.

Eco, Umberto. (1986), *Travels in Hyperreality*, trans. William Weaver, London: Picador.

Eeckhout, Bart and Lesley Janssen. (2014), "Making the Visible A Little Hard to See: D. J. Waldie's Aesthetic Challenge to American Urban Studies in *Holy Land: A Suburban Memoir*," *Anglia: Journal of English Philology*, 132 (1), April: 78–97.

Egan, John J. (1958), "Trojan Horse in Our Cities," America, March 1958, Series 11: Committee on Slum Clearance, Box 116: 1955–57, Folder 1, Robert Moses Papers, Manuscripts and Archives Division, The New York Public Library, New York, New York, accessed April 6, 2015.

Elkind, Sarah S. (2012), "Oil in the City: The Fall and Rise of Oil Drilling in Los Angeles," *The Journal of American History*, 99 (1): 82–90.

Epstein-Deutsch, Eli. (2009), "Jonathan Lethem and LJ Davis Bring Back *A Meaningful Life*," *The Village Voice*, 1 April. Available online: http://www.villagevoice.com/arts/jonathan-lethem-and-lj-davis-bring-back-a-meaningful-life-7133212 (accessed May 16, 2016).

Estrada, Gilbert. (2005), "If You Build It, They Will Move: The Los Angeles Freeway System and the Displacement of Mexican East Los Angeles, 1944–1972," *Southern California Quarterly*, 87 (3): 287–315.

Everson, William. (1976), *Archetype West: The Pacific Coast as a Literary Region*, Berkeley: Oyez.

Ferlinghetti, Lawrence. ([1955] 1958), *A Coney Island of the Mind*, New York: New Directions.

Fine, David. (1984), "Introduction," in David Fine (ed.), *Los Angeles in Fiction: A Collection of Original Essays*, 1–26, Albuquerque: University of New Mexico Press.

Fine, David. (1989/1990), "Nathanael West, Raymond Chandler, and the Los Angeles Novel," *California History*, 68 (4): 196–201.

Fine, David. (1991), "Running out of Space: Vanishing Landscapes in California Novels," *Western American Literature*, 26 (3): 209–18.

Fine, David. (2004), *Imagining Los Angeles: A City in Fiction*, Reno and Las Vegas: University of Nevada Press.

Fine, Richard. (2015), Personal interview, May 14.

Fishman, Robert. (2005), "*Holy Land: A Suburban Memoir* by D. J. Waldie," *Journal of the Society of Architectural Historians*, 64 (4): 562–6.

Fitch, James Marston. (1974), "Special Aspects of Urbanism", Introduction, Conference Guide: Back to the City - A Guide to Urban Preservation, New York City, September 13–16: 4–9, Back to the City collection, 1991.036, Box 1, Folder: Back to the City Conference – New York City, 1974, Brooklyn Historical Society, accessed May 14, 2015.

Fitzpatrick, John, ed. (2009), *The Idea of the City: Early-Modern, Modern and Post-Modern Locations and Communities*, Newcastle-upon-Tyne: Cambridge Scholars Publishing.

Fogelson, Robert. (1993), *The Fragmented Metropolis: Los Angeles, 1850–1930*, Berkeley, Los Angeles, and London: University of California Press.

Foucault, Michel. (1980), "The Eye of Power," in Colin Gordon (trans. and ed.), *Power/Knowledge: Selected Interviews and Other Writings 1972–1977*, 146–65, New York: Pantheon Books.

Fox, Paula. ([1970] 2003), *Desperate Characters*, London: Flamingo/HarperCollins Publishers.

Fox, Paula. (2015), "'The Truth of Life': Paula Fox on the Re- (Re-) Release of Her 1970 Novel," Interview by Sari Botton, *Longreads*, July. Available online: https://longreads.com/2015/07/27/the-truth-of-life-paula-fox-on-the-re-re-release-of-her-1970-novel/ (accessed June 9, 2018).

Fox, William L. (2007), "Tracking Tar," *Orion*, January/February. Available online: www.orionmagazine.org/index.php/articles/article/93/ (accessed March 21, 2018).

Freeman, Ira Henry. (1958), "Brooklyn Slums Shock Officials," *New York Times*, November 19. Available online: https://www.nytimes.com/1958/11/19/archives/brooklyn-slums-shock-officials-district-attorney-silver-cuts-short.html (accessed July 2, 2020).

Freeman, Lance. (2006), *There Goes the Hood: Views of Gentrification from the Ground Up*, Philadelphia: Temple University Press.

French, Warren. (1961), *John Steinbeck*, New York: Twayne Publishers.

Freud, Sigmund. ([1919] 2003), "The Uncanny," *The Uncanny*, trans. David McLintock, 121–62, London: Penguin.

Freud, Sigmund. ([1930] 1961), *Civilization and Its Discontents*, trans. James Strachey, New York: W.W. Norton.

Friedberg, Anne. (1993), *Window Shopping: Cinema and the Postmodern*, Berkeley, Los Angeles, and London: University of California Press.

Frommer, Myrna Katz and Harvey Frommer. (1993), *It Happened in Brooklyn: An Oral History of Growing Up in the Borough in the 1940s, 1950, and 1960s*, Wisconsin: The University of Wisconsin Press.

Gamboa, Manazar. (1996), *Memories around a Bulldozed Barrio: Book One*. Los Angeles: published by the author.

Gill, Jo. (2013), *The Poetics of the American Suburbs*, New York: Palgrave Macmillan.

Gilmore, Leigh. (1994), *Autobiographics: A Feminist Theory of Women's Self-Representation*, Ithaca and London: Cornell University Press.

Gissen, David. (2013), *Manhattan Atmospheres: Architecture, the Interior Environment, and Urban Crisis*, Minneapolis and London: University of Minnesota Press.

Glaab, Charles N. and A. Theodore Brown. (1967), *A History of Urban America*. New York: Macmillan Company.

Glaeser, Edward. (2011), *Triumph of the City*, London: Pan Books.

Glass, Ruth. (1964), "Introduction," in The Centre for Urban Studies (ed.), *London: Aspects of Change*, xiii–xlii, London: MacGibbon and Kee.

Gleason, Gene and Fred J. Cook. (1959), "The Shame of New York," *The Nation*, 189 (14): Series 11: Committee on Slum Clearance, Box 118, Folder: Committee on Slum Clearance 1957, Robert Moses Papers, Manuscripts and Archives Division, The New York Public Library, New York, New York, accessed April 6, 2015.

Goldberger, Paul. (1981), "Obituary: Robert Moses, Master Builder, Is Dead at 92," *The New York Times*, July 30. Available online: http://www.nytimes.com/learning/general/onthisday/bday/1218.html (accessed May 15, 2015).

Goldberger, Paul. ([1999] 2000), "Foreword," in Albert LaFarge (ed.), *The Essential William H. Whyte*, vii–ix, New York: Fordham University Press.

Goldberger, Paul. (2007), "Eminent Dominion," *The New Yorker*, February 5. Available online: https://www.newyorker.com/magazine/2007/02/05/eminent-dominion (accessed April 10, 2015).

Gomel, Elana. (2014), *Narrative Space and Time: Representing Impossible Topologies in Literature*, London and New York: Routledge.

Gonzalez, David. (2008), "City Room Blog: The Bronx Transformed, Through One Artist's Lens," *The New York Times*, September 15. Available online: https://cityroom.blogs.nytimes.com/2008/09/15/the-bronx-transformed-through-one-artists-lens/ (accessed July 22, 2020).

Gornick, Vivian. ([1987] 2015), *Fierce Attachments*, London: Daunt Books.

Gornick, Vivian. (1996), *Approaching Eye Level*, Boston: Beacon Press.

Gornick, Vivian. (2001), "My Neighborhood: Its Fall and Rise," *The New York Times*, June 24. Available online: https://www.nytimes.com/2001/06/24/nyregion/my-neighborhood-its-fall-and-rise.html (accessed June 21, 2016).

Gornick, Vivian. (2015), Personal interview, May 15.
Halbwachs, Maurice. ([1952] 1980), *The Collective Memory*, trans. Francis J. Ditter, Jr. and Vida Yazdi Ditter, New York: Harper & Row.
Hamill, Pete. (1969), "Brooklyn: The Sane Alternative", *New York Magazine*, 2 (28): 24–33.
Handbook of General Information. (1955), Los Angeles: Housing Authority of the City of Los Angeles.
Handler, Richard. (1986), "Authenticity," *Anthropology Today*, 2 (1), February: 2–4.
Hareven, Tamara K. and Randolph Langenbach. (1981), "Living Places, Work Places and Historical Identity," in David Lowenthal and Marcus Binney (eds.), *Our Past Before Us: Why Do We Save It?* 109–23, London: Temple Smith.
Haughton, Hugh. (2003), "Introduction," in *The Uncanny*, by Sigmund Freud, trans. David McLintock, vii–lx, London: Penguin.
Hayden, Dolores. (1995), *The Power of Place: Urban Landscapes as Public History*, Cambridge, MA and London: The MIT Press.
Heise, Thomas. (2011), *Urban Underworlds: A Geography of Twentieth-Century American Literature and Culture*, New Brunswick and London: Rutgers University Press.
Hellman, Peter. (1969), "The Consequences of Brownstone Fever," *New York Magazine*, 31 March: 22–32.
Henderson, George L. ([1998] 2003), *California and the Fictions of Capital*, Philadelphia: Temple University Press.
Highmore, Ben. (2002), *Everyday Life and Cultural Theory: An Introduction*, London and New York: Routledge.
Highmore, Ben. (2005), *Cityscapes: Cultural Readings in the Material and Symbolic City*, Hampshire and New York: Palgrave Macmillan.
Holland, Gale. (2011), "Lessons of 'Arborgeddon'," *The Los Angeles Times*, December. Available online: https://www.latimes.com/local/la-xpm-2011-dec-15-la-me-1215-holland-20111215-story.html (accessed June 29, 2020).
Home-Buyer's Guide to New York City Brownstone Neighborhoods (2nd edition), Brownstone Revival Committee, 1974, Back to the City collection, 1991.036, Box 1, Folder: Back to the City Conference – New York City, 1974, Brooklyn Historical Society, accessed May 14, 2015.
Hsy, Hsuan L. (2010), *Geography and the Production of Space in Nineteenth-Century American Literature*, Cambridge: Cambridge University Press.
Huxtable, Ada Louise. (1963), "Farewell to Penn Station," *The New York Times*, October 30. Available online: https://nycarchitectureandurbanism.files.wordpress.com/2015/03/huxtable-farewell-to-penn-station-1963.pdf (accessed February 20, 2016).
Huxtable, Ada Louise. ([1968] 2008), "Where Did We Go Wrong?", in *On Architecture: Collected Reflections on a Century of Change*, 413–17, New York: Walker & Company.
Huxtable, Ada Louise. (1997), *The Unreal America: Architecture and Illusion*, New York: The New Press.

Huxtable, Ada Louise. ([2007] 2008), "The Man Who Remade New York", in *On Architecture: Collected Reflections on a Century of Change*, 338–42, New York: Walker & Company.
Huyssen, Andreas. (2003), *Present Pasts: Urban Palimpsests and the Politics of Memory*. Stanford: Stanford University Press.
Isenstadt, Sandy. (2006), *The Modern American Home*, New York: Cambridge University Press.
Isherwood, Christopher. ([1964] 2010), *A Single Man*, London: Vintage Books.
Jackson, Kenneth T. (1985), *Crabgrass Frontier: The Suburbanization of the United States*, New York and Oxford: Oxford University Press.
Jackson, Kenneth T. (2004), *The Neighborhoods of Brooklyn*, 2nd edn, New Haven and London: Yale University Press.
Jackson, Kenneth T. and Stanley K. Schultz, eds. (1972), *Cities in American History*, New York: Alfred A. Knopf.
Jackson Ford, Karen. (1997), *Gender and the Poetics of Excess: Moments of Brocade*, Jackson: University Press of Mississippi.
Jacobs, Jane. ([1961] 1965), *The Death and Life of Great American Cities*, London: Pelican Books.
James, Henry. ([1907] 1994), *The American Scene*, New York: Penguin.
Jameson, Fredric. (1988), "Cognitive Mapping," in Cary Nelson and Lawrence Grossberg (eds.), *Marxism and the Interpretation of Culture*, 347–57. Urbana and Chicago: University of Illinois Press.
Jameson, Fredric. ([1995] 1999), "Marx's Purloined Letter," in Michael Sprinker (ed.), *Ghostly Demarcations: A Symposium on Jacques Derrida's Specters of Marx*, 26–67, London and New York: Verso.
Jameson, Fredric. (2016), *Raymond Chandler: The Detections of Totality*, London and New York: Verso.
Jarvis, Brian. (1998), *Postmodern Cartographies: The Geographical Imagination in Contemporary American Culture*, London: Pluto Press.
Jensen, Robert, ed. (1979), *Devastation/Resurrection: The South Bronx*, New York: The Bronx Museum of the Arts.
Johnson, Gaye Theresa. (2014), "Spatial Entitlement: Race, Displacement, and Sonic Reclamation in Postwar Los Angeles," in Josh Kun and Laura Pulido (eds.), *Black and Brown in Los Angeles: Beyond Conflict and Coalition*, 316–40, Berkeley: University of California Press.
Johnson, George. (1991), *In the Palaces of Memory: How We Build the Worlds Inside Our Heads*, New York: Knopf.
Jonnes, Jill. (2002), *South Bronx Rising: The Rise, Fall, and Resurrection of an American City*, New York: Fordham University Press.
Kaminsky, Howard. (2015), Personal interview, 18 April.
Kayden, Jerold S. (2000), *New York City Department of City Planning and Municipal Art Society of New York, Privately Owned Public Space: The New York City Experience*, New York: John Wiley and Sons.

Kazin, Alfred. (1951), *A Walker in the City*, New York: Harcourt, Brace & Co.
Kimmelman, Michael. (2015), "Panel: Redefining Preservation for the 21st Century", in The Museum of the City of New York Symposium, The New York Academy of Medicine, New York, April 20.
Klein, Norman M. (2008), *The History of Forgetting: Los Angeles and the Erasure of Memory*, London and New York: Verso.
Konigsberg, Eric. (2009), "For a Brooklyn Tale, and Its Author, a Second Chance at a First Impression," *The New York Times*, April 5. Available online: https://www.nytimes.com/2009/04/06/books/06davis.html (accessed September 6, 2016).
Koolhaas, Rem. ([1978] 1994), *Delirious New York: A Retroactive Manifesto for Manhattan*, New York: The Monacelli Press.
Koppelman, Lee. (2015), Personal interview, July 9.
Kostof, Spiro. (1991), *The City Shaped: Urban Patterns and Meanings Through History*, London: Thames and Hudson.
Kouwenhoven, John A. ([1961] 1988), *The Beer Can by the Highway: Essays on What's American about America*, Baltimore and London: The Johns Hopkins University Press.
Krauss, Rosalind. (1979), "Grids," *October*, 9 (Summer): 50–64.
Krell, David Farrell. (1990), *Of Memory, Reminiscence, and Writing*, Bloomington and Indianapolis: Indiana University Press.
Krieg, Joann P., ed. (1989), *Robert Moses: Single-Minded Genius*, New York: Heart of the Lakes Publishing.
Krisher, Bernard. (1957), "A View of the Heights: Newcomers Like Link with Past, Feel Area is Symbol of Frontier," *World Daily News*, January 25, Clinton Hill Folder 2, Brooklyn Collection, Brooklyn Public Library, Central Library at Grand Army Plaza, Brooklyn, New York, accessed April 8, 2016.
Kunstler, James Howard. (1993), *The Geography of Nowhere*, New York: Simon & Schuster.
Laslett, John H. M. (2015), *Shameful Victory: The Los Angeles Dodgers, the Red Scare, and the Hidden History of Chavez Ravine*, Tucson: University of Arizona Press.
"Latino/a Writers of Los Angeles and Southern California" (2016), *Los Angeles Literature*, October 4. Available online: https://losangelesliterature.wordpress.com/2016/10/04/latinoa-writers-of-los-angeles-and-southern-california/ (accessed June 29, 2020).
Lefebvre, Henri. (1991), *The Production of Space*, trans. Donald Nicholson-Smith, Malden: Blackwell.
Lefebvre, Henri. ([1992] 2004), *Rhythmanalysis: Space, Time and Everyday Life*, trans. Stuart Elden and Gerald Moore, London and New York: Continuum.
Lefebvre, Henri. (1996), *Writings on Cities*, ed. and trans. Eleonore Kofman and Elizabeth Lebas, Cambridge, MA and Oxford: Blackwell.
Lehan, Richard. (1967), "The American Novel: A Survey of 1966," *Wisconsin Studies in Contemporary Literature*, 8 (3): 437–49.
Lehan, Richard. (1998), *The City in Literature: An Intellectual and Cultural History*, Berkeley: California University Press.

Levy, Lawrence. (2015), Personal interview, May 6.
Liebling, Abbott Joseph (2008), "Apology for Breathing," in Phillip Lopate (ed.), *Writing New York: A Literary Anthology*, 626–31, New York: Library of America.
Lindsey, Robert. (1976), "Inner City Houses in Demand as Costs Soar in the Suburbs," *The New York Times*, June 28. Available online: http://query.nytimes.com/gst/a bstract.html?res=9804EFDC143FE334BC4051DFB066838D669EDE&legacy=true (accessed October 19, 2016).
Lipsitz, George. (1990), *Time Passages: Collective Memory and American Popular Culture*, Minneapolis: University of Minnesota Press.
Lopate, Phillip. (2008), *Writing New York: A Literary Anthology*, New York: Library of America.
Los Angeles: A Guide to the City and Its Environs. (1941), Compiled by Workers of the Writers' Program of the Work Projects Administration in Southern California, American Guide Series, New York: Hastings House.
Lowenthal, David. (1985), *The Past is a Foreign Country*, Cambridge: Cambridge University Press.
Lowenthal, David and Marcus Binney, eds. (1981), *Our Past Before Us: Why Do We Save It?* London: Temple Smith.
Lurie, Alison. ([1965] 1994), *The Nowhere City*, London: Minerva.
Lurie, Alison. (n.d.), "Alison Lurie: The Nowhen City," Interview by Ron Martinetti, *American Legends.com*. Available online: http://www.americanlegends.com/inte rviews/alison-lurie-the-nowhen-city.html (accessed September 12, 2014).
Lynch, Kevin. (1960), *The Image of the City*, Cambridge, MA and London: MIT Press.
Lynch, Kevin. (1972), *What Time Is This Place?* Cambridge, MA and London: MIT Press.
Madley, Benjamin. (2016), *An American Genocide: The United States and the California Indian Catastrophe, 1846–1873*, New Haven and London: Yale University Press.
Mahler, Jonathan. (2005), *Ladies and Gentlemen, the Bronx is Burning*, New York: Picador.
Malamud, Bernard. ([1950] 1985), "The Cost of Living," in *Selected Stories*, 183–92, Harmondsworth: Penguin.
Malamud, Bernard. (n.d.), Note in Letter from HA to RG, Farrar, Straus & Giroux, Inc., Series 1: Author Files, 1899–1998, Box 570, Folder: Malamud, Bernard, General correspondence 1979–1992, Manuscripts and Archives Division, The New York Public Library, New York, New York, accessed May 5, 2015.
Mallon, Thomas. (1984), "The Limits of History in the Novels of Joan Didion," in Ellen G. Friedman (ed.), *Joan Didion: Essays & Conversations*, 60–7, Princeton: Ontario Review Press.
Man, Paul de. (1983), *Blindness and Insight: Essays in the Rhetoric of Contemporary Criticism*, 2nd edn, Minneapolis: University of Minnesota Press.
Marcuse, Peter. (1984), *Gentrification, Abandonment, and Displacement in New York City*, New York: Columbia University, Graduate School of Architecture and Planning.

Marlin, George J. (2010), "Postscript: Opinions & Ideas – 'Tale of Two Pities,'" *The New York Post*, October 3. Available online: https://nypost.com/p/news/opinion/opedcolumnists/tale_of_two_pities_buffalo_and_the_JenvfKYTOLTovZ4trqFVfM (accessed April 28, 2016).

Marling, William. (2010), "City of Sleuths," in Kevin R. McNamara (ed.), *Cambridge Companion to the Literature of Los Angeles*, 111–22, Cambridge: Cambridge University Press.

Marot, Sebastien. (2003), *Sub-urbanism and the Art of Memory*, ed. Pamela Johnston, trans. Brian Holmes, London: Architectural Association.

Marshall, John C. and David M. Fryer. (1978), "'Speak, Memory!' An Introduction to Some Historic Studies of Remembering and Forgetting," in Michael M. Gruneberg and Peter Morris (eds.), *Aspects of Memory*, 1–25, London: Methuen.

Marshall, Paule. ([1959] 1982), *Brown Girl, Brownstones*, London: Virago Press.

Marx, Karl and Friedrich Engels. ([1848] 1992), "*The Communist Manifesto*," ed. David McLellan, Oxford: Oxford University Press.

Marx, Leo. (1964), *The Machine in the Garden*, Oxford and London: Oxford University Press.

Mason, Randall. (2009), *The Once and Future New York: Historic Preservation and the Modern City*, Minneapolis: University of Minnesota Press.

Mayo, Morrow. (1933), *Los Angeles*, New York: Alfred A. Knopf.

McWilliams, Carey. ([1946] 1973), *Southern California: An Island on the Land*, Salt Lake City: Gibbs-Smith Publisher, Peregrine Smith.

Merrill, James. ([1962] 2008), "An Urban Convalescence," in D. McClatchy and Stephen Yenser (eds.), *Selected Poems*, 21–3, New York: Knopf.

Morrone, Francis. (2016), Personal interview, May 4.

Moses, Robert. (1942), "What Happened to Haussmann?" *Architectural Forum*, 77 (July): 57–66.

Moses, Robert. (1954), "The City of New York," Address by Robert Moses before the National Education Association at Madison Square Garden, New York City, 28 June, Series 2: Triborough Bridge and Tunnel Authority, Box 73, Folder: Library – Robert Moses Correspondence – January 1, 1954 to December 31, 1954, Robert Moses Papers, Manuscripts and Archives Division, The New York Public Library, New York, New York, accessed April 24, 2015.

Moses, Robert. (1957a), "Memo to Mr Spargo," July 19, Series 11: Committee on Slum Clearance, Box 116, Folder: Committee on Slum Clearance 1957, Robert Moses Papers, Manuscripts and Archives Division, The New York Public Library, New York, New York, accessed April 6, 2015.

Moses, Robert. (1957b), Statement by Robert Moses, Chairman of the City Slum Clearance Committee on the Occasion of the Opening of North Harlem Houses, September 11, 1957, Series 11: Committee on Slum Clearance, Box 116, Folder 2: 1957, Robert Moses Papers, Manuscripts and Archives Division, The New York Public Library, New York, New York, accessed April 6, 2015.

Moses, Robert. (1977), *PBS WNET Reports*, Interview by Robert Sam Anson, PBS WNET, April 5.

Moskowitz, Peter. (2017), *How to Kill a City: Gentrification, Inequality, and the Fight for the Neighborhood*, New York: Nation Books.

Mosser, Jason. ([2011] 2012), *The Participatory Journalism of Michael Herr, Norman Mailer, Hunter S. Thompson, and Joan Didion: Creating New Reporting Styles*, Lewiston, Queenston, and Lampeter: The Edwin Mellen Press.

Mumford, Lewis. ([1937] 2004), "What Is a City?" in Malcolm Miles, Tim Hall, and Iain Borden (eds.), *The City Cultures Reader*, 28–32, London and New York: Routledge, Taylor and Francis Group.

Mumford, Lewis. ([1938] 1940), *The Culture of Cities*, London: Secker & Warburg.

Mumford, Lewis. (1968), *The Urban Prospect*, London: Secker & Warburg.

Murphy, Bernice M. (2009), *The Suburban Gothic in American Popular Culture*, Basingstoke: Palgrave Macmillan.

Nabokov, Vladimir. (1969), *Ada, or Ardor: A Family Chronicle*, New York and Toronto: McGraw-Hill.

Nadel, Alan. (1992), "Failed Cultural Narratives: America in the Postwar Era and the Story of Democracy," *Boundary 2*, 19 (1): 95–120.

Nadel, Alan. (1995), *Containment Culture: American Narratives, Postmodernism, and the Atomic Age*, Durham and London: Duke University Press.

Nadell, Martha. (2010), "Writing Brooklyn," in Cyrus RK Patell and Bryan Waterman (eds.), *The Cambridge Companion to the Literature of New York*, 109–20, Cambridge: Cambridge University Press.

Nash, Roderick Frazier. ([1967] 2014), *Wilderness and the American Mind*, New Haven: Yale University Press.

Newman, Judie. (2000), *Alison Lurie: A Critical Study*, Amsterdam: Rodopi.

New York: A Documentary Film. (1999), [Documentary] Dir. Ric Burns, USA: Public Broadcasting Service (PBS).

Nicolaides, Becky M. (2002), *My Blue Heaven: Life and Politics in the Working-Class Suburbs of Los Angeles, 1920–1965*, Chicago and London: University of Chicago Press.

Nicolaides, Becky M. (2003), "Suburbia and the Sunbelt," *OAH Magazine of History*, 18 (1): 21–6.

Osman, Suleiman. (2011), *The Invention of Brownstone Brooklyn: Gentrification and the Search for Authenticity in Postwar New York*, New York: Oxford University Press.

Ovnick, Merry. (2002), "The San Fernando Valley: America's Suburb by Kevin Roderick; Holy Land: A Suburban Memoir by D. J. Waldie," Review of *Holy Land*, by D. J. Waldie, *Southern California Quarterly*, 84 (¾): 284–6.

Page, Max. (1999), *The Creative Destruction of Manhattan, 1900–1940*, Chicago: University of Chicago Press.

Paletta, Anthony. (2016), "Story of cities #32: Jane Jacobs v Robert Moses, Battle of New York's Urban Titans," *The Guardian*, April 28. Available online: https://www.theguard

ian.com/cities/2016/apr/28/story-cities-32-new-york-jane-jacobs-robert-moses (accessed July 23, 2020).
Paley, Grace. (1987), "Somewhere Else," in *Later the Same Day*, 47–60, Harmondsworth: Penguin.
Paley, Grace. (1994), "The Long-Distance Runner," *The Collected Stories*, 242–59, New York: Farrar, Straus and Giroux.
Park, Robert E. (1967), "The City: Suggestions for the Investigation of Human Behavior in the Urban Environment," in Robert E. Park, Ernest W. Burgess, and Roderick D. McKenzie (eds.), *The City*, 1–46, Chicago and London: University of Chicago Press.
Parson, Don. (2005), *Making a Better World: Public Housing, the Red Scare, and the Direction of Modern Los Angeles*, Minneapolis and London: University of Minnesota Press.
Paz, Octavio. (1973), *Alternating Current*, trans. Helene R. Lane, New York: The Viking Press.
Peacock, James. (2015), *Brooklyn Fictions: The Contemporary Urban Community in a Global Age*, London: Bloomsbury Academic.
Pearlman, Mickey, ed. (1989), *American Women Writing Fiction: Memory, Identity, Family, Space*, Kentucky: The University Press of Kentucky.
Pearlman, Mickey. (1990), "Alison Lurie," in Mickey Pearlman and Katherine Usher Henderson (eds.), *Inter/View: Talks with America's Writing Women*, 9–14, Kentucky: The University Press of Kentucky.
"Pentimento – Glossary Entry." *National Gallery*. Available online: https://www.national gallery.org.uk/paintings/glossary/pentimento (accessed December 2, 2017).
Phillips-Fein, Kim. (2017), *Fear City: New York's Fiscal Crisis and the Rise of Austerity Politics*, New York: Metropolitan Books, Henry HOH and Co.
Price, Jenny. (2006), "Thirteen Ways of Seeing Nature in L.A," *The Believer*, 4 (6). Available online: https://believermag.com/thirteen-ways-of-seeing-nature-in-la/ (accessed March 21, 2018).
Pulido, Laura, Laura Barraclough, and Wendy Chend. (2012), *A People's Guide to Los Angeles*, Berkeley, Los Angeles, and London: University of California Press.
Pyke Jr., John S. (1969), "Landmark Preservation," Everett and Evelyn Ortner papers and photographs ARC.306, Series 6: Brooklyn and Historic Preservation general files, circa 1880-2008, Box 41, Folder 7, Brooklyn Historical Society, accessed September 25, 2015.
Raban, Jonathan. ([1974] 2017), *Soft City*, London: Picador.
Radley, Alan. (1990), "Artefacts, Memory and a Sense of the Past," in David Middleton and Derek Edwards (eds.), *Collective Remembering*, 46–59, London, Newbury Park, and New Delhi: Sage Publications.
Rasmussen, Cecilia. (1989), "Los Angeles Street Names," *Los Angeles Times*, July 5. Available online: https://www.latimes.com/archives/la-xpm-1989-07-05-me-3186-s tory.html (accessed June 20, 2020).

Rau, Petra. (2009), *English Modernism, National Identity and the Germans, 1890–1950*, Farnham: Ashgate Publishing Limited.

Rauam, Naima. (2015), Personal interview, May 4.

Rehak, Melanie. (2001), "The Life and Death And Life of Paula Fox," *The New York Times*, March 4. Available online: https://www.nytimes.com/2001/03/04/magazine/the-life-and-death-and-life-of-paula-fox.html?pagewanted=all (accessed April 1, 2016).

Revell, Keith D. (1992), "Regulating the Landscape: Real Estate Values, City Planning, and the 1916 Zoning Ordinance," in David Ward and Olivier Zunz (eds.), *The Landscape of Modernity: Essays on New York City, 1900–1940*, 19–45, New York: Russell Sage Foundation.

Reynolds, Malvina. ([1962] 2000), "Little Boxes," in *Ear to the Ground*. Smithsonian Folkways.

Rosen, Joe. (2016), Personal interview, 25 April.

Rosenblum, Constance. (2009a), *Boulevard of Dreams: Heady Times, Heartbreak, and Hope along the Grand Concourse in the Bronx*, New York: New York University Press.

Rosenblum, Constance. (2009b), "Grand, Wasn't It?" *The New York Times*, August 20. Available online: http://www.nytimes.com/2009/08/21/arts/design/21concourse.html (accessed April 1, 2016).

Rotella, Carlo. (1998), *October Cities: The Redevelopment of Urban Literature*, Berkeley and London: University of California Press.

Rowe, Colin and Fred Koetter. (1979), *Collage City*, Cambridge, MA: The MIT Press.

Royden Winchell, Mark. (1980), *Joan Didion*, Boston: Twayne Publishers.

Rubenstein, Roberta. (2001), *Home Matters: Longing and Belonging, Nostalgia and Mourning in Women's Fiction*, New York: Palgrave.

Sanneh, Kelefa. (2016), "Is Gentrification Really A Problem?" *New Yorker*, July 11. Available online: https://www.newyorker.com/magazine/2016/07/11/is-gentrification-really-a-problem (accessed May 16, 2018).

Satz, Martha. (1986), "A Kind of Detachment: An Interview with Alison Lurie," *Southwest Review*, 71 (2): 194–202.

Saul, Alice. (1957), Letter to Robert Moses, August 1957, Series 11: Committee on Slum Clearance, Box 116, Folder 2: 1957, Robert Moses Papers, Manuscripts and Archives Division, The New York Public Library, New York, New York, accessed April 6, 2015.

Saving Place Exhibition. April 2015–January 2016, Museum of the City of New York, New York.

Schaeffer, Susan Fromberg. (1985), *Mainland*, London: Pan Books.

Schaeffer, Susan Fromberg. (1986), *The Injured Party*, London: Hamish Hamilton.

Schlichtman, John Joe, Jason Patch, and Marc Lamont Hill. (2017), *Gentrifier*, Toronto, Buffalo, and London: University of Toronto Press.

Schwartz, Alexandra. (2017), "Rereading Paula Fox's 'Desperate Characters,'" *New Yorker*, March 9. Available online: https://www.newyorker.com/culture/cultural-comment/rereading-paula-foxs-desperate-characters (accessed May 16, 2018).

Schwartz, Lynne Sharon. (1989), *Leaving Brooklyn*, Boston: Houghton Mifflin Company.
Schwartz, Lynne Sharon. (2016), Personal interview, April 14.
Schwartz, Lynne Sharon. (2017), *No Way Out But Through*, Pittsburgh: University of Pittsburgh Press.
Sclan, Shellie. (2016), Personal interview, 25 April.
Sclan, Shellie. (2017), "Introduction," Section VII: The Romance of Public Space, in David Marcus and Shellie Sclan (eds.), *Modernism in the Streets: A Life and Times in Essays*, by Marshall Berman, 335-7, London and New York: Verso.
Scobey, David M. (2002), *Empire City: The Making and Meaning of the New York City Landscape*, Philadelphia: Temple University Press.
Shaw, Philip. (2006), *The Sublime*, London and New York: Routledge.
Shoop, Casey. (2011), "Corpse and Accomplice Fredric Jameson, Raymond Chandler, and the Representation of History in California," *Cultural Critique*, 77: 205-38.
Silver, Nathan. (2000), *Lost New York*, Boston: Houghton Mifflin.
Simmel, Georg. ([1903] 2002), "The Metropolis and Mental Life," trans. Edward Shils, in Gary Bridge and Sophie Watson (eds.), *The Blackwell City Reader*, 11-19, Oxford: Blackwell Publishing.
Simon, Kate. (1982), *Bronx Primitive: Portraits in a Childhood*, New York: The Viking Press.
Sinclair, Upton. ([1926] 2008), *Oil!* London: Penguin Classics.
Skenazy, Paul. (1984), "Behind the Territory Ahead," in David Fine (ed.), *Los Angeles in Fiction: A Collection of Original Essays*, 85-107, Albuquerque: University of New Mexico Press.
Sleeper, Jim. (1982), Draft version of: "Gentrification: Towards a New Apartheid?" Dissent, Winter (January 1982), H. Dickson McKenna collection, ARC.060, Box 2, Folder 10, Brooklyn Historical Society, accessed September 25, 2015.
Slotkin, Richard. (1973), *Regeneration Through Violence: The Mythology of the American Frontier, 1600-1860*, Norman: University of Oklahoma Press.
Smith, Betty. ([1943] 1974), *A Tree Grows in Brooklyn*, London: Heinemann.
Smith, Neil. (1996), *The New Urban Frontier: Gentrification and the Revanchist City*, London and New York: Routledge.
Soja, Edward. (1989), *Postmodern Geographies: The Reassertion of Space in Critical Social Theory*, London and New York: Verso.
Soja, Edward. (1996), *Thirdspace*, Cambridge: Blackwell.
Soja, Edward. (1999), "Thirdspace: Expanding the Scope of the Geographical Imagination," in Doreen Massey, John Allen, and Phil Sarre (eds.), *Human Geography Today*, 260-78, Cambridge: Polity.
Solnit, Rebecca. (2002), *Hollow City: The Siege of San Francisco and the Crisis of American Urbanism*, London and New York: Verso.
Solomon, Geri. (2015), Personal interview, April 29.
Sontag, Susan. (1979), "Introduction," in *One-Way Street*, by Walter Benjamin, 7-28, London: New Left Books.

Sontag, Susan. (n.d.), "Special Report: 'Electric Weather' Brownstones," *The Brownstone Hunters Guide*, ConEdison, no date, H. Dickson McKenna collection, ARC.060, Box 1, Folder 8. Brooklyn Historical Society, accessed May 14, 2015.

Spiegel, Samuel A. (1959), *The Forgotten Man in Housing*, August 1959, Series 11: Committee on Slum Clearance, Box 118, Folder: Committee on Slum Clearance 1959, Robert Moses Papers, Manuscripts and Archives Division, The New York Public Library, New York, New York, accessed April 6, 2015.

Spivak, Gayatri Chakravorty. ([1967] 1997), "Translator's Preface," in *Of Grammatology* by Jacques Derrida, trans. Gayatri Chakravorty Spivak, ix–lxxxix, Baltimore: John Hopkins University Press.

Staley, Willy. (2018), "When Gentrification Isn't About Housing," *The New York Times Magazine*, January 23. Available online: https://www.nytimes.com/2018/01/23/magazine/when-gentrification-isnt-about-housing.html (accessed May 16, 2018).

Starr, Kevin. (1985), *Inventing the Dream: California Through the Progressive Era*, Oxford and New York: Oxford University Press.

Starr, Kevin. (1990), *Material Dreams: Southern California Through the 1920s*, Oxford and New York: Oxford University Press.

Starr, Kevin. (1997), *The Dream Endures: California Enters the 1940s*. Oxford, New York: Oxford University Press.

Starr, Kevin. (2005), *California: A History*, New York: Random House.

Starr, Kevin. (2009), *Golden Dreams: California in an Age of Abundance, 1950–1963*, Oxford and New York: Oxford University Press.

Starr, Roger. (1979), The Editorial Notebook: "Thoughts on Eggshells on the Beach," *The New York Times*, June 4. Available online: http://www.nytimes.com/1979/06/04/archives/the-editorial-notebook-thoughts-of-eggshells-on-the-beach.html (accessed May 5, 2016).

Steigman, K. (2012), "Cold War Intimacies: Joan Didion and the Critique of Postcolonial Reason," in Steven Belletto and Daniel Grausam (eds.), *American Literature and Culture in an Age of Cold War: A Critical Reassessment*, 109–32, Iowa City: University of Iowa Press.

Stein, Samuel. (2019), *Capital City: Gentrification and the Real Estate State*, London and New York: Verso.

Steiner, Rodney. (1981), *Los Angeles, the Centrifugal City*, Dubuque and Iowa: Kendall/Hunt Publishing Company.

Stephens, Suzanne. (2013), "Obituary: Ada Louise Huxtable, 1921–2013," *Architectural Record*, January 18. Available online: https://www.architecturalrecord.com/articles/2780-obituary-ada-louise-huxtable-1921-2013 (accessed July 21, 2020).

Stern, Robert A. M., Thomas Mellins, and David Fishman. (1997), *New York 1960: Architecture and Urbanism Between the Second World War and the Bicentennial*, Köln: Evergreen.

Stilgoe, John R. (1988), *Borderland: Origins of the American Suburb, 1820–1939*, New Haven and London: Yale University Press.

Stratton, Jim. (1977), *Pioneering in the Urban Wilderness*, New York: Urizen.
Streitfeld, David. (1992), "The Subjective Observer," *New York Newsday*, August 7.
Sutcliffe, Anthony. (1981), *Towards the Planned City: Germany, Britain, the United States and France, 1780–1914*, New York: St Martin's Press.
Talese, Gay. ([1964] 2003), *The Bridge*, New York: Walker & Company.
Tauber, Gilbert. (2015), Personal interview, May 3.
Taylor, Gordon O. (1983), *Studies in Modern American Autobiography*, New York: Macmillan.
The Bible. (2014), New International Version, London: Hodder and Stoughton.
"The Lakewood Story Begins." (2011), *Lakewood Online*, City of Lakewood. Available online: http://www.lakewoodcity.org/about/history/history/ch1.asp (accessed May 4, 2018).
"The New Brooklyn: Business and Community Directory." (1973), The Brooklyn Chamber of Commerce, Carroll Gardens Neighbourhood Folder 5, Brooklyn Collection, Brooklyn Public Library, Central Library at Grand Army Plaza, Brooklyn, New York, accessed April 8, 2016.
Thomas, Piri. ([1967] 1997), *Down These Mean Streets*, New York: Vintage.
Thompson, Hunter S. ([1973] 2012), *Fear and Loathing on the Campaign Trail '72*, New York: Simon & Schuster.
Thrift, Nigel. (2004), "Driving in the City," *Theory, Culture & Society*, 21 (4–5): 41–60.
Tierney, John. (1994), "The Winner, Axles Down," *The New York Times*, April 3. Available online: http://www.nytimes.com/1994/04/03/magazine/the-winner-axles-down-the-winner-axles-down.html (accessed July 24, 2020).
Tochterman, Brian. (2017), *The Dying City: Postwar New York and the Ideology of Fear*, Chapel Hill: University of North Carolina Press.
Trilling, Lionel. ([1971] 1972), *Sincerity and Authenticity*, Cambridge, MA and London: Harvard University Press.
Tversky, Barbara. (2000), "Remembering Spaces," in Endel Tulving and Fergus I. M. Craik (eds.), *The Oxford Handbook of Memory*, 363–78, Oxford: Oxford University Press.
Ulin, David. (2006), "Unshakeable Memories," *Los Angeles Times*, April 16. Available online: http://articles.latimes.com/2006/apr/16/opinion/op-ulin16 (accessed April 16, 2018).
Ulin, David. (2015), "Fifteen Takes on California," *Virginia Quarterly Review*, 91 (3): 28–36.
Usher Henderson, Katherine. (1981), *Joan Didion*, New York: Frederick Ungar Publishing Co.
Van Dover, James Kenneth (1995), *The Critical Response to Raymond Chandler*, Westport and London: Greenwood Press.
Venturi, Robert, Denise Scott Brown, and Steven Izenour. (1972), *Learning from Las Vegas*, London: MIT Press.

Vidler, Anthony. (1992), *The Architectural Uncanny: Essays in the Modern Unhomely*, Cambridge, MA: MIT Press.

Villa, Raúl Homero. (1999), "Ghosts in the Growth Machine: Critical Spatial Consciousness in Los Angeles Chicano Writing," *Social Text*, 58 (Spring): 111–31.

Viramontes, Helena Maria. (2007), *Their Dogs Came With Them. A Novel*, New York: Atria Books.

Virilio, Paul. (1998), "Dromoscopy, or The Ecstasy of Enormities," trans. Edward R. O' Neill, *Wide Angle*, 20 (3): 10–22.

Virilio, Paul. (2005), *Negative Horizon: An Essay in Dromoscopy*, London and New York: Continuum.

Waldie, Donald J. (1996), *Holy Land: A Suburban Memoir*, New York: St Martin's Press.

Waldie, Donald J. (2004), *Where We Are Now: Notes from Los Angeles*, Santa Monica: Angel City Press.

Waldie, Donald J. (2010a), "How Do We Make Our Home Here?," *Los Angeles Times*, A31.

Waldie, Donald J. (2010b), "L.A.'s Crooked Heart," *Los Angeles Times*, October 24. Available online: http://articles.latimes.com/2010/oct/24/opinion/la-oe-waldie-maps-20101024 (accessed May 17, 2018).

Waldie, Donald J. (2011a), "How We Got This Way," *KCET*, December 12. Available online: https://www.kcet.org/shows/lost-la/how-we-got-this-way-los-angeles-has-always-been-suburban (accessed July 11, 2020).

Waldie, Donald J. (2011b), "Public Policy/Private Lives," in Patricia Hampl and Elaine Tyler May (eds.), *Tell Me True: Memoir, History, and Writing a Life*, 203–18, Minnesota: Borealis.

Waldie, Donald J. (2015), "How to Look at Los Angeles: A Conversation with D.J. Waldie, Lynell George and Josh Kun," Interview by Carolina A. Miranda, *Los Angeles Times*, July 24. Available online: http://www.latimes.com/entertainment/arts/miranda/la-et-cam-how-to-see-los-angeles-dj-waldie-lynell-george-and-josh-kun-20150721-column.html (accessed March 28, 2018).

Waldie, Donald J. (2016), "How I Found Los Angeles," *KCET*, March 10. Available online: https://www.kcet.org/shows/lost-la/how-i-found-los-angeles (accessed June 10, 2018).

Waldie, Donald J. and Neil Campbell. (2011), "An Assemblage of Habits," D. J. Waldie and Neil Campbell - A Suburban Conversation, *Western American Literature*, 46 (3): 228–49.

Wallis, Michael. (2017), *The Best Land Under Heaven: The Donner Party in the Age of Manifest Destiny*, New York: Liveright.

Ward, David and Olivier Zunz, eds. (1992), *The Landscape of Modernity: Essays on New York City, 1900–1940*, New York: Russell Sage Foundation.

Warnock, Mary. (1987), *Memory*, London and Boston: Faber and Faber.

Wasserburg, Charles. (1989), "Raymond Chandler's Great Wrong Place," *Southwest Review*, 74 (4): 534–45.

Waterman, Bryan and Cyrus R. K. Patell, eds. (2010), *Cambridge Companion to the Literature of New York*, Cambridge: Cambridge University Press.

Weinstein, Richard S. (1998), "The First American City," in Allen J. Scott and Edward Soja (eds.), *The City: Los Angeles and Urban Theory at the End of the Twentieth Century*, 22–46, Berkeley, Los Angeles, and London: University of California Press.

West-Pavlov, Russell. (2009), *Space in Theory: Kristeva, Foucault, Deleuze*, Amsterdam and New York: Rodopi.

Wheeler, Elizabeth A. (1996), "A Concrete Island: Hisaye Yamamoto's Postwar Los Angeles," *Southern California Quarterly*, 78 (1): 19–50.

White, Elwyn Brooks. ([1949] 1999), *Here Is New York*, New York: The Little Bookroom.

Whitehead, Colson. (2003), *The Colossus of New York*, New York: Anchor Books.

Whyte, William H. ([1988] 2000), "From *City: Rediscovering the Center*," in Albert LaFarge (ed.), *The Essential William H. Whyte*, 269–340, New York: Fordham University Press.

Widdicombe, Toby. (2001), *A Reader's Guide to Raymond Chandler*, Connecticut and London: Greenwood Press.

Wilcox, Leonard. (1984), "Narrative Technique and the Theme of Historical Continuity in the Novels of Joan Didion," in Ellen G. Friedman (ed.), *Joan Didion: Essays & Conversations*, 68–80, Princeton: Ontario Review Press.

Willett, Martha. (1974), "Back-to-City Convention Spells Out Advantages, How-to's of Restoration," *PHOENIX*, September 19, Back to the City collection, 1991.036, Box 1, Folder: Back to the City Conference – New York City, 1974, Brooklyn Historical Society, accessed May 14, 2015.

Winterson, Jeanette. ([2011] 2012), *Why Be Happy When You Could Be Normal?* London: Vintage.

Wolfe, Tom. (1972), "'The Birth of 'The New Journalism'; Eyewitness Report by Tom Wolfe," *New York Magazine*, February 14. Available online: http://nymag.com/news/media/47353/ (accessed December 15, 2019).

Wolfe, Tom. ([1987] 2010), *The Bonfire of the Vanities*, London: Vintage Books.

Worth, Robert. (1999), "Guess Who Saved the South Bronx?" *Washington Monthly*, April. Available online: https://washingtonmonthly.com/1999/04/01/guess-who-saved-the-south-bronx/ (accessed May 13, 2017).

Wright, Frank Lloyd. ([1928] 2008), "In the Cause of Architecture IV: The Meaning of Materials – Glass," in Bruce Brooks Pfeiffer (ed.), *The Essential Frank Lloyd Wright: Critical Writings on Architecture*, 137–40, Princeton and Oxford: Princeton University Press.

Wroe, Nicholas. "Young at Heart." Author profile of Alison Lurie. *The Guardian*, October 25, 2003, https://www.theguardian.com/books/2003/oct/25/featuresreviews.guardianreview15

Wyatt, David. (1986), *The Fall into Eden: Landscape and Imagination in California*, Cambridge and New York: Cambridge University Press.

Wyatt, David. (2010), "LA Fiction through Mid-century," in Kevin R. McNamara (ed.), *Cambridge Companion to the Literature of Los Angeles*, 35–48, Cambridge: Cambridge University Press.

Yamamoto, Hisaye. ([1950] 1998), "Wilshire Bus," *Seventeen Syllables and Other Stories*, 34–8, New Jersey and London: Rutgers University Press.

Yamamoto, Hisaye. (1976), "I Still Carry It Around," *RIKKA* 3 (4): 11–19.

Yates, Francis. ([1966] 1978), *The Art of Memory*, Harmondsworth: Penguin.

Yeats, William Butler ([1920] 1994), "The Second Coming," *The Collected Poems of W. B. Yeats*, 158–9, Ware: Wordsworth Editions.

Yogi, Stan. (1989), "Legacies Revealed: Uncovering Buried Plots in the Stories of Hisaye Yamamoto," *Studies in American Fiction*, 17 (Autumn): 169–81.

"You Can Have Your Brownstone…And Rent It, Too." (1974), *The Brownstoner*, Special Conference Issue, 5 (6), Back to the City collection, 1991.036, Box 1, Folder: Back to the City Conference – New York City, 1974, Brooklyn Historical Society, accessed May 14, 2015.

Zimmerman, Lee. (1999), "Public and Potential Space: Winnicott, Ellison, and DeLillo," *The Centennial Review*, 43 (3): 565–74.

Zipp, Samuel. (2010), *Manhattan Projects: The Rise and Fall of Urban Renewal in Cold War New York*, New York: Oxford University Press.

Zukin, Sharon. (1987), "Gentrification: Culture and Capital in the Urban Core," *Annual Review of Sociology*, 13: 129–47.

Zukin, Sharon. (2008), "Consuming Authenticity: From Outposts of Difference to Means of Exclusion," *Cultural Studies*, 22 (5): 724–48.

Zukin, Sharon. ([2009] 2010), *Naked City: The Death and Life of Authentic Urban Places*, New York and Oxford: Oxford University Press.

Index

Adams, Henry   112
alienation   4, 11, 39, 57, 92, 96, 123, 126, 130
All That is Solid Melts into Air (Berman)   2, 6, 9, 14, 17, 108, 109, 117–19, 123, 125, 128, 130, 132, 133, 136, 178, 180, 182
America. *See* United States
America (Baudrillard)   90
American Housing Act (1949)   115, 118, 119
American Scene, The (James)   112, 179
"Angel of History" (Benjamin)   188
anxiety   5, 6, 34, 57, 177
Arcades (Benjamin)   3, 185, 187
Architectural Record   5, 93
Arroyo Seco Parkway   34
Art of Memory, The (Yates)   52, 53
Austin, Mary   20, 71
authenticity   12, 138–46, 159, 169
autobiographical memory. *See* external memory
autophilia   87
Avella, Steven   73
Avila, Eric   27

Bachelard, Gaston   52, 53
Back to the City Conference   122, 144
Banham, Reyner   22, 27, 88, 92, 97
Barthes, Roland   27, 28, 80
Baudrillard, Jean   90
Bed-Stuy neighborhood   140
Benjamin, Walter   2, 3, 16, 93, 94, 130, 185, 187–9
"A Berlin Chronicle" (Benjamin)   2, 189
Berman, Marshall   2, 4, 5, 8, 10, 13–15, 17, 36, 74, 96, 100, 104, 108–10, 115–21, 123–8, 130–6, 140, 146, 153, 168, 171, 176–80, 182, 183, 186–8, 194 n.20

Big Sleep, The (Chandler)   4, 11, 17, 18, 40–65, 99, 100, 124, 135, 167, 178, 180, 187–8
Borderland (Stilgoe)   25
Boyar, Louis   24
Boyer, M. Christine   15, 16, 81, 127–8, 169, 170, 171, 183, 189
Boyle Heights   11, 35, 37
Bridge, The (Talese)   116
Bronx   4, 10, 13, 14, 104, 108, 117, 118, 120–9, 133–6, 140, 177, 178, 188. *See also* South Bronx
Bronx Mural   130, 171
Brooklyn, New York City   4, 10, 15, 131, 137–41, 143, 146, 148, 155–7, 160–2, 165, 166, 168, 170–2, 178, 180, 186
Brooklyn Chamber of Commerce   149
Brooklyn Dodgers   35, 138
Brooklyn Eagle   138
Brooklyn Fictions (Peacock)   146
Brooklyn Heights   143, 148–9
Brooklyn Heights Promenade   149
Brooklyn Navy Yard   138, 161
Brooklyn Queens Expressway   149
Brown Girl, Brownstones (Marshall)   15, 138, 140–1, 170, 186
Brownstone Revival Committee   144
brownstoner movement   138, 142, 145
Bruckner Expressway   118, 124, 128
"Bureaucrats" (Didion)   87, 88

Caillois, Roger   61
California Division of Highways   36
Calvino, Italo   126
Capital City (Stein)   9, 111, 141
Caro, Robert   107, 109, 114, 116, 121
Chandler, Raymond   3–6, 10–12, 14, 15, 17–19, 33, 34, 38, 41–3, 46–8, 51, 53, 55–9, 62, 64, 65, 94, 99, 104, 105, 123, 135, 161, 163, 165, 176, 180, 188

Chavez Ravine   11, 35, 36, 37
City Beautiful movement   116
City of Collective Memory, The
   (Boyer)   15, 171
City Terrace   11, 36
Civilian Exclusion Order number 69
   (1942)   95
Civilization and its Discontents
   (Freud)   18, 122, 126
Clinton Hill   161–3
"Cognitive Mapping" (Jameson)   130
Collective Memory, The (Halbwachs)   108, 127
Colonial Williamsburg, Virginia   168
Committee on Slum Clearance   114
Communist Manifesto, The (Marx and
   Engels)   109
Co-op City   193 n.11
Corona Ash Dumps   107
Cross-Bronx Expressway   4, 6, 101, 116, 118, 119, 121, 122, 124–31, 136, 178
crossing story   13, 14, 65, 68, 70, 75, 76, 78, 89, 91, 158, 179
Cuadros, Gil   5, 6, 11, 36, 176, 188
cultural mourning   151–2, 156
Culture of Cities, The (Mumford)   4

Davis, L. J.   5, 6, 15, 137, 142, 158, 159, 161
Davis, Mike   19, 22, 87
Death and Life of Great American Cities, The (Jacobs)   119, 186
de Certeau, Michel   28, 29, 107, 128, 131
deindustrialization   117, 141
Delirious New York (Koolhaas)   29, 150, 163
Democracy (Didion)   67, 68
Derrida, Jacques   7, 8
Desperate Characters (Fox)   15, 137, 138, 145–55, 165, 184
Didion, Joan   3–6, 9, 13–15, 24, 31, 39, 40, 46, 48, 63, 65–82, 84, 87–91, 99, 100, 103, 104, 117, 132, 137, 154, 158, 161, 177, 179, 180, 183, 188
Dillon, Sarah   80, 96
Dines, Martin   18, 26

discontinuity   7, 17, 175, 182, 183, 188, 189
displacement   7, 14, 35, 118, 154, 169
Dodger Stadium   35, 37
Donner Lake from the Summit
   (Bierstadt)   78
Donner Memorial State Park   76
Donner Pass   70, 76, 78
Donner-Reed party   76

East Los Angeles Freeway System   36

façades   10, 46, 47, 93, 95, 169
Farewell, My Lovely (Chandler)   11, 17, 18, 34, 39–41, 60, 178–9
Federal Aid Highway Act (1956)   115, 118
Federal Housing Administration   24, 115
Federal Housing Authority Loans   35
Fine, David   40, 43, 44, 47, 62, 65, 90, 97, 98, 101
Fort Greene   160, 161
Foucault, Michel   110
Fox, Paula   5, 15, 137, 146–9, 158, 165
Freeman, Lance   148, 157, 162
freeway system   34–6, 92, 101, 161, 178
Freud, Sigmund   7, 17, 18, 42, 43, 46, 47, 50, 85, 122, 126, 167, 168, 175, 183
frontier   12, 24, 44, 54, 68–70, 72, 76, 89, 90, 100, 103, 146, 156

Gamboa, Manazar   6, 11, 36, 176
Garnett, William   27, 28
gentrification and gentrifiers   7, 15, 138, 142–5, 157, 158, 162, 168, 169, 175, 179, 182, 183, 188, 195 n.3
G. I. Bill   24, 35
Gill, Jo   23, 27
Glass, Ruth   142
glass in modern buildings   93–4
"Goodbye to All That" (Didion)   180
Gornick, Vivian   121, 126, 128, 129, 131, 135, 181–2
Grand Boulevard and Concourse   6, 120, 125, 127, 128, 133
"Grids" (Krauss)   27

grid system   6, 10, 11, 20–1, 26–29, 39, 60, 100, 111, 170
grief   11, 30, 32, 74, 135, 151, 152, 177

Haight-Ashbury district, San Francisco   66
Halbwachs, Maurice   19, 59, 108, 127, 135, 185
haunted spaces   7, 14, 131
hauntology   7, 8
Hayden, Dolores   18, 65, 108
Highmore, Ben   7, 48, 111, 118
highway construction   14, 115
High Window, The (Chandler)   11, 17, 33–4, 40, 42, 48, 49, 53, 54, 62–3
historical memory   127, 144, 185
history   3–6, 9–15, 18, 21, 32, 86, 89, 105, 108, 127–9, 131, 170, 174–6
History of Forgetting, The (Klein)   21, 46, 122
Holy Land: A Suburban Memoir (Waldie)   9, 10, 15, 18, 25–33, 52, 79, 100, 104, 135, 178, 183
Home Owners Loan Corporation   24, 141
homesickness   4, 133, 153, 177
"How I Found Los Angeles" (Waldie)   37
"How We Got This Way" (Waldie)   22
Huxtable, Ada Louise   5, 107, 113, 168
Huyssen, Andreas   8, 9, 80

Idle Valley   33
imago   46, 47, 49, 53, 86
interior spaces   13, 15, 47–9, 146, 147, 163, 164, 178
Interstate 78   113
Interstate 405   101
Interstate Highway System   114–25
"In the Forest of Symbols: Some Notes on Modernism in New York" (Berman)   108
Invention of Brownstone Brooklyn, The (Osman)   142
Invisible Cities (Calvino)   126, 135
irrigation   11, 20, 22, 34, 72

Jackson, Helen Hunt   77
Jackson, Kenneth T.   22, 23, 141
Jacobs, Jane   28, 119, 144, 186

James, Henry   57, 112, 179
Jameson, Fredric   8, 38, 41, 44, 48, 56, 58–60, 65, 127, 130

Kaminsky, Howard   121, 125, 129, 135, 182, 194 n.15
Kazin, Alfred   5, 15, 138, 139, 178, 183
Kinney, Abbot   103, 105
Klein, Norman M.   21, 46, 49, 52, 86, 119, 122, 176, 177, 184
Koolhaas, Rem   29, 150, 163, 170
Krell, David Farrell   51, 55, 56, 61
Kunstler, James Howard   20, 25, 100

Lafayette Avenue   160, 162
Lakewood, California   4, 9–11, 18, 24–30, 32, 178, 188
Landmarks Preservation Commission   114
language   7, 8, 29, 38, 58, 65, 66, 117
"L.A.'s Crooked Heart" (Waldie)   20, 21
Lefebvre, Henri   87, 130
liminal spaces   25, 40, 61, 184, 185, 188
Lincoln Center for the Performing Arts   116
London: Aspects of Change (Glass)   142
Los Angeles, California   3, 5, 6, 8–13, 17–23, 26, 27, 30, 33–40, 42, 44–6, 51, 52, 55, 56, 59, 64, 65, 72, 82, 83, 86–8, 91, 92, 94, 96–105, 161, 169, 176–8, 180, 184, 187–9
Los Angeles Aqueduct   19
Los Angeles Dodgers. *See* Brooklyn Dodgers
"Los Angeles Notebook" (Didion)   40
Los Angeles River   20, 64
loss   7, 11, 16, 35, 66–8, 81, 91, 110, 121, 135, 139, 152–3, 177, 179
Lowenthal, David   78, 113, 156, 175
Lower Manhattan Expressway   114
Lurie, Alison   5, 6, 11, 12, 20, 40, 65, 91, 96, 98, 99, 101, 105, 135, 161, 180, 192 n.12
Lynch, Kevin   169, 170, 177

Machine in the Garden (Marx)   34
McWilliams, Carey   19, 20, 32, 77
Manhattan, New York City   111–14, 143

Manhattan Projects (Zipp)   117
"manifest destiny"   44, 159
Marshall, Paule   5, 15, 138, 140
Mar Vista   11, 40, 103, 104, 177
Marx, Karl   109
Marx, Leo   34, 37
Mason, Randall   112, 144, 145
Mayo, Morrow   37, 72, 103
Meaningful Life, A (Davis)   6, 15, 124, 137, 138, 142, 145, 155–70, 178, 182, 183, 186
memories   3–7, 10, 11, 13–15, 16, 18, 27, 30–2, 46, 49, 51–3, 55–6, 62, 78, 90, 108, 122, 126, 127, 131, 135, 139, 152, 169, 170, 174–7, 188. *See also individual entries*
Memories Around a Bulldozed Barrio (Gamboa)   37
memory palaces   52, 53, 176–7
"metaphorical city". *See* "mobile city"
"The Metropolis and Mental Life" (Simmel)   183
Mexican-American War   43, 44
Mexican Revolution   36
Mitchell, Joseph   194 n.18
mnemotechnics   52, 176
"mobile city"   127, 128, 135, 179
modern city   5–7, 9, 16, 18, 63, 93, 107–8, 119, 123, 177, 179, 181, 182, 189
modernity/modernization   4, 8, 9, 11, 12, 14, 15, 17, 18, 64, 105, 109–12, 115, 117, 122, 123, 132, 135, 143, 145, 174, 176, 182, 184
Moses, Robert   4, 5, 14, 15, 101, 107–20, 125, 127, 128, 135, 136, 145, 149, 161, 182, 185, 188, 193 n.6
Mulholland, William   19
Mulholland Highway/Drive   34
Mumford, Lewis   4, 101, 104, 175, 176
"My Aztlan: White Place" (Cuadros)   36, 124

Naked City (Zukin)   112, 115
National Historic Preservation Act (1966)   113
national identity   67, 72, 75
Native Americans   35, 44, 76, 77
natural world   34, 41, 58–60, 64, 143

New Deal   24, 115
New York Calling: From Blackout to Bloomberg (Berman)   14, 123, 133
New York City, New York   4–6, 8–10, 13, 14, 34, 65, 70, 101, 107–9, 111–15, 117, 119, 128, 135, 141, 142, 171, 176–81, 184–7, 189, 194 n.14
New York City Landmarks Law (1965)   113
New York Times   5, 108, 113, 129, 142, 144, 162, 169, 183
Nicolaides, Becky   18, 23
nonfiction   5, 13, 67, 78, 79, 81
non-space   60, 124
nostalgia   3, 12, 47, 57, 73, 74, 77, 78, 131, 133, 138, 141, 156, 160, 175, 181–3, 189
"Notes from a Native Daughter" (Didion)   6, 14, 68–70, 81, 100, 180
Nowhere City, The (Lurie)   6, 11–13, 20, 40, 65, 91, 96–105, 124, 135, 137–8, 178, 180–1, 187

Oil! (Sinclair)   23, 45
oil fields   17, 18, 41, 44–6, 50, 57, 62–4, 124
Once and Future New York, The (Mason)   112
"On Going Home" (Didion)   14
"On Keeping a Notebook" (Didion)   78, 79
On the Town: One Hundred Years of Spectacle in Times Square (Berman)   14, 134
Organization Man, The (Whyte)   186
Osman, Suleiman   140, 142, 145
Owens Valley   20

Pacific Electric Railroad   22
palimpsest   4, 11, 80, 92, 96, 113, 172
pentimento   171
Play It As It Lays (Didion)   6, 13, 15, 31, 39, 46, 54, 63–5, 67, 68, 75, 79, 81–6, 88–91, 104, 177, 179
postwar period   9, 35, 115, 118, 119, 141, 153

Power Broker, The (Caro)   107, 121
Practice of Everyday Life, The (de Certeau)   28, 107
Present Pasts (Huyssen)   8
preservation   2, 5, 6, 12, 18, 53, 101, 112, 113, 122, 138, 143–5, 169, 179, 188
pre-urban spaces   12, 18, 41
private spaces   43, 49, 51, 93, 168
Production of Space, The (Lefebvre)   87
public housing   108, 115, 120
public spaces   22, 93, 108, 128, 142, 161
Pyke, John S., Jr.   113

Raúl Homero Villa   36
restoration   6, 138, 145, 162, 168, 169, 182
Rhythmanalysis (Lefebvre)   87–8
romanticism   68, 71, 77
Run River (Didion)   70–1, 84

Sacramento, California   3, 9, 69–71, 73, 74, 81, 179
San Bernardino freeway   36
San Fernando Valley   20
San Francisco-Oakland Bay Bridge   34
Santa Ana Freeway   35
Schaeffer, Susan Fromberg   171
Schwartz, Lynne Sharon   128, 138, 171, 194 n.19
Sclan, Shellie   129, 185
Second World War   4, 13, 18, 24, 71, 95, 114, 122, 138, 140
Serviceman's Readjustment Act. See G. I. Bill
Seventeen Syllables and Other Stories (Yamamoto)   13, 91
Simmel, Georg   183
Sincerity and Authenticity (Trilling)   143
Sinclair, Upton   23, 45
Slouching Towards Bethlehem (Didion)   13, 14, 48, 65–7, 81, 85, 99, 117, 154, 188
slum clearance   7, 14, 111, 115–17, 120
Slum Clearance Committee   161
Smith, Betty   137, 140, 163, 172, 180
Social Life of Small Urban Spaces , The (Whyte)   186
"soft city"   127, 128, 194 n.17

Soja, Edward   8, 56, 101, 191 n.1
"Some Dreamers of the Golden Dream" (Didion)   180
South Bronx   2, 118, 124, 132, 134
Southern California   12, 18–20, 22, 23, 27, 32, 34, 35, 38, 40, 43, 45, 46, 56, 59, 63–5, 77, 87, 92, 100, 101, 124
Southern Pacific Railroad   22
spatial incongruity   40, 101
spatial transformation   117, 180
Starr, Kevin   19, 20, 70, 92, 100
Starr, Roger   116
Stein, Samuel   9, 21, 77, 111, 141, 159
storytelling   71, 77, 80, 81
suburbs   10, 11, 15, 18, 22–7, 141
"Sunset" (Didion)   71

Talese, Gay   116, 182
Their Dogs Came With Them (Viramontes)   36
thirdspace   8
Thirdspace (Soja)   191 n.1
Tree Grows in Brooklyn, A (Smith)   137, 171, 182
Trilling, Lionel   143, 169
"the uncanny"   7, 9, 12, 14, 50, 64, 123, 151, 168, 175, 179
"The Uncanny" (Freud)   17, 85, 133, 167

Unisphere   107
United States   9, 11, 16, 24, 44, 67, 70, 72, 75, 114, 156
urban crisis (1960s)   115, 141, 143, 153
urbanization   4, 7, 8, 11, 12, 17, 45, 63, 188
urban planning   30, 117, 150
urban renewal   5, 7, 14, 16, 65, 108, 111, 115, 116, 141, 145, 161, 174
urban spaces   3–6, 9, 15–17, 27, 37, 46, 57, 58, 61, 87, 92, 101, 104, 111, 113, 116, 117, 122, 130, 144, 174, 176, 180, 184, 189

Venice Beach   103, 188
Verrazano-Narrows Bridge   116, 182, 116
Vidler, Anthony   12, 62, 63, 89, 110, 114, 123, 126, 132, 179, 183

"Views from the Burning Bridge" (Berman) 124
Viramontes, Helena Maria 11, 36

Waldie, D. J. 4–6, 8–11, 14, 15, 18–22, 24–32, 37, 46, 52, 72, 79, 81, 82, 100, 104, 112, 135, 166, 177, 178, 181, 183, 184, 188
Walker in the City, A (Kazin) 15, 138–40
Where I Was From (Didion) 3, 6, 13–15, 24, 67–72, 74–6, 79–85, 89, 91, 100, 132, 180
Whyte, William H. 186–7
Wilderness and the American Mind (Nash) 60

Wilshire Boulevard 92, 96
"Wilshire Bus" (Yamamoto) 6, 8, 9, 13, 65, 91–6, 184
Wolfe, Tom 79, 124
World's Fair
   1939–40 107
   1964–5 107, 109
Wyatt, David 12, 33, 34, 37

Yamamoto, Hisaye 5, 6, 8, 13, 65, 91–6, 182
Yates, Frances 52, 53, 176, 177
Yeats, W. B. 117

Zoning Resolution (1916) 112
Zukin, Sharon 112, 115, 143, 145

www.ingramcontent.com/pod-product-compliance
Lightning Source LLC
Chambersburg PA
CBHW062218300426
44115CB00012BA/2116